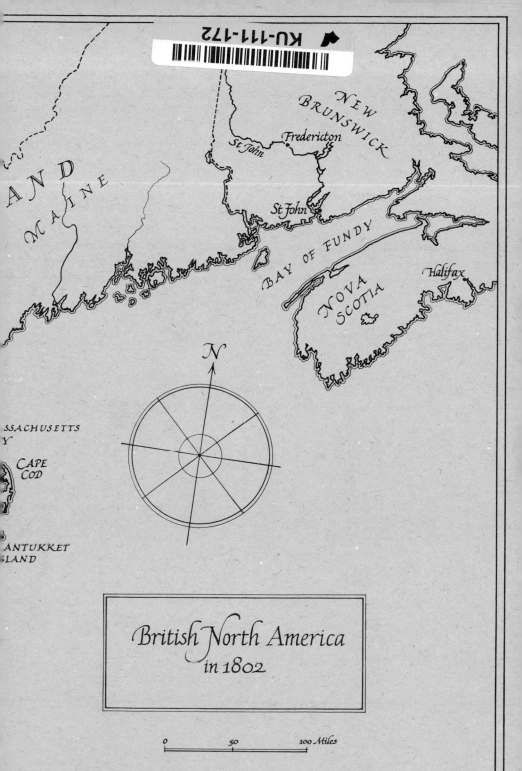

NEW
BRUNSWICK

Fredericton

St John

AND

MAINE

St John

BAY OF FUNDY

NOVA
SCOTIA

Halifax

N

SSACHUSETTS
Y

CAPE
COD

ANTUKKET
SLAND

British North America
in 1802

0    50    100 Miles

EX LIBRIS
A J Bisset

FOLIO SOCIETY

# COBBETT'S

# AMERICA

*William Cobbett*

# Cobbett's America

A SELECTION

FROM THE WRITINGS

OF WILLIAM COBBETT

EDITED WITH AN INTRODUCTION

BY J. E. MORPURGO

THE FOLIO SOCIETY

LONDON

1985

PRINTED AND BOUND

BY BUTLER & TANNER LTD, FROME

SET IN 11 POINT EHRHARDT

LEADED ONE POINT

PRINTED ON SUNNINGDALE OPAQUE

AND BOUND IN QUARTER CLOTH

WITH PRINTED PAPER SIDES

PRINTED IN GREAT BRITAIN

# CONTENTS

# ILLUSTRATIONS

# *ACKNOWLEDGMENTS*

---

The editor acknowledges, with gratitude, assistance from Thad Tate, Director of the Institute of Early American History and Culture, from the Keeper of the Brotherton Collection, the University of Leeds, and from Cathy Feeny, Research Assistant at Vanderbilt University. He is, as ever, deeply conscious of the part played by his wife and by his secretary, Debbie Brown, in the arduous business of making order out of a complex text.

# *INTRODUCTION*

---

If there is regret in Heaven for vanished earthly fame few there can suffer as bitterly as does the shade of William Cobbett. In life he was always noticeable, generally notable and, even by his many enemies, never offered the insult which he would have resented above all others: a passport to oblivion. At times a scourge and often a favourite son to two nations, he was also in both Great Britain and the United States, and for long periods, variously a hero and a villain to conservatives and to radicals. Before he was thirty, by the vigour and impudence of his assault on institutions which it cherished, he had earned the animosity of the hierarchy in Britain; within ten years he had become the darling of these same men and in so doing had entered the nightmares of decades of their American equivalents. For the last thirty years of his long life, as the most notorious and most articulate defector from the Tory cause, he was yet again a principal target for the malice of British conservatives and, on both sides of the Atlantic, honoured as an apostle by all who battled for reform.

Even in an age not yet besotted with specialisation Cobbett's versatility was remarkable. Soldier, agronomist, grammarian, moral counsellor, historian, popular educator, editor, journalist, parliamentarian, author: he was all of these and such was his genius for controversy and such his boldness that in none could he be ignored.

A hundred and fifty years after his death the echoes from his contemporary fame and notoriety are for the most part inaudible. His reforming zeal has slipped from the record, his contribution to political discourse has been relegated to the bottom of the page, a footnote in the more exhaustive histories. From all his diverse activities, even from his huge bibliography, only *Rural Rides* retains a sure hold upon the respect and affection of posterity, its persisting reputation sustained, not by the academy, not by those who customarily guard the entrance to the literary pantheon, but by succeeding generations of unprofessional admirers. Cobbett's great writer-contemporaries – Wordsworth, Coleridge, Byron, Shelley, Carlyle, Jane Austen and Hazlitt among them – are freshly remembered not merely because the grandeur of their achievement is inescapable but also because their quality is resurrected for each new generation of readers by the pertinent attention of critics and biographers and by the impertinent demands of the examination syllabus. Cobbett, even for *Rural Rides*, has been generally and ungenerously denied the benefits of this immortalising process.

If the decline of Cobbett's reputation among the British is sad and inexcusable, his exclusion from the hagiology of the United States is amazing to the point of being inexplicable. Half his adult life was passed in North America. His interventions in the political debates of the new nation were sturdy and at the time more influential than those of many Americans-born who still stand as ikons for American worship. With Tom Paine he was rare in that he was truly an Anglo-American, a qualification he shares with very few; among the great figures only with Henry James, T.S. Eliot and, perhaps, W.H. Auden.

In the half-century that followed the Revolution the fascination was intense that lured British writers across the Atlantic. For some, it seemed that the Declaration of Independence was the opening chapter in a new version of British history, a happier story not marred by past failures and distant tragedies but still plush with the rich blessings of an unshakeably British tradition. For others, it was the American continent that set the lure; that vast, mysterious and uncluttered map which promised opportunity to any who dared to seize it.

For those decades, the last of the eighteenth century and the first four of the nineteenth, the bibliography of British writing about America is more abundant, and the names of the authors included more eminent, than for the whole of the two preceding centuries of American history.

Two of the major figures of the period, William Hazlitt and James Henry Leigh Hunt, had close family ties with America, but neither showed any inclination to return to that country. Their close friends, Coleridge, Southey and even Charles Lamb, dreamed briefly of peace to come and Heaven on earth on the banks of the Susquehanna, but soon awoke to the realisation that they were utterly unsuited to the task of establishing a Utopia on those dangerous frontiers, and stayed at home instead.

Harriet Martineau, Frances Trollope, Captain Marryat, Richard Cobden, a swarm of lesser scribblers and one much greater, Charles Dickens, set out for America seeking instant impressions and quick royalties. They came, they saw – and they returned home as quickly as possible to pass on to a British readership their generally caustic and captious comments about the poverty of American culture and the miserable state of American political life.

In all this resplendent parade Cobbett stands out, certainly not for elegance but because he alone carries a pack made heavy by experience. In America he was never, as were so many of his distinguished contemporaries, an itinerant. He lived as an American and worked, as he saw it, always for the good of the people of America. Even when he was back in England he did not discard the especial qualities of perception that he had acquired from his years in America; he could still view the events of those times through American eyes. So it was that when, in 1812, the United States brought down upon itself the hatred of all parties and all classes in Britain by allying itself with Napoleon, Cobbett, alone among British writers, set himself boldly to the task of presenting to his countrymen a lucid and vehement defence of actions which seemed to all others in Britain at best inexplicable and at worst unmitigated treachery to a world threatened by despotism – an irrevocable breach of the very democratic principles on which the United States itself had been established.

Cobbett's immediate contribution to the development of American society and, above all, to American political activity was greater than that of any other Englishman save only, again, Tom Paine. It is nevertheless undeniable that even when he was writing as an American – especially in Philadelphia when he was most active as an American editor and as an American journalist – Cobbett never shook off characteristics inherited from rural England nor did he ever attempt to disguise from his American neighbours his distaste for those of their number who, by his lights, were denying to the new nation the fulfilment of those ambitions which he believed to be the common property of the American and the British people. It was not contrariness and most certainly not sentimentality that worked for Cobbett the paradox that he was never so blatantly an Englishman as he was when he was living in America and never so openly sympathetic to Americanism as he was after he had returned to Britain. His apparent perverseness was in truth symptomatic of his independent spirit, of his determination to hold himself free of the mores and prejudices of his neighbours, of his zest for the task of passing on to his two countries awareness of the failings common to both and knowledge of the benefits they could acquire if only each would take on some of the virtues of the other. But among his American contemporaries his obdurate Englishness and his impertinent iconoclasm led him often into conflict with those who saw themselves as appointed guardians of truths that were self-evident only to Americans – even though his doubts about the perfection of the United States were much the same as those voiced by the Father of American Literature, James Fenimore Cooper (and with no less vehemence by the second President, John Adams).

Unusually for the time, Cobbett made his way to distinction without the initial advantage of an elaborate education. Shelley, Byron and Macaulay built their artistic and intellectual achievements upon patrician foundations; Coleridge, Wordsworth, Carlyle, Lamb, Leigh Hunt, De Quincey and even Hazlitt upon sound schooling. Cobbett had little formal education:

I do not remember the time, when I did not earn my living ... I have some faint recollection of going to school to an old woman who, I believe, did not succeed in learning me my letters ... my father learnt us all to read and write, and gave us a pretty tolerable knowledge of arithmetic. Grammar he did not perfectly understand himself, and therefore his endeavours to learn us that, necessarily failed; for, though he thought he understood it, and made us get the rules by heart, we learnt nothing at all of the principles.

This was the sort of education: and I am perfectly satisfied that had I not received such an education ... I should have been at this day as great a fool, as inefficient a mortal, as any of those

frivolous idiots that are turned out from Winchester or Westminster School or from any of those dens of dunces called Colleges and Universities.

From the teaching of his father and his father's fellow-
labourers Cobbett learned that intimacy with the land which later
he was to dedicate to the service of America. It was also through
them that he was first touched by affection and respect for the
United States.

Even at a time when it seemed inevitable that George III
would soon chastise his rebellious subjects, Cobbett's father was
outspoken in support of the Revolutionary cause.

My father was a partizan of the Americans: he used frequently
to dispute on the subject, with the gardener of a nobleman who
lived near us. This was generally done with good humour, over
a pot of our best ale; yet the disputants sometimes grew warm,
and gave way to language that could not fail to attract our attention. My father was worsted without doubt, as he had for antagonist, a shrewd and sensible old Scotchman, far his superior in
political knowledge; but he pleaded before a partial audience: we
thought there was but one wise man in the world, and that that
one was our father.

His country wisdom Cobbett inherited from generations of
unspectacular ancestors; his morality, his earnestness and, to
some extent, his political truculence, were fashioned by his father;
his intellectual equipment he acquired for himself in his teens;
and for much of the rest of his life he devoted a great part of his
extraordinary energy to passing on to others, as disadvantaged as
he himself had been in youth, the benefits that he had won by
stubborn and lonely effort.

Cobbett's age when first, like Don Quixote, he sallied forth to
seek adventures is uncertain. Throughout his life he made himself
out to be younger than he was. He claimed that he was born in
March 1766; his son gave his father's birthday as 9 March 1762;
the Farnham parish register, though vague, seems to indicate a
date some time in 1763. But whether he was seventeen, twenty-
one or twenty on that day in May 1783 when he quit the country
for London Cobbett was still, by city standards, an immature

yokel and unsuited, by all except his clear handwriting, for the first job he found, as 'an understrapping quill-driver ... perched upon a great high stool, in an obscure chamber in Gray's Inn'.

His second attempt to break with the bucolic tradition of his forefathers came close to foundering into farce. Already earlier, tempted by his first view of the sea, Cobbett had tried to sign on aboard a ship of the navy and had been charitably rejected – by a captain and an admiral! Seeking still a life at sea Cobbett enlisted in the marines – and found himself mustered instead into the 54th Regiment of Foot. Then, and for the rest of his days, he set down this subversion of his intentions as a typical example of administrative incompetence and of the careless way of the authorities with the innocent and humble.

Most of what is known about Cobbett's nine years in the army comes from his own telling and the manner of the tale makes the record embarrassing to an advocate for his reputation. Modesty was never prominent among Cobbett's qualities but the smugness and conceit of his portrait of William Cobbett as soldier is virtually untouched by the geniality and charity that adds decent humanity to the pride in his own achievements which is general to his other autobiographical writings.

He was without doubt intelligent, diligent and efficient but he was also obsessively concerned to prove himself better than his equals and far superior to those set above him who were 'in everything except mere authority, my inferiors; and ought to have been commanded by me'. He pitied his subordinates, but despised them for seeking compensation for the harshness of their existence in drink and riotousness:

... As I never disguised my dislikes, or restrained my tongue, I should have been broken and flogged for fifty different offences, had they not been kept in awe by my inflexible sobriety, impartiality and integrity.

Cobbett's unmitigated distaste for the 'epaulet gentry', as he called them, led eventually to the disastrous end of his military career. Thereafter, his disdain for aristocratic pretensions wherever he found them (whether in Britain or in avowedly egalitarian America) spilled acid into all his journalism, and fuelled his political career. Yet he remained throughout his life,

*The Jolly Farmer at Farnham where Cobbett was born*

*An officer and two soldiers of Cobbett's regiment, the 54th Foot*

for all his fervent radicalism, in some sense unmistakably a warrant officer, conservative after the fashion of his rank, a guardian of tradition, eager to preserve what he found to be good even if it meant condoning some evils, reluctant to overturn the past lest in doing so he deprived the future of stability.

It was Cobbett's army service in New Brunswick which taught him to question the validity of his incipient republicanism. For him, as for so many of his sensitive contemporaries – Coleridge, Wordsworth, Southey and even Beethoven among them – the brutal despotism practised in the name of democracy by the French completed his change of heart, but the first doubts were sowed by an American Revolution which blasphemed against fraternity, liberty and equality. Cobbett may have been an insufferable soldier, but he made friends among the civilians of the Province. He admired their courage, their will to survive the harsh climate of the Maritimes, and their determination to hew a new and happy society from that grim unpromising soil. They were Loyalists to a man, and as Cobbett's admiration for them grew, so did his doubts about the perfection of the New Republic to the South which persecuted them in the name of a new freedom.

But there was an even more significant factor in the development of William Cobbett's character: in New Brunswick this unlovable soldier found love.

Anna Reid (known to her friends and to Cobbett as Nancy) was the daughter of a sergeant of artillery and only thirteen years old when first they met. His reaction was typical of the solemn man he then was:

That I thought her beautiful is certain, for that I had always said should be an indispensable qualification; but I saw in her what I deemed marks of that sobriety of conduct ... which has been by far the greatest blessing of my life ... As to beauty, though men may fall in love with girls at play, there is nothing to make them stand to their love like seeing them at work.

When Cobbett first set eyes on Nancy Reid, 'it was hardly light, but she was out in the snow, scrubbing out a washing-tub.'

They were married on 8 February 1792. Cobbett demanded a great deal of a wife:

With regard to young women . . . attending to the affairs of the house; to the washing, the baking, the brewing, the preservation and cooking of victuals, the management of the poultry and the garden; these are their proper occupations.

All these responsibilities Nancy took upon herself: she was a hard worker, a superb manager and in time a sensible and loving mother; but she also gave to her husband something he had hitherto lacked – warmth of spirit, ease of heart and sensitivity. Cobbett would never be sentimental; his capacity for rage always outstripped his benevolence; but the gentle perceptions which were to make him in the end so much greater than the mere roaring journalist he might otherwise have been, he learnt from Nancy. In *Rural Rides*, that miraculous amalgam of loving observation and sharp protest, Nancy Cobbett's influence merits reverence.

At this point, however, he was still a serving soldier and he was undoubtedly looking for trouble. He found it when he discovered that the quartermaster of the 54th was selling a quarter of the supplies destined for the regiment. Regardless of the fact that this was a time-honoured custom, a practice common to all regiments (and indeed all armies), Cobbett decided that it was a scandal that must be exposed. He spent night after night copying incriminating evidence from the regimental accounts and returned to England with his Case against Corruption complete. Securing his discharge – an honourable one, as he would forever insist – he forwarded his case to the War Office.

It was a most unwise move. All ranks immediately closed to block the assault of this pious upstart. A Court of Enquiry found Cobbett's villains to be honourable men. Still hurling abuse at the authorities, Cobbett left England with his new wife and went to live in France.

His humiliation did not teach him either caution or moderation; indeed, it made irreversible his contempt for those who held and abused power wherever they might be found. He was ordained into a ministry, which he never abandoned, whose responsibility it was to attack the blasphemies of injustice and political malpractice wherever they might be heard. But, from his miserable experience with the military hierarchy Cobbett learnt that the obscure are helpless. From then on he was determined to make himself so notable, and if need be so notorious, that his demands for reform could never again be drowned by the chorus of the complacent plutocrats.

That he chose France is in no way surprising.

> *Bliss was it in that dawn to be alive*
> *But to be young was very Heaven*

The French Revolution offered to him, as to Wordsworth, a promise of vital and practical democracy. Though later he was to claim that he had moved across the Channel for no other reason than to master the French language, Cobbett was almost certainly seeking confirmation of his conviction that, somehow, liberty could be achieved without bloodshed, fraternity without disorder, and equality without loss of pride. The six months that the Cobbetts spent near St Omer he came to remember as the happiest of his life.

Then came the Terror. The French revolutionaries were the first to betray the French Revolution. As one of Cobbett's earliest American apologists wrote, some twenty years later:

Instead of liberty [the Revolution] carried with it the stamp of licentiousness; and under the toga of Roman eloquence, breathing virtue and self-devotion, was a dagger concealed, yet warm with blood and thirsting for further victims.

The Cobbetts left France in August 1792, and sailed for America.

That Cobbett chose to emigrate to the United States, the country that had persecuted, dispossessed and driven into exile his United Empire Loyalist friends, seems at first sight more paradoxical than his initial choice of France as place of refuge, but there was then for him, a discredited warrant officer, no hope that he could make a career in England; America was still the land of opportunity; no Englishman then (or for many years thereafter) quite believed that the United States was a foreign country; no Englishman then (or for many years thereafter) quite accepted that in America he would be an alien. The Americans spoke, wrote, and (most important for Cobbett) read English.

Also adding weight to Cobbett's decision, was the very fact that he had been comfortable among the United Empire Loyalists, and he was convinced that he would find the same contentment among the Yankees south of the border as had been his when living as neighbour to their compatriots in New Brunswick.

In the next eight years, after a tentative and humble beginning as teacher and bookseller, this self-educated, self-trained and largely self-financed neophyte journalist became – under the name of Peter Porcupine – one of the best known and most scurrilous pamphleteers in the United States. He was also the founder, proprietor, editor and sole correspondent of some of the most widely circulated journals and one of the most influential newspapers.

Once settled in America, he moved almost immediately from Delaware to Philadelphia – proof indeed of his shrewdness and of his eagerness to be in the middle of the ring – and fighting. Philadelphia was still the capital. It had its own aristocracy, heirs to a long line of Philadelphia notables. More importantly, at 'public times' there came to the city that brilliant generation of Americans who had led the nation out of colonial subservience. Not surprisingly, Philadelphia was a city of Anglophobes, and the many Irish residents, together with the swarms of French émigrés, only served to fuel the fires of anti-British feeling. All this was meat and drink to Cobbett.

There is nothing more common [wrote a contemporary], than to confound the terms of the American Revolution with those of the late American war. The American war is over but this is far from being the case with the American Revolution. On the contrary, nothing but the first act of the great drama is closed.

The second act was played out almost before Cobbett's eyes, as Federalists and anti-Federalists struggled to produce a party-political system. The former saw the new nation as little more than a confederation of otherwise independent states, while the latter favoured vigorous centralism, and it seemed at times as if accommodation between the two was impossible.

It was James Madison who contributed most to the temporary victory of the Federalists with a superb display of casuistical arguments designed to demonstrate that a defence of the privileges of property was also a defence of the rights of western settlements:

There is no maxim [he wrote in 1786] which is more likely to be misapplied and which therefore needs more elucidation, than the current one, that the interest of the majority is the political standard of right and wrong. Taking the word 'interest' as synonymous with ultimate happiness, in which sense it is qualified with every moral ingredient, it is no doubt true. But taking it in the popular sense, as referring to the immediate augmentation of property and wealth, nothing can be more false. In the latter sense it would be in the interest of the majority, in every community, to despoil and enslave the minority of individuals.

Certainly, though the War of Independence was fought and won by Americans of all conditions, the leadership was predominantly aristocratic, consisting of men who, in their cultural, social and economic prejudices, were not so very different from their British adversaries. They opposed British dominion, and destroyed it with courage and skill, but they lived in fear lest by their own exertions they replaced the suzerainty of George III with the rule of the mob, lest independence be a prelude to egalitarianism.

To Cobbett, with his view of an ordered society inherited from generations of English countrymen, and reinforced, despite his skirmish with officialdom, by his service in that most hierarchical of all societies, the British Army, the views of Madison and his fellow-Federalists were inevitably attractive but, almost as he arrived in the United States, events in Europe made his intervention in American affairs imperative. His own Britain went to war with Revolutionary France. The philosophical argument over the future of the United States was now translated into a wrangle more immediate in its quality: which side should have the support, tacit or active, of the new nation?

Enduring Anglophobia and thankfulness for the part played by France in the victory over Britain not unnaturally predisposed Americans to the French cause, but the American people were not *sans-culottes*. American independence had been won in honourable battle, with some bitterness but without the shame of massacre. Even Jefferson, an eager Francophil, could not

condone the Terror and, on the other side, the merchant-class
and the landowners, most of them Federalists, felt

the winds of hate ... blowing from the Place de la Guillotine ...
They looked uneasily around them. Perhaps the American
Revolution would be continued through the French, and they,
who had led the way to the overthrow of British aristocratic rule,
would be themselves the next victims of mob hatred.

Had all the patron-saints of scribblers combined together to
perform miracles for his especial advantage, they could hardly
have contrived a more convenient set of circumstances for Cobbett's entry into American political journalism. A Federalist by
conviction he may have been; and he advanced this cause by
flavouring his pamphlets, whenever possible, with the spices of
American parochial political controversy; but a patriot – a British
patriot – he was, and without reserve. He saw it as his patriotic
duty to turn his American neighbours away from any fealty to
France.

During the first years of his residence in the United States
ex-Sergeant-Major Cobbett proved himself more useful than a
couple of infantry divisions. When he began his campaign the
tricolour was flown frequently above the houses of American
citizens; before he left again for England

I lived to see, in the same city of Philadelphia, a public celebration of the feats of England over those of France, and to hear
George III a favourite toast; a change which my friends, certainly
too partial, ascribed *wholly* to my exertions, but to which those
exertions did assuredly greatly contribute.

And, though war between the United States and France was
never declared, Cobbett lived (still in America) for long enough
to see the United States Navy at sea against the French.

Other controversialists played their part: President Washington
himself, the unquestioned and unquestionable Messiah of the
United States, could not tolerate the bestiality of the Terror. The
extravagant follies of French émigrés on behalf of the Revolutionary
cause, and above all the lunacies of Citizen Genet, the French

representative in Philadelphia, disgusted even Thomas Jefferson, who resented Genet's impertinent infringements of diplomatic privilege and of American sovereignty. The American people, too, though many among them sentimentally always inclined to prefer their old ally to their old enemy, were not slow to realise that the Terror, the Directory and the Consulate set the French Revolution out of key with its own proclaimed principles and made it shriekingly discordant with the tones of American national morality.

But, if Cobbett's role was not unique, it was considered so valuable that, acting on the instructions of his government, Sir Robert Liston, the British Minister in Washington, offered him a salary.

Cobbett needed the money but he was too shrewd to accept. He voiced his rejection of Liston's invitation in noble terms: 'When a man hears his country reviled,' he wrote, 'does it require that he should be paid for speaking in its defence?'

Even more symptomatic of his growing importance was a sidling approach from the French, in the person of Talleyrand, then temporarily in Philadelphia. As one accustomed to negotiating with gentlemen, Talleyrand buried the true purpose of the interview in a morass of polite conversation. At one point he asked Cobbett whether he had been educated at Oxford or Cambridge! As well suggest to Cobbett that he had been reared in a brothel as make evident that eloquence such as his must prove a background in one of those 'dens of dunces'.

Hitherto [wrote Cobbett] I had kept my countenance pretty well; but this abominable stretch of hypocrisy, and the placid mien and silver accent with which it was pronounced, would have forced a laugh from a Quaker in the midst of meeting. I don't recollect what reply I made him, but this I recollect well, I gave him to understand that I was no trout, and consequently was not to be caught by tickling.

The contemporary effectiveness of Cobbett's American pamphleteering can be measured by these advances from representatives of the two most powerful nations in the world, the contenders for the affections of the American Government and people, but the potency of his propaganda lay not so much in the force of his arguments as in the manner in which they were presented.

*The Federalist* papers, superb examples of American political journalism in that era, were study-born and generally study-read: Cobbett was seeking a larger constituency, a readership that did not own studies or large libraries, an audience that had not been raised under the tutelage of that brilliant generation of educators, men like Wythe at William and Mary or Witherspoon at Princeton, which had done so much to prepare the way for the leaders of the American Revolution.

Because he was of their sort, Cobbett knew how to approach an intelligent but unintellectual readership. Instinctively, and perhaps also because of his familiarity with 'the Americans' of New Brunswick, he knew how to attract their attention. He was prolific to a degree that was unmatched even in that era of extravagant literary energy, but he was always direct, vehement and, often, explosive. What he believed he said without equivocation and with no thought to the sensitivity of individuals, without respect even for the most sacred cows. He could make a *cause célèbre* out of a whisper and the merest rumour he could turn into a sensational exposé. He ranted, abused, proclaimed as unimpeachable verity what was often no more than personal prejudice or undocumented hearsay, but the simplicity and the force of his writing made it difficult, almost impossible, for honest men to question his integrity, even if they did not always accept his conclusions. His bluntness and his freedom from casuistry appealed to that considerable section in American society which had come to suspect the high tones, the sophistries and the aristocratic pretensions common in American political leaders; and conferred upon his writings a quality acceptable to those many Americans who were seeking a new species of national hero more coarse-grained than the Cocked Hats of Virginia or the Brahmins of Massachusetts.

Cobbett's enthusiasm for firing off volleys of rage did much to make his influence burgeon and to improve the circulation of his pamphlets and journals but it also induced high blood-pressure in his influential targets.

A sardonic reference to the King of Spain might have passed unnoticed in America had not the Spanish Ambassador sued for libel. Cobbett found himself before a judge notorious for his

Anglophobia (who was also soon to be His Excellency's son-in-law). Judge McKean's summation would have persuaded most juries to convict the Archangel Gabriel of rape but this jury honoured itself and American justice by acquitting Cobbett - if only by the slimmest majority. Immediately Cobbett turned on the judge. He excoriated McKean as a numskull, a hired man and a traducer and, not satisfied with his attack on the man's professional competence, went on to reveal all manner of salacious details about his private life.

Then Judge McKean became Governor of Pennsylvania.

It was time for Cobbett to leave. He chose New York, already well-established as the commercial and cultural capital of the United States, and rapidly developing another role that it has never lost, as the centre of American publishing.

But Cobbett could not escape the reach of McKean's vindictiveness. Faced with another suit for libel, taken against him this time by Benjamin Rush, a person much-honoured as doctor and as political worthy, whom Cobbett had savaged, he found himself this time before one of Governor McKean's closest friends. Judge Shippen was a member of a long-established and well-known Philadelphia family, but he was also necessarily and energetically engaged in erasing from American folk-memory his kin's slippery record during the American Revolution. The family home, one of the most elegant in the city, had been a regular haunt of British officers during the occupation, and it was there that the most beautiful and the most notorious of all the Shippens, Edward's daughter Peggy, had met 'the amiable spy' John André, whose death at the end of an American hangman's rope still burdened the conscience of the nation.

Shippen demonstrated his now unflagging patriotism - and repaid his many obligations to McKean - by handing down in the Rush case a verdict so ambiguous and yet so unfriendly that it brought Cobbett once more close to financial ruin. All that remained to him of his Philadelphia property was sequestrated. The sheets of a new collection of his Peter Porcupine works were impounded and sold as waste-paper. Costs in the sum of 3,000 dollars were awarded to the plaintiff and Cobbett was fined an additional 5,000 dollars.

Even so Cobbett might have stayed on in New York, where he had established a newspaper which had achieved already a circulation which came close to matching that of any other American paper. Friends and admirers answered readily an appeal for a public subscription to meet the inequitable charges imposed upon him by Judge Shippen. But he was now less sure than sometimes he pretended of the good-will towards Britain of the Federalists. The new President, John Adams, in particular he mistrusted, both because of his uncertain attitude to America's role in the quarrel between Britain and France and because Adams made no secret of his antipathy for all he classed as brash and plebeian, among them Cobbett. Adams had even talked of having him deported.

Well-wishers suggested that Cobbett could guard himself against this, to that moment the most vicious of all threats to his security, by taking American citizenship but, changeable though he was in matters of opinion, refuge under a foreign passport was inconceivable to the man described by Carlyle as 'the pattern John Bull of his century'. Cobbett left America before Adams could throw him out.

Yet again opportunism informed his decision as much as necessity. Official America thought to rid itself of a malevolent alien; official Britain held its arms wide to embrace a patriotic hero. All memory of the petty offences of Sergeant-Major Cobbett had been mislaid in admiration for the services of Peter Porcupine.

Cobbett's American writings had been reprinted and widely read in Britain almost as soon as they appeared on the far side of the Atlantic. The government, unconvinced by his rejection of Liston's offer, wanted him still as a hired propagandist. No sooner did he reach London than he was dined by Pitt and Canning. Thereafter he was invited to take entire editorial responsibility for the government news-sheet, the *New Briton*.

Cobbett enjoyed the dinner, was flattered by the proposal, and refused the bait. Peter Porcupine must be re-born in England but he did not intend that his quills be blunted by ministerial supervision. Even Cobbett knew himself too well, saw too clearly that his own capacity was in destruction, to believe that he would be of much use as a hired man.

In the next years, and with increasing intensity after Pitt's resignation, Cobbett set about the British political hierarchy with the same vigour which previously he had directed against the leaders of the democrats. The grass in Britain was not as green as he had thought it to be when in exile. As in America so also in Britain there were wrongs to be righted and institutions that needed to be pulled down. No less than their American counterparts the leaders of Britain were arrogant bumblers who must be attacked and, if possible, removed lest their follies undermine the undoubted virtues of the people, lest their blindness lead the nation away from its antique virtues to disaster.

Cobbett's vehemence suited the times. His fame spread and with it, in some quarters, his infamy. His popularity blossomed and, because he chose his enemies well but not wisely, so too did the detestation in which he was held by those he reviled. His career progressed, upwards from 'plough-boy' towards his goal, 'a seat in Parliament'.

He who had been an arch-Tory came to be pre-eminent among the Reformers.

As his stance in British politics shifted so too did his view of his own past. But no experience was ever lost to Cobbett. He did not forget America.

Cobbett's sturdy defence of the propriety of the intervention of the United States in the Napoleonic Wars was yet one more added to the list of his offences against those in power at Westminster, but even to them it was a trifle when compared to all his other misdemeanours. It was not Cobbett's justification of America's alliance with Napoleon which at last brought down upon him the full frenzy of official revenge, but the fact that his fire was coming too close to the fuse under an explosive electorate.

Before the end of the Napoleonic Wars Cobbett had faced and won some libel-suits, faced and lost others but, whether won or lost, court-actions and even imprisonment served but to increase the number of his readers. Hazlitt described him as 'a kind of fourth estate', and, looking back at his influence at this time, Harriet Martineau wrote of him that 'never before had any single writer in England wielded such power'. He owned, edited and wrote a newspaper, the *Political Register*, which had a circulation almost equal to that of *The Times*, a paper which was read not only by those who took *The Times* but also by many who were deaf to the thunder over Printing House Square.

Power so blatant could not be tolerated. The administration

had driven Napoleon into exile on St Helena, now it would force Cobbett into exile in America but it had other and seemingly greater problems on its hands. As Cobbett himself wrote after the signing of the Treaty of Amiens:

The alliterative words, peace and plenty, sound well in a song or make a pretty transparency in the window of an edict; but the things which these harmonious words represent are not always in unison.

Those 'things' were 300,000 demobilised soldiers and sailors, a National Debt amounting to almost two thirds of the country's revenues; an economy long-battered by Napoleon's Berlin Decree and now no longer bolstered by huge orders for the materials of war. To all these causes for discontent Cobbett served as irritant.

Early in 1817, faced by disturbances for which many held Cobbett primarily responsible, the administration suspended *Habeas Corpus*. Undesirables could now be imprisoned without trial, and Cobbett was to the government the least desirable of all Englishmen. He could not be shouted down; there was no one on the Tory side capable of out-writing him. Again an attempt was made to buy him; the price of his silence £10,000 a year. But with the bribe went a threat: Keep quiet or else... !

Angrily Cobbett turned away from temptation, but the threat he heeded. For the second and final time he fled to America.

It was a capitulation entirely out of character, for it is doubtful if the government would or could have made good its threat and, had it done so, Cobbett as martyr must have seen his authority enhanced as indisputable leader of the Radicals. Others of his contemporaries, less obviously public figures than he (for example, Leigh Hunt), had been promoted to hero-status by a vindictive prison sentence. Perhaps even Cobbett was tired after almost thirty years of battle but more likely, in this moment of personal danger Cobbett at last made his choice between the two careers which had always divided his ambition; he settled for farming instead of politics. Certainly it was of all the decisions of his life the most foolish and the one example of inept timing. When, a year later, the Peterloo Massacre aroused even the middle-class to the need for change Cobbett was three thousand miles away and the Radicals an army without a general. The leadership of the Reform crusade fell into the hands of the Whigs, gradualists to a man, and so it was that many of the reforms for which he fought, and which at the moment of his flight seemed so close to achievement, were not implemented until long after his death.

When, little more than a year later, he returned to England he had lost much of his power over British public opinion. Though he came at last to Parliament his career as a Member did not fulfil the promise of the long years of apprenticeship. He was a journalist, not an orator, the niceties of Parliamentary convention were foreign to his nature, he lacked both enthusiasm and capacity for lobby conniving and so, though there stands to the credit of his Westminster record the ground-work for the eventual revision of the Poor Law Acts, most of his interventions in formal political life were ineffectual.

Nor can it be claimed that there was compensation for his failure to seize his chance to build 'Jerusalem in England's green and pleasant land' in any true revival of his previous formidable status in the United States. His sensational career as Peter Porcupine had slipped from American memory. The Americans knew little and cared not at all for the struggles of British Radicals. In the hectic years which separated him from himself when young he had romanticised his earlier existence in American and now he seemed content to perpetuate the idyll created by retrospection.

It is difficult to imagine Cobbett resigning himself to life on a Long Island farm, and indeed his placidity was short-lived. For a few months he indulged two of his great loves – observation of the rural scene and writing – but soon the pastoral palled:

Here are many birds in summer, and some of very beautiful plumage. There are some wild flowers, some English flowers in the best gardens. But generally speaking, they are birds without song, and flowers without smell.

*The Journal of a Year's Residence in the United States* is in many respects a dreary work. Intended primarily as a hand-book for agricultural immigrants, it shows Cobbett still capable of pungency, but the vivacity so characteristic of most of his work is generally absent.

However, whenever in *A Year's Residence* Cobbett revealed his growing restlessness, the old Cobbett returned, his sharpness, his capacity to record in simple, athletic English all that he saw was revived. And, once restlessness became compulsive and Cobbett took to the road to make his rural ride through the Atlantic Seaboard States, there is in *A Year's Residence* not only much that is reminiscent of Cobbett the shrewd journalist but also a foretaste of the greater Cobbett still to come, the author of *Rural Rides*.

In that year Cobbett was deprived of his other two loves. Nancy was in England and he had no platform for political activity.

He was not yet ready to bring Nancy to join him (only one of his sons had accompanied him to America) and, for all his pro-testations of pleasure in the American polity, he was somehow dissatisfied with the United States. This nation had changed; it was no longer possible to believe that the United States would ever become what once he had hoped he could help to make it, the apotheosis of the tradition of Britain. He was, too, disturbed in his conscience. Living in ease on Long Island he looked at himself and saw a deserter, a traitor to the cause of English liberty. His attempt to edit his *Political Register* by correspond-ence across the Atlantic was futile and no salve to his bruised honour.

*Agnosco veteris vestigia flammae.* The ancient spark was blown to flame by home-sickness. This time it was not expedience but a sense of obligation – and a longing for Nancy and family – which set him once more on the ocean, bound for England (reverentially taking with him the bones of his old enemy, Tom Paine).

He lived through almost two more decades of frenetic political and journalistic activity. He settled at Botley in Hampshire and later opened a seed-farm in Kensington. In 1830 he published *Rural Rides* and in 1832 he was elected Member of Parliament for Oldham.

William Cobbett died on 18 June 1835, his age uncertain.

He, the most English of Englishmen, had contributed more than most Americans to American society and from his American experience he had gleaned more than any other of his many contemporaries who visited the United States. There is, in the General Preface to *A Year's Residence*, written at a time when he

*Cobbett returns from America with the bones of Tom Paine,*
*his old enemy*

*A satirical dig at Cobbett's frenetic political career*
*Two illustrations from* The Book of Wonders *by G. Cruikshank*

was a fugitive from Britain, a phrase which can stand as his epitaph, 'I am bound to England for life', but the valediction needs enlargement and that too he himself provided. In 1800, when he was hounded out of the United States, he wrote a paragraph which, more than all his baying and bellowing, measures the depth of his Anglo-Americanism and which, by generalised application, is exegesis of the strange, perverse and unique relationship between the British and the Americans; nation to nation, mutual admiration and mutual suspicion, immediate recognition and immediate incomprehension; but individual to individual, understanding and, above all else, affection:

If no man ever had so many and such malignant foes, no one ever had more friends, and those more kind, more sincere and more faithful ... If the ravages of the city have scared my children in their cradle, those children have, for their father's sake, been soothed and caressed by the affectionate, the gentle, the generous inhabitants of the country, under whose hospitable roofs I have spent some of the happiest days of my life.

*PRELUDE:*
*YOUTH RECALLED*

*(1763?-1784)*

# YOUTH RECALLED

---

To be descended from an illustrious family certainly reflects honour on any man, in spite of the *sans-culotte* principles of the present day. This is, however, an honour that I have no pretensions to. All that I can boast of in my birth is, that I was born in Old England; the country from whence came the men who explored and settled North America; the country of Penn, and of all those to whom this country is indebted.

With respect to my ancestors, I shall go no further back than my grandfather, and for this plain reason, that I never heard talk of any prior to him. He was a day-labourer; and I have heard my father say, that he worked for one farmer from the day of his marriage to that of his death, upwards of forty years. He died before I was born, but I have often slept beneath the same roof that had sheltered him, and where his widow dwelt for several years after his death. It was a little thatched cottage, with a garden before the door. It had but two windows; a damson tree shaded one, and a clump of filberts the other. Here I and my brothers went every Christmas and Whitsuntide to spend a week or two, and torment the poor old woman with our noise and dilapidations. She used to give us milk and bread for breakfast, an apple pudding for our dinner, and a piece of bread and cheese for supper. Her fire was made of turf, cut from the neighbouring heath, and her evening light was a rush dipped in grease.

How much better is it, thus to tell the naked truth, than to descend to such miserable shifts as Doctor Franklin has had recourse to, in order to persuade people that his forefathers were men of wealth and consideration. Not being able to refer his reader to the herald's office for proofs of the fame and antiquity

of his family, he appeals to the etymology of his name, and points
out a passage in an obsolete book, whence he has the conscience
to insist on our concluding, that, in the Old English language, a
*Franklin* meant a man of *good reputation and of consequence.*
According to Dr Johnson, a Franklin was what we now call a
gentleman's steward or land-bailiff, a personage one degree above
a bumbailiff, and that's all.

Everyone will, I hope, have the goodness to believe, that my
grandfather was no philosopher. Indeed he was not. He never
made a lightning-rod, nor bottled up a single quart of sunshine,
in the whole course of his life. He was no almanack-maker, nor
quack, nor chimney-doctor, nor soap-boiler, nor ambassador, nor
printer's devil: neither was he a deist, and all his children were
born in wedlock. The legacies he left, were, his scythe, his
reap-hook, and his flail; he bequeathed no old and irrecoverable
debts to an hospital: he never *cheated the poor during his life*, nor
*mocked them in his death.* He has, it is true, been suffered to sleep
quietly beneath the green sord; but, if his descendants cannot
point to his statue over the door of a library, they have not the
mortification to hear him daily accused of having been a whore-
master, a hypocrite, and an infidel.

My father, when I was born, was a farmer. The reader will
easily believe, from the poverty of his parents, that he had received no very brilliant education: he was, however, learned, for
a man in his rank of life. When a little boy, he drove plough for
two pence a day; and these his earnings, were appropriated to the
expenses of an evening school. What a village school-master could
be expected to teach, he had learnt; and had, besides, considerably improved himself, in several branches of the mathematics.
He understood land-surveying well, and was often chosen to draw
the plans of disputed territory: in short, he had the reputation of
possessing experience and understanding, which never fails, in
England, to give a man in a country place, some little weight
with his neighbours. He was honest, industrious, and frugal; it
was not, therefore, wonderful, that he should be situated in a
good farm, and happy in a wife of his own rank, like him,
beloved and respected.

So much for my ancestors, from whom, if I derive no
honour, I derive no shame.

I had (and I hope I yet have) three brothers: the eldest is a shopkeeper; the second a farmer, and the youngest, if alive, is in the service of the Honourable East India Company, a private soldier, perhaps, as I have been in the service of the king. I was born on the 9th of March, 1766: the exact age of my brothers, I have forgotten; but I remember having heard my mother say, that there was but three years and three quarters difference between the age of the oldest and that of the youngest.

A father like ours, it will be readily supposed, did not suffer us to eat the bread of idleness. I do not remember the time, when I did not earn my living. My first occupation was, driving the small birds from the turnip-seed, and the rooks from the peas. When I first trudged a-field, with my wooden bottle and my satchel swung over my shoulders, I was hardly able to climb the gates and stiles; and, at the close of the day, to reach home, was a task of infinite difficulty. My next employment was weeding wheat, and leading a single horse at harrowing barley. Hoeing peas followed, and hence, I arrived at the honour of joining the reapers in harvest, driving the team, and holding plough. We were all of us strong and laborious, and my father used to boast, that he had four boys, the eldest of whom was but fifteen years old, who did as much work as any three men in the parish of Farnham. Honest pride, and happy days!

I have some faint recollection of going to school to an old woman, who, I believe, did not succeed in learning me my letters. In the winter evenings, my father learnt us all to read and write, and gave us a pretty tolerable knowledge of arithmetic. Grammar he did not perfectly understand himself, and therefore his endeavours to learn us that, necessarily failed; for, though he thought he understood it, and though he made us get the rules by heart, we learnt nothing at all of the principles.

Our religion was that of the Church of England, to which I have ever remained attached; the more so, perhaps, as it bears the name of my country. As my ancestors were never persecuted for their religious opinions, they never had an opportunity of giving such a singular proof of their faith, as Doctor Franklin's grandfather did, when' he kept his Bible under the lid of a close-stool. (What a book-case!) If I had been in the place of Doctor Franklin, I never would have related this ridiculous circumstance, especially as it must be construed into a boast of his grandfather's having an extraordinary degree of veneration for a book, which, it is well known, he himself *durst* not believe in.

As to politics, we were like the rest of the country people in England; that is to say, we neither knew nor thought anything about the matter. The shouts of victory, or the murmurs at a defeat, would now and then break in upon our tranquillity for a moment; but I do not remember ever having seen a newspaper in the house; and, most certainly, that privation did not render us less industrious, happy, or free.

After, however, the American war had continued for some time, and the cause and nature of it began to be understood, or rather misunderstood, by the lower classes of the people in England, we became a little better acquainted with subjects of this kind. It is well known, that the people were, as to numbers, nearly equally divided in their opinions, concerning that war, and their wishes respecting the result of it. My father was a partizan of the Americans: he used frequently to dispute on the subject, with the gardener of a nobleman who lived near us. This was generally done with good humour, over a pot of our best ale; yet the disputants sometimes grew warm, and gave way to language that could not fail to attract our attention. My father was worsted, without doubt, as he had for antagonist, a shrewd and sensible old Scotchman, far his superior in political knowledge; but he pleaded before a partial audience: we thought there was but one wise man in the world, and that that one was our father. He who pleaded the cause of the Americans, had an advantage, too, with young minds: he had only to represent the king's troops as sent to cut the throats of a people, our friends and relations, merely because they would not submit to oppression; and his cause was gained. Speaking to the passions, is ever sure to succeed on the uninformed.

Men of integrity are generally pretty obstinate, in adhering to an opinion once adopted. Whether it was owing to this, or to the weakness of Mr Martin's arguments, I will not pretend to say; but he never could make a convert of my father: he continued an American, and so staunch a one, that he would not have suffered his best friend to drink success to the king's arms at his table. I cannot give the reader a better idea of his obstinacy in this respect, and of the length to which this difference in sentiment was carried in England, than by relating the following instance.

My father used to take one of us with him every year, to the great hop-fair at Wey Hill. The fair was held at Old Michaelmas-tide, and the journey was, to us, a sort of reward for the labours of the summer. It happened to be my turn to go thither, the very year that Long Island was taken by the British. A great company of hop-merchants and farmers were just sitting down to supper as the post arrived, bringing in the *Extraordinary Gazette*, which announced the victory. A hop-factor from London took the paper, placed his chair upon the table, and began to read with an audible voice. He was opposed, a dispute ensued, and my father retired, taking me by the hand, to another apartment, where we supped with about a dozen others of the same sentiments. Here Washington's health, and success to the Americans, were repeatedly toasted, and this was the first time, as far as I can recollect, that I ever heard the general's name mentioned. Little did I then dream, that I should ever see the man, and still less, that I should hear some of his own countrymen reviling and execrating him.

Let not the reader imagine, that I wish to assume any merit from this mistaken prejudice of an honoured and beloved parent. Whether he was right or wrong, is not now worth talking about: that I had no opinion of my own is certain; for, had my father been on the other side, I should have been on the other side too; and should have looked upon the company I then made a part of as malcontents and rebels. I mention these circumstances, merely to show that I was not 'nursed in the lap of aristocracy', and that I did not imbibe my principles, or prejudices, from those who were the advocates of blind submission. If my father had any fault, it was not being submissive enough, and I am much afraid, my acquaintance have but too often discovered the same fault in his son.

It would be as useless as unentertaining, to dwell on the occupations and sports of a country boy; to lead the reader to fairs, cricket-matches, and hare-hunts. I shall therefore come at once to the epoch, when an accident happened, that gave that turn to my future life, which at last brought me to the United States.

Towards the autumn of 1782, I went to visit a relation who

lived in the neighbourhood of Portsmouth. From the top of Portsdown, I, for the first time, beheld the sea, and no sooner did I behold it, than I wished to be a sailor. I could never account for this sudden impulse, nor can I now. Almost all English boys feel the same inclination: it would seem that, like young ducks, instinct leads them to rush on the bosom of the water.

But it was not the sea alone that I saw: the grand fleet was riding at anchor at Spithead. I had heard of the wooden walls of Old England: I had formed my ideas of a ship, and of a fleet; but, what I now beheld, so far surpassed what I had ever been able to form a conception of, that I stood lost between astonishment and admiration. I had heard talk of the glorious deeds of our admirals and sailors, of the defeat of the Spanish Armada, and of all those memorable combats, that good and true Englishmen never fail to relate to their children about a hundred times a year. The brave Rodney's victories over our natural enemies, the French and Spaniards, had long been the theme of our praise, and the burden of our songs. The sight of the fleet brought all these into my mind; in confused order, it is true, but with irresistible force. My heart was inflated with national pride. The sailors were my countrymen; the fleet belonged to my country, and surely I had my part in it, and in all its honours; yet, these honours I had not earned; I took to myself a sort of reproach, for possessing what I had no right to, and resolved to have a just claim by sharing in the hardships and dangers.

I arrived at my uncle's late in the evening, with my mind full of my sea-faring project. Though I had walked thirty miles during the day, and consequently was well wearied, I slept not a moment. It was no sooner day-light, than I arose and walked down towards the old castle, on the beach of Spithead. For a sixpence given to an invalid, I got permission to go upon the battlements; here I had a closer view of the fleet, and at every look my impatience to be on board increased. In short, I went from the castle to Portsmouth, got into a boat, and was in a few minutes on board the *Pegasus* man-of-war.

The captain had more compassion than is generally met with in men of his profession: he represented to me the toils I must undergo, and the punishment that the least disobedience or neglect would subject me to. He persuaded me to return home, and towards me at a merry rate. The notion of going to London, never entered my mind, till this very moment, yet the step was completely determined on, before the coach came to the spot where I stood. Up I got, and was in London about nine o'clock in the evening.

It was by mere accident, that I had money enough to defray the expenses of this day. Being rigged out for the fair, I had three or four crown and half-crown pieces (which most certainly I did not intend to spend), besides a few shillings and half-pence. This, my little all, which I had been years in amassing, melted away, like snow before the sun, when touched by the fingers of the innkeepers and their waiters. In short, when I arrived at Ludgate Hill, and had paid my fare, I had but about half a crown in my pocket.

By a commencement of that good luck, which has hitherto attended me, through all the situations in which fortune has placed me, I was preserved from ruin. A gentleman, who was one of the passengers in the stage, fell into conversation with me at dinner, and he soon learnt that I was going, I knew not whither, nor for what. This gentleman was a hop-merchant in the borough of Southwark, and, upon closer inquiry, it appeared that he had often dealt with my father at Wey Hill. He knew the danger I was in; he was himself a father, and he felt for my parents. His house became my home; he wrote to my father, and endeavoured to prevail on me to obey his orders, which were to return immediately home. I am ashamed to say that I was disobedient. It was the first time I had ever been so, and I have repented of it from that moment to this. Willingly would I have returned; but pride would not suffer me to do it. I feared the scoffs of my acquaintances more than the real evils that threatened me.

My generous preserver, finding my obstinacy not to be overcome, began to look out for an employment for me. He was preparing an advertisement for the newspaper, when an acquaintance of his, an attorney, called in to see him. He related my adventure to this gentleman, whose name was Holland, and who, happening to want an understrapping quill-driver, did me the honour to take me into his service, and the next day saw me perched upon a great high stool, in an obscure chamber in Gray's Inn, endeavouring to decipher the crabbed draughts of my employer.

I could write a good plain hand, but I could not read the pot-hooks and hangers of Mr Holland. He was a month in learn-ing me to copy without almost continual assistance, and even then I was of but little use to him; for, besides that I wrote a snail's pace, my want of knowledge in orthography, gave him infinite trouble: so that, for the first two months, I was a dead weight upon his hands. Time, however, rendered me useful; and Mr Holland was pleased to tell me, that he was very well satis-fied with me, just at the very moment when I began to grow extremely dissatisfied with him.

No part of my life has been totally unattended with pleasure, except the eight or nine months I passed in Gray's Inn. The office (for so the dungeon where I wrote was called) was so dark, that, on cloudy days, we were obliged to burn candle. I worked like a galley-slave from five in the morning till eight or nine at night, and sometimes all night long. How many quarrels have I assisted to foment and perpetuate between those poor innocent fellows, John Doe and Richard Roe! How many times (God forgive me!) have I sent them to assault each other with guns, swords, staves and pitchforks, and then brought them to answer for their misdeeds before our Sovereign Lord the King seated in His Court of Westminster! When I think of the *saids* and *soforths*, and the counts of tautology that I scribbled over; when I think of those sheets of seventy-two words, and those lines two inches apart, my brain turns. Gracious heaven! if I am doomed to be wretched, bury me beneath Iceland snows, and let me feed on blubber; stretch me under the burning line, and deny me thy propitious dews; nay, if it be thy will, suffocate me with the infected and pestilential air of a democratic club-room; but save me from the desk of an attorney!

Mr Holland was but little in the chambers himself. He always went out to dinner, while I was left to be provided for by the *laundress*, as he called her. Those gentlemen of the law, who have resided in the Inns of Court in London, know very well what a *laundress* means. Ours was, I believe, the oldest and ugliest of the sisterhood. She had age and experience enough to be Lady Ab-bess of all the nuns in all the convents of Irish Town. It would be wronging the witch of Endor to compare her to this hag, who was the only creature that deigned to enter into conversation with me. All except the name, I was in prison, and this weird sister was my keeper. Our chambers were, to me, what the subterraneous cavern was to Gil Blas: his description of the Dame Leonarda exactly suited my laundress; nor were the professions, or rather the practice, of our masters altogether dissimilar.

I never quitted this gloomy recess except on Sundays, when I usually took a walk to St James's Park, to feast my eyes with the sight of the trees, the grass, and the water. In one of these walks I happened to cast my eye on an advertisement, inciting all loyal young men, who had a mind to gain riches and glory, to repair to a certain rendezvous, where they might enter into His Majesty's marine service, and have the peculiar happiness and honour of being enrolled in the Chatham Division. I was not ignorant enough to be the dupe of this morsel of military bombast; but a change was what I wanted: besides, I knew that marines went to sea, and my desire to be on that element had rather increased than diminished by my being penned up in London. In short, I resolved to join this glorious corps; and, to avoid all possibility of being discovered by my friends, I went down to Chatham and enlisted, into the marines as I thought, but the next morning I found myself before a captain of a marching regiment. There was no retreating: I had taken a shilling to drink His Majesty's health, and his further bounty was ready for my reception.

When I told the captain (who was an Irishman, and who has since been an excellent friend to me) that I thought myself engaged in the marines: 'By Jasus! my lad,' said he, 'and you have had a narrow escape.' He told me, that the regiment into which I had been so happy as to enlist, was one of the oldest and boldest in the whole army, and that it was at that moment serving in that fine, flourishing, and plentiful country, Nova Scotia. He dwelt long on the beauties and riches of this terrestrial paradise, and dismissed me, perfectly enchanted with the prospect of a voyage thither.

I enlisted early in 1784, and, as peace had then taken place, no great haste was made to send recruits off to their regiments. I remained upwards of a year at Chatham, during which time I was employed in learning my exercise, and taking my tour in the duty of the garrison. My leisure time, which was a very considerable portion of the twenty-four hours, was spent, not in the dissipations common to such a way of life, but in reading and study. In the course of this year I learnt more than I had ever done before. I subscribed to a circulating library at Brompton, the greatest part of the books in which I read more than once over. The library was not very considerable, it is true, nor in my reading was I directed by any degree of taste or choice. Novels, plays, history, poetry, all were read, and nearly with equal avidity.

Such a course of reading could be attended with but little profit: it was skimming over the surface of everything. One branch of learning, however, I went to the bottom with, and that the most essential branch too, the grammar of my mother tongue. I had experienced the want of a knowledge of grammar during my stay with Mr Holland; but it is very probable that I never should have thought of encountering the study of it, had not accident placed me under a man whose friendship extended beyond his interest. Writing a fair hand procured me the honour of being copyist to Colonel Debeig, the commandant of the garrison. I transcribed the famous correspondence between him and the Duke of Richmond, which ended in the good and gallant old colonel being stripped of the reward, bestowed on him for his long and meritorious servitude.

Being totally ignorant of the rules of grammar, I necessarily made many mistakes in copying, because no one can copy letter by letter, nor even word by word. The colonel saw my deficiency, and strongly recommended study. He enforced his advice with a sort of injunction, and with a promise of reward in case of success.

I procured me a Lowth's grammar, and applied myself to the study of it with unceasing assiduity, and not without some profit; for, though it was a considerable time before I fully comprehended all that I read, still I read and studied with such unremitted attention, that, at last, I could write without falling into any very gross errors. The pains I took cannot be described: I wrote the whole grammar out two or three times; I got it by heart; I repeated it every morning and every evening, and, when on guard, I imposed on myself the task of saying it all over once every time I was posted sentinel. To this exercise of my memory I ascribe the retentiveness of which I have since found it capable, and to the success with which it was attended, I ascribe the perseverance that has led to the acquirement of the little learning of which I am master.

This study was, too, attended with another advantage: it kept me out of mischief. I was always sober, and regular in my attendance; and, not being a clumsy fellow, I met with none of those reproofs, which disgust so many young men with the service.

# COBBETT IN CANADA
## (*1784-1791*)

# SERGEANT-MAJOR COBBETT

As promotion began to dawn, I grew impatient to get to my regiment, where I expected soon to bask under the rays of royal favour. The happy day of departure at last came: we set sail from Gravesend, and, after a short and pleasant passage, arrived at Halifax in Nova Scotia. When I first beheld the barren, not to say hideous, rocks at the entrance of the harbour, I began to fear that the master of the vessel had mistaken his way; for I could perceive nothing of that fertility that my good recruiting captain had dwelt on with so much delight.

Nova Scotia had no other charm for me than that of novelty. Everything I saw was new: bogs, rocks and stumps, musquitoes and bull-frogs. Thousands of captains and colonels without soldiers, and of squires without stockings or shoes. In England, I had never thought of approaching a squire without a most respectful bow: but, in this new world, though I was but a corporal, I often ordered a squire to bring me a glass of grog, and even to take care of my knapsack.

We staid but a few weeks in Nova Scotia, being ordered to St John's, in the province of New Brunswick. Here, and at other places in the same province, we remained till the month of September, 1791, when the regiment was relieved and sent home.

There is no situation where merit is so sure to meet with reward as in a well-disciplined army. Those who command are obliged to reward it for their own ease and credit. I was soon raised to the rank of corporal, a rank which, however contemptible it may appear in some people's eyes, brought me in a clear twopence *per diem*, and put a very clever worsted knot upon my shoulder too.

In a very short time, the whole of the business, in that way, fell into my hands; and at the end of about a year, neither adjutant, paymaster, or quartermaster, could move an inch without my assistance. The accounts and letters of the paymaster went through my hands; or, rather, I was the maker of them. All the returns, reports, and other official papers were of my drawing-up.

The *military* part of the regiment affairs fell under my care in like manner. About this time [1788] the new *discipline*, as it was called; that is to say, the mode of handling the musket, and of marching, etc., called '*Dundas's System*', was sent out to us, in little books, which were to be studied by the officers of each regiment, and the rules of which were to be immediately conformed to. Though any old woman might have written such a book; though it was excessively foolish from beginning to end; still, it was to be complied with; it ordered and commanded a *total change*, and this change was to be completed before the next annual review took place. To make this change was left to me, who was not then twenty years of age, while not a single officer in the regiment paid the least attention to the matter; so that when the time came for the annual review, I, then a *corporal*, had to give lectures of instruction to the officers themselves, the colonel not excepted; and, for several of them, if not for all of them, I had to make out, upon large cards, which they bought for the purpose, little plans of the position of the regiment, together with lists of the words of command, which they had to give in the field. There was I, at the review, upon the flank of the Grenadier Company, with my worsted shoulder-knot, and my great, high, coarse, hairy cap; confounded in the ranks amongst other men, while those who were commanding me to move my hands or my feet, thus or thus, were, in fact, uttering words which I had taught them; and were, in everything excepting mere authority, my inferiors; and ought to have been commanded by me. It was impossible for reflections of this sort not to intrude themselves; and, as I advanced in experience, I felt less and less respect for those whom I was compelled to obey.

I remember a set of *commissioners* being sent out from England, a part of whose business it was to make a statement and report of the population, etc., etc., of the provinces. They lived about our quarters for some time; they had some jovial carousings with our officers; but *it was I* who made out their statement, and *drew*

*The north aspect of Halifax, Nova Scotia, scene of Cobbett's first few weeks in Canada*

*Fredericton, New Brunswick, one of the postings for Cobbett's regiment*

*up their report* to be sent home to the king; for which, by the by, they never even gave me their thanks. This statement, which, as was the case with everything that I meddled with, was done in so clear, correct, and, in point of penmanship, so beautiful a manner, that, I have been told, the Duke of Kent, when he afterwards became commander-in-chief of those provinces, had it copied, and took away the original as a curiosity. This was the way in which I did everything. I was, of course, very much envied and hated by the weak and the wicked, and, as was natural to expect, I did not, amongst people whom, though my superiors in rank, I could not help despising, bear myself with much moderation. From nineteen to twenty-seven is not much of an age for moderation, especially with those who must necessarily despise all around them.

But, I had a very delicate part to act with those gentry; for, while I despised them for their gross ignorance and their vanity, and hated them for their drunkenness and rapacity, I was fully sensible of their power. My path was full of rocks and pitfalls; and, as I never disguised my dislikes, or restrained my tongue, I should have been broken and flogged for fifty different offences, had they not been kept in awe by my inflexible sobriety, impartiality, and integrity, by the consciousness of their inferiority to me, and by the real and almost indispensable necessity of the use of my talents. They, in fact, resigned all the discipline of the regiment to me, and I very freely left them to swagger about and to get roaring drunk.

To describe the various instances of their ignorance, and the various tricks they played to disguise it from me, would fill a volume. It is the custom in regiments to give out orders every day from the officer commanding. These are written by the adjutant, to whom the sergeant-major is a sort of deputy. The man whom I had to do with was a keen fellow, but wholly illiterate. The orders, which he wrote, most cruelly murdered our mother-tongue. But, in his absence, or, during a severe drunken fit, it fell to my lot to write orders. As we both wrote in the same book, he used to look at these. He saw commas, semi-colons, colons, full points, and paragraphs. The questions he used to put to me, in an obscure sort of way, in order to know why I made these divisions, and yet, at the same time, his attempts to disguise his object, have made me laugh a thousand times. He, at last, fell upon this device: he made me write, while he pretended to dictate! Imagine to yourself, me sitting, pen in hand, to put upon paper the precious offspring of the mind of this stupid curmudgeon! But, here, a greater difficulty than any former arose. He that could not write good grammar, could not, of course, dictate good grammar. Out would come some gross error, such as I was ashamed to see in my handwriting. I would stop; suggest another arrangement; but, this I was, at first, obliged to do in a very indirect and delicate manner. But, this course could not continue long; and he put an end to it in this way; he used to tell me his story, and leave me to put it upon paper; and this we continued to the end of our connection.

But the fame of my services and talents ran through the whole country. Every good man respected me. I was invited to visit people in all parts of the provinces. While we lay at Frederickton in New Brunswick, I had the settling, or rather the preventing, of eight or nine law-suits. I had the affairs of a whole regiment to attend to; all its accounts, its parades, its guards, its everything. I found, however, time for studying English and French grammar; I learnt geometry and fortifications; I built a barrack for four hundred men, without the aid of either draughtsman, carpenter, or bricklayer; the soldiers under me cut down the timber and dug the stones, and I was the architect; I went through a track of woods, of about a hundred miles, where no man had ever ventured before to go alone; and this I did for the purpose of putting a stop to desertion, by showing the regiment that I *myself* was able to follow the fugitives, and, accordingly, after that we had no more desertions to the United States. With all these occupations (of which I mention only a few particulars that occur to me at the moment) I found time for skating, fishing, shooting, and all the other sports of the country, of which, when I left it, I had seen, and knew, more than any other man.

*Toujours prêt* was the motto of a famous French general; and pray, let it be yours: be *always ready*; and never, during your whole life, have to say, '*I cannot go till I be shaved and dressed.*' Do the whole at once for the day, whatever may be your state of life; and then you have a day unbroken by those indispensable performances. Begin thus, in the days of your youth, and, having felt the superiority which this practice will give you over those in all other respects your equals, the practice will stick by you to the end of your life. Till you be shaved and dressed for the day, you cannot set steadily about any business; you know that you must presently quit your labour to return to the dressing affair; you, therefore, put it off until that be over; the interval, the precious interval, is spent in lounging about; and, by the time that you are ready for business, the best part of the day is gone.

Trifling as this matter appears upon *naming* it, it is, in fact, one of the great concerns of life; and, for my part, I can truly say, that I owe more of my great labours to my strict adherence to the precepts that I have here given you, than to all the natural abilities with which I have been endowed; for these, whatever may have been their amount, would have been of comparatively little use, even aided by great sobriety and abstinence, if I had not, in early life, contracted the blessed habit of husbanding well my time. To this, more than to any other thing, I owed my very extraordinary promotion in the army. I was *always ready*: if I had to mount guard at *ten*, I was ready at *nine*: never did any man, or any thing, wait one moment for me. Being, at an age *under twenty years*, raised from corporal to sergeant major *at once*, over the heads of thirty sergeants, I naturally should have been an object of envy and hatred; but this habit of early rising and of rigid adherence to the precepts which I have given you, really subdued these passions; because every one felt, that what I did he had never done, and never could do. Before my promotion, a clerk was wanted to make out the morning report of the regiment. I rendered the clerk unnecessary; and, long before any other man was dressed for the parade, my work for the morning was all done, and I myself was on the parade, walking, in fine weather, for an hour perhaps. My custom was this: to get up, in summer, at day-light, and in winter at four o'clock, shave, dress, even to the putting of my sword-belt over my shoulder, and having my sword lying on the table before me, ready to hang by my side. Then I ate a bit of cheese, or pork, and bread. Then I prepared my report, which was filled up as fast as the companies brought me in the materials. After this I had an hour or two to read, before the time came for any duty out of doors, unless when the regiment or part of it went out to exercise in the morning. When this was the case, and the matter was left to me, I always had it on the ground in such time as that the bayonets glistened in the *rising sun*, a sight which gave me delight, of which I often think, but which I should in vain endeavour to describe. If the *officers* were to go out, eight or ten o'clock was the hour, sweating the men in the heat of the day, breaking in upon the time for cooking their dinner, putting all things out of order, and all men out of humour. When I was commander, the men had a long day of leisure before them: they could ramble into the town or into the woods; go to get raspberries, to catch birds, to catch fish, or to pursue any other recreation, and such of them as chose, and were qualified, to work at their trades. So that here, arising solely from the early habits of one very young man, were pleasant and happy days given to hundreds.

Then I became sergeant-major to the regiment, which brought me in close contact at every hour, with the whole of the epaulet gentry, whose profound and surprising ignorance I discovered in a twinkling. The military part of the regiment's affairs fell under my care.

In my regiment I was everything; the whole corps was under my control; I rendered services, not only in the regiment, but in the provinces where we were stationed, such as no one but myself would have thought of.

# COURTSHIP AND MARRIAGE

By the word SOBRIETY, in a young woman, I mean a great deal more than even a rigid abstinence from that love of *drink*, which I am not to suppose, and which I do not believe, to exist anything like generally amongst the young women of this country. I mean a great deal more than this; I mean *sobriety of conduct*. The word *sober*, and its derivatives, do not confine themselves to matters of *drink*: they express *steadiness, seriousness, carefulness, scrupulous propriety of conduct*; and they are thus used amongst country people in many parts of England. When a Somersetshire fellow makes too free with a girl, she reproves him with, 'Come! be *sober!*' And when we wish a team, or anything, to be moved on *steadily* and with *great care*, we cry out to the carter, or other operator, '*Soberly, soberly.*' Now, this species of sobriety is a great qualification in the person you mean to make your wife. Skipping, capering, romping, rattling girls are very amusing where all costs and other consequences are out of the question; and they *may* become *sober* in the Somersetshire sense of the word. But while you have *no certainty* of this, you have a presumptive argument on the other side. To be sure, when girls are *mere children*, they are to play and romp like children. But, when they arrive at that age which turns their thoughts towards that sort of connexion which is to be theirs for life; when they begin to think of having the command of a house, however small or poor, it is time for them to cast away the levity of the child. It is natural, nor is it very wrong, that I know of, for children to like to gad about and to see all sorts of strange sights, though I do not approve of this even in children: but, if I could not have found a *young woman* (and I am sure I never should have married an *old* one) who I was not *sure* possessed *all* the qualities expressed by the word sobriety, I should have remained a bachelor to the end of that life, which, in that case, would, I am satisfied, have terminated without my having performed a thousandth part of those labours which have been, and are, in spite of all political prejudice, the wonder of all who have seen, or heard of, them. Scores of gentlemen have, at different times, expressed to me their surprise, that I was *always in spirits*; that nothing *pulled me down*; and the truth is, that, throughout nearly forty years of troubles, losses, and crosses, assailed all the while by more numerous and powerful enemies than ever man had before to contend with, and performing, at the same time, labours greater than man ever before performed; all those labours requiring mental exertion, and some of them mental exertion of the highest order; the truth is, that, throughout the whole of this long time of troubles and of labours, I have never known a single hour of *real anxiety*; the troubles have been no troubles to me; I have not known what *lowness of spirits* meaned; have been more gay, and felt less care, than any bachelor that ever lived. 'You are *always in spirits*, Cobbett!' To be sure; for why should I not? *Poverty* I have always set at defiance, and I could, therefore, defy the temptations of riches; and, as to *home* and *children*, I had taken care to provide myself with an inexhaustible store of that *sobriety*, which I am so strongly recommending my reader to provide himself with; or, if he cannot do that, to deliberate long before he ventures on the life-enduring matrimonial voyage. This sobriety is a title to *trustworthiness*; and *this*, young man, is the treasure that you ought to prize far above all others. Miserable is the husband, who, when he crosses the threshold of his house, carries with him doubts and fears and suspicions. I do not mean suspicions of the *fidelity* of his wife, but of her care, frugality, attention to his interests, and to the health and morals of his children. Miserable is the man, who cannot leave *all unlocked*, and who is not *sure*, quite certain, that all is as safe as if grasped in his own hand. He is the happy husband, who can go away, at a moment's warning, leaving his house and his family with as little anxiety as he quits an inn, not more fearing to find, on his return, anything wrong, than he would fear a discontinuance of the rising and setting of the sun, and if, as in my case, leaving books and papers all lying about at sixes and sevens, finding them arranged in proper order, and the room, during the lucky interval, freed from the effects of his and his ploughman's or gardener's dirty shoes. Such a man has no *real cares*; such a man has *no troubles*; and this is the sort of life that I have led. I have had all the numerous and indescribable delights of home and children, and, at the same time, all the bachelor's freedom from domestic cares; and, to this cause, far more than to any other, my readers owe those labours, which I never could have performed, if even the slightest degree of want of confidence at home had ever once entered into my mind.

But, in order to possess this precious *trustworthiness*, you must, if you can, exercise your *reason* in the choice of your partner. If she be vain of her person, very fond of dress, fond of *flattery* at all, given to gadding about, fond of what are called *parties of pleasures*, or coquetish, though in the least degree; if either of these, she never will be trustworthy: she cannot change her nature; and, if you marry her, you will be *unjust* if you expect trustworthiness at her hands. But, besides this, even if you find in her that innate *sobriety*, of which I have been speaking, there requires, on your part, and that at once too, confidence and trust without any limit. Confidence is, in this case, nothing unless it be reciprocal. To have a trustworthy wife, you must begin by showing her, even before you are married, that you have no suspicions, no fears, no doubts, with regard to her. Many a man has been discarded by a virtuous girl, merely on account of his querulous conduct. All women despise jealous men; and, if they marry such, their motive is other than that of affection. Therefore, *begin* by proofs of unlimited confidence; and, as *example* may serve to assist precept, and as I never have preached that which I have not practised, I will give you the history of my own conduct in this respect.

When I first saw my wife, she was *thirteen years old*, and I was within about a month of *twenty-one*. She was the daughter of a sergeant of artillery, and I was the sergeant-major of a regiment of Foot, both stationed in forts near the city of St John, in the province of New Brunswick. I sat in the same room with her, for about an hour, in company with others, and I made up my mind that she was the very girl for me. That I thought her beautiful is certain, for that I had always said should be an indispensable qualification; but I saw in her what I deemed marks of that *sobriety of conduct* of which I have said so much, and which has been by far the greatest blessing of my life. It was now dead of winter, and, of course, the snow several feet deep on the ground, and the weather piercing cold. It was my habit, when I had done my morning's writing, to go out at break of day to take a walk on a hill at the foot of which our barracks lay. In about three mornings after I had first seen her, I had, by an invitation to breakfast with me, got up two young men to join me in my walk; and our road lay by the house of her father and mother. It was hardly light, but she was out on the snow, scrubbing out a washing-tub. 'That's the girl for me,' said I, when we had got out of her hearing. One of these young men came to England soon afterwards; and he, who keeps an inn in Yorkshire, came over to Preston, at the time of the election, to verify whether I were the same man. When he found that I was, he appeared surprised; but what was his surprise, when I told him that those tall young men, whom he saw around me, were the *sons* of that pretty little girl that he and I saw scrubbing out the washing-tub on the snow in New Brunswick at daybreak in the morning!

From the day that I first spoke to her, I never had a thought of her ever being the wife of any other man more than I had a thought of her being transformed into a chest of drawers; and I formed my resolution at once to marry her as soon as we could get permission, and to get out of the army as soon as I could. So that this matter was, at once, settled as firmly as if written in the book of fate. At the end of about six months my regiment, and I along with it, were removed to Frederickton, a distance of a *hundred miles* up the river of St John; and, which was worse, the artillery was expected to go off to England a year or two before our regiment! The artillery went, and she along with them; and now it was that I acted a part becoming a real and sensible lover. I was aware that, when she got to that gay place Woolwich, the house of her father and mother, necessarily visited by numerous persons not the most select, might become unpleasant to her, and I did not like, besides, that she should continue to *work hard*. I had saved a *hundred and fifty guineas*, the earnings of my early hours, in writing for the paymaster, the quartermaster, and others, in addition to the savings of my own pay. *I sent her all my money* before she sailed; and wrote to her to beg of her, if she found her home uncomfortable, to hire a lodging with respectable people: and, at any rate, not to spare the money, by any means, but to buy herself good clothes, and to live without hard work, until I arrived in England; and I, in order to induce her to lay out the money, told her that I should get plenty more before I came home.

As the malignity of the devil would have it, we kept abroad *two years longer* than our time, Mr Pitt (England not being so tame then as she is now) having knocked up a dust with Spain about Nootka Sound. Oh, how I cursed Nootka Sound, and poor bawling Pitt too, I am afraid! At the end of *four years*, however, home I came, landed at Portsmouth, and got my discharge from the army by the great kindness of poor Lord Edward Fitzgerald, who was then the major of my regiment. I found my little girl *a servant of all work* (and hard work it was), *at five pounds a year*, in the house of a Captain Brisac; and, without hardly saying a word about the matter, she put into my hands *the whole of my hundred and fifty guineas unbroken!*

Need I tell the reader what my feelings were? Need I tell kind-hearted English parents what effect this anecdote *must* have produced on the minds of our children? Need I attempt to describe what effect this example ought to have on every young woman who shall do me the honour to read this book? Admiration of her conduct, and self-gratulation on this indubitable proof of the soundness of my own judgment were now added to my love of her beautiful person.

Now, I do not say that there are not many young women of this country who would, under similar circumstances, have acted as my wife did in this case; on the contrary, I hope, and do sincerely believe, that there are. But when *her age* is considered; when we reflect, that she was living in a place crowded, literally *crowded*, with gayly-dressed and handsome young men, many of whom really far richer and in higher rank than I was, and scores of them ready to offer her their hand; when we reflect that she was living amongst young women who put upon their backs every shilling that they could come at; when we see her keeping the bag of gold untouched, and working hard to provide herself with but mere necessary apparel, and doing this while she was passing from *fourteen to eighteen years of age*; when we view the whole of the circumstances, we must say that here is an example, which, while it reflects honour on her sex, ought to have weight with every young woman whose eyes or ears this relation shall reach.

If any young man imagine, that this great *sobriety of conduct* in young women must be accompanied with seriousness approaching to *gloom*, he is, according to my experience and observation, very much deceived. The *contrary* is the fact; for I have found that as, amongst men, your jovial companions are, except over the bottle, the dullest and most insipid of souls; so, amongst women, the gay, the rattling and laughing are, unless some party of pleasure, or something out of domestic life, is going on, generally in the dumps and blue-devils. Some *stimulus* is always craved after by this description of women; some sight to be seen, something to see or to hear other than what is to be found *at home*, which, as it affords no incitement, nothing *to raise and keep up the spirits*, is looked upon merely as a place *to be at* for want of a better; merely a place for eating and drinking, and the like; merely a hiding place, whence to sally in search of enjoyments. A greater curse than a wife of this description, it would be somewhat difficult to find; and, in your character of Lover, you are to provide against it. I hate a dull, melancholy, moping thing: I could not have existed in the same house with such a thing for a single month. The mopers are, too, all giggle at other times: the gaiety is for others, and the moping for the husband, to comfort him, happy man, when he is alone: plenty of smiles and of badinage for others, and for him to participate with others; but the moping is reserved exclusively for him. One hour she is capering about, as if rehearsing a jig; and, the next, sighing to the motion of a lazy needle, or weeping over a novel: and this is called *sentiment*! Music, indeed! Give me a mother singing to her clean and fat and rosy baby, and making the house ring with her extravagant and hyperbolical encomiums on it. That is the music which is '*the food of love*'; and not the formal, pedantic noises, an affectation of skill in which is nowadays the ruin of half the young couples in the middle rank of life. Let any man observe, as I so frequently have, with delight, the excessive fondness of the labouring people for their children. Let him observe with what pride they dress them out on a Sunday, with means deducted from their own scanty meals. Let him observe the husband, who has toiled all the week like a horse, nursing the baby, while the wife is preparing the bit of dinner. Let him observe them both abstaining from a sufficiency, lest the children should feel the pinchings of hunger. Let him observe, in short, the whole of their demeanour, the real mutual affection, evinced, not in words, but in unequivocal deeds. Let him observe these things, and, having then cast a look at the lives of the great and wealthy, he will say, with me, that, when a man is choosing his partner for life, the dread of poverty ought to be cast to the winds. A labourer's cottage, on a Sunday; the husband or wife having a baby in arms, looking at two or three older ones playing between the flower-borders going from the wicket to the door, is, according to my taste, the most interesting object that eyes ever beheld; and, it is an object to be beheld in no country upon earth but England. In France, a labourer's cottage means a *shed* with a *dungheap* before the door; and it means much about the same in America, where it is wholly inexcusable.

An *ardent-minded* young man (who, by-the-by, will, as I am afraid, have been wearied by this rambling digression) may fear, that this great *sobriety of conduct* in a young woman, for which I have been so strenuously contending, argues a want of that *warmth*, which he naturally so much desires; and, if my observation and experience warranted the entertaining of this fear, I should say, had I to live my life over again, give me the *warmth*, and I will stand my chance as to the rest. But, this observation and this experience tell me the contrary; they tell me that *levity* is, ninety-nine times out of a hundred, the companion of *a want of ardent feeling*. Prostitutes never *love*, and, for the far greater part, never did. Their passion, which is more *mere animal* than anything else, is easily gratified; they, like rakes, change not only without pain, but with pleasure; that is to say, pleasure as great as they can enjoy. Women of *light minds* have seldom any *ardent* passion; love is a mere name, unless confined to one object; and young women, in whom levity of conduct is observable, will not be thus restricted. I do not, however, recommend a young man to be *too severe* in judging, where the conduct does not go beyond *mere levity*, and is not bordering on *loose* conduct; for something depends here upon constitution and animal spirits, and something also upon the manners of the country. That levity, which, in a French girl, I should not have thought a great deal of, would have frightened me away from an English or an American girl.

There are, however, certain cases in which you deceive, or nearly deceive, *yourself*; cases in which you are, by degrees and by circumstances, deluded into something very nearly resembling sincere love for a second object, the first still, however, maintaining her ground in your heart; cases in which you are not actuated by vanity, in which you are not guilty of injustice and cruelty; but cases in which you, nevertheless, *do wrong*; and as I once did a wrong of this sort myself, I will here give a history of it, as a warning to every young man; that being the best and, indeed, the only atonement, that I can make, or ever could have made, for this only *serious sin* that I ever committed against the female sex.

The province of New Brunswick, in North America, in which I passed my years from the age of eighteen to that of twenty-six, consists, in general, of heaps of rocks, in the interstices of which grow the pine, the spruce, and various sorts of fir trees, or, where the woods have been burnt down, the bushes of the raspberry or those of the huckleberry. The province is cut asunder lengthwise, by a great river, called the St John, about two hundred miles in length, and, at half way from the mouth full a mile wide. Into this main river run innumerable smaller rivers, there called CREEKS. On the sides of these creeks the land is, in places, clear of rocks; it is, in these places, generally good and productive; the trees that grow here are the birch, the maple, and others of the deciduous class; natural meadows here and there present themselves; and some of these spots far surpass in rural beauty any other that my eyes ever beheld; the creeks, abounding towards their sources in water-falls of endless variety, as well in form as in magnitude, and always teeming with fish, while water-fowl enliven their surface, and while wild-pigeons, of the gayest plumage, flutter, in thousands upon thousands, amongst the branches of the beautiful trees, which, sometimes, for miles together, form an arch over the creeks.

I, in one of my rambles in the woods, in which I took great delight, came to a spot at a very short distance from the source of one of these creeks. Here was everything to delight the eye, and especially of one like me, who seem to have been born to love rural life, and trees and plants of all sorts. Here were about two hundred acres of natural meadow, interspersed with patches of maple trees in various forms and of various extent; the creek (there about thirty miles from its point of joining the St John) ran down the middle of the spot, which formed a sort of dish, the high and rocky hills rising all around it, except at the outlet of the creek, and these hills crowned with lofty pines: in the hills were the sources of the creek, the waters of which came down in cascades, for any one of which many a nobleman in England would, if he could transfer it, give a good slice of his fertile estate; and in the creek, at the foot of the cascades, there were, in the season, salmon the finest in the world, and so abundant, and so easily taken, as to be used for manuring the land.

If nature, in her very best humour, had made a spot for the express purpose of captivating me, she could not have exceeded the efforts which she had here made. But I found something here besides these rude works of nature; I found something in the fashioning of which *man* had had something to do. I found a large and well-built log dwelling house, standing (in the month of September) on the edge of a very good field of Indian corn, by the side of which there was a piece of buck-wheat just then mowed. I found a homestead, and some very pretty cows. I found all the things by which an easy and happy farmer is surrounded: and I found still something besides all these; something that was destined to give me a great deal of pleasure and also a great deal of pain, both in their extrcme degree; and both of which, in spite of the lapse of forty years, now make an attempt to rush back into my heart.

Partly from misinformation, and partly from miscalculation, I had lost my way; and, quite alone, but armed with my sword and a brace of pistols, to defend myself against the bears, I arrived at the loghouse in the middle of a moonlight night, the hoar frost covering the trees and the grass. A stout and clamorous dog, kept off by the gleaming of my sword, waked the master of the house, who got up, received me with great hospitality, got me something to eat, and put me into a feather-bed, a thing that I had been a stranger to for some years. I, being very tired, had tried to pass the night in the woods, between the trunks of two large trees, which had fallen side by side, and within a yard of each other. I had made a nest for myself of dry fern, and had made a covering by laying boughs of spruce across the trunk of the trees. But unable to sleep on account of the cold; becoming sick from the great quantity of water that I had drank during the heat of the day, and being, moreover, alarmed at the noise of the bears, and lest one of them should find me in a defenceless state, I had roused myself up, and had crept along as well as I could. So that no hero of eastern romance ever experienced a more enchanting change.

I had got into the house of one of those YANKEE LOYAL-
ISTS, who, at the close of the revolutionary war (which, until it
had succeeded, was called a rebellion) had accepted of grants of
land in the King's Province of New Brunswick; and who, to the
great honour of England, had been furnished with all the means
of making new and comfortable settlements. I was suffered to
sleep till breakfast time, when I found a table, the like of which
I have since seen so many in the United States, loaded with good
things. The master and the mistress of the house, aged about
fifty, were like what an English farmer and his wife were half a
century ago. There were two sons, tall and stout, who appeared
to have come in from work, and the youngest of whom was about
my age, then twenty-three. But there was *another member* of the
family, aged nineteen, who (dressed according to the neat and
simple fashion of New England, whence she had come with her
parents five or six years before) had her long light-brown hair
twisted nicely up, and fastened on the top of her head, in which
head were a pair of lively blue eyes, associated with features of
which that softness and that sweetness, so characteristic of American girls, were the predominant expressions, the whole being set
off by a complexion indicative of glowing health, and forming,
figure, movements, and all taken together, an assemblage of beauties, far surpassing any that I had ever seen but *once* in my life.
That *once* was, too, *two years agone*; and, in such a case and at
such an age, two years, two whole years, is a long, long while! It
was a space as long as the eleventh part of my then life! Here
was the *present* against the *absent*: here was the power of the *eyes*
pitted against that of the *memory*: here were all the senses up in
arms to subdue the influence of the thoughts: here was vanity,
here was passion, here was the spot of all spots in the world, and
here were also the life, and the manners and the habits and the
pursuits that I delighted in: here was everything that imagination
can conceive, united in a conspiracy against the poor little bru-
nette in England! What, then, did I fall in love at once with this
bouquet of lilies and roses? Oh! by no means. I was, however, so
enchanted with *the place*; I so much enjoyed its tranquillity, the
shade of the maple trees, the business of the farm, the sports of
the water and of the woods, that I stayed at it to the last possible
minute, promising, at my departure, to come again as often as I
possibly could; a promise which I most punctually fulfilled.

Winter is the great season for jaunting and *dancing* (called *frolicking*) in America. In this province the river and the creeks were the only *roads* from settlement to settlement. In summer we travelled in *canoes*; in winter in *sleighs* on the ice or snow. During more than two years I spent all the time I could with my Yankee friends: they were all fond of me: I talked to them about country affairs, my evident delight in which they took as a compliment to themselves: the father and mother treated me as one of their children; the sons as a brother; and the daughter, who was as modest and as full of sensibility as she was beautiful, in a way to which a chap much less sanguine than I was would have given the tenderest interpretation; which treatment I, especially in the last-mentioned case, most cordially repaid.

It is when you meet in company with others of your own age that you are, in love matters, put, most frequently, to the test, and exposed to detection. The next door neighbour might, in that country, be ten miles off. We used to have a frolic, sometimes at one house and sometimes at another. Here, where female eyes are very much on the alert, no secret can long be kept; and very soon father, mother, brothers and the whole neighbourhood looked upon the thing as certain, not excepting herself, to whom I, however, had never once even talked of marriage, and had never even told her that I *loved* her. But I had a thousand times done these by *implication*, taking into view the interpretation that she would naturally put upon my looks, appellations and acts; and it was of this, that I had to accuse myself. Yet I was not a *deceiver*; for my affection for her was very great: I spent no really pleasant hours but with her: I was uneasy if she showed the slightest regard for any other young man: I was unhappy if the smallest matter affected her health or spirits: I quitted her in dejection, and returned to her with eager delight: many a time, when I could get leave but for a day, I paddled in a canoe two whole succeeding nights, in order to pass that day with her. If this was not love, it was first cousin to it; for as to any *criminal* intention I no more thought of it, in her case, than if she had been my sister. Many times I put to myself the questions: 'What am I at? Is not this wrong? *Why do I go?*' But still I went.

Then, farther in my excuse, my *prior engagement*, though carefully left unalluded to by both parties, was, in that thin population, and owing to the singular circumstances of it, and to the great talk that there always was about me, *perfectly well known* to her and all her family. It was matter of so much notoriety and conversation in the province, that GENERAL CARLETON (brother of the late Lord Dorchester), who was the governor when I was there, when he, about fifteen years afterwards, did me the honour, on his return to England, to come and see me at my house in Duke Street, Westminster, asked, before he went away, to see my *wife*, of whom *he had heard so much* before her marriage. So that here was no *deception* on my part: but still I ought not to have suffered even the most distant hope to be entertained by a person so innocent, so amiable, for whom I had so much affection and to whose heart I had no right to give a single twinge. I ought, from the very first, to have prevented the possibility of her ever feeling pain on my account. I was young, to be sure; but I was old enough to know what was my duty in this case, and I ought, dismissing my own feelings, to have had the resolution to perform it.

The *last parting* came; and now came my just punishment! The time was known to everybody, and was irrevocably fixed; for I had to move with a regiment, and the embarkation of a regiment is an *epoch* in a thinly settled province. To describe this parting would be too painful even at this distant day, and with this frost of age upon my head. The kind and virtuous father came forty miles to see me just as I was going on board in the river. *His* looks and words I have never forgotten. As the vessel descended, she passed the mouth of *that creek* which I had so often entered with delight; and though England, and all that England contained, were before me, I lost sight of this creek with an aching heart.

On what trifles turn the great events in the life of man! If I had received a *cool* letter from my intended wife; if I had only heard a rumour of anything from which fickleness in her might have been inferred; if I had found in her any, even the smallest, abatement of affection; if she had but let go any one of the hundred strings by which she held my heart: if any of these, never would the world have heard of me. Young as I was; able as I was as a soldier; proud as I was of the admiration and commendations of which I was the object; fond as I was, too, of the command, which, at so early an age, my rare conduct and great natural talents had given me; sanguine as was my mind,

*Anna Cobbett, always referred to by her husband as 'Nancy'*

and brilliant as were my prospects: yet I had seen so much of the meannesses, the unjust partialities, the insolent pomposity, the disgusting dissipations of that way of life, that I was weary of it: I longed, exchanging my fine laced coat for the Yankee farmer's home-spun, to be where I should never behold the supple crouch of servility, and never hear the hectoring voice of authority, again; and, on the lonely banks of this branch-covered creek, which contained (she out of the question) every thing congenial to my taste and dear to my heart, I, unapplauded, unfeared, unenvied and uncalumniated, should have lived and died.

It does very well in bantering songs, to say that the bachelor's life is *devoid of care*. My observation tells me the contrary, and reason concurs, in this regard, with experience. The bachelor has no one on whom he can in all cases rely. When he quits his home, he carries with him cares that are unknown to the married man. If, indeed, like the common soldier, he have merely a lodging-place, and a bundle of clothes, given in charge to some-one, he may be at his ease; but if he possess anything of a home, he is never sure of its safety; and this uncertainty is a great enemy to cheerfulness. And as to *efficiency* in life, how is the bachelor to equal the married man? In the case of farmers and tradesmen, the latter have so clearly the advantage over the former, that one need hardly insist upon the point; but it is, and must be, the same in all the situations of life. To provide for a wife and children is the greatest of all possible spurs to exertion. Many a man, naturally prone to idleness, has become active and industrious when he saw children growing up about him; many a dull sluggard has become, if not a bright man, at least a bustling man, when roused to exertion by his love. Dryden's account of the change wrought in CYMON, is only a strong case of the kind. And, indeed, if a man will not exert himself for the sake of a wife and children, he can have no exertion in him; or he must be deaf to all the dictates of nature.

Perhaps the world never exhibited a more striking proof of the truth of this doctrine than that which is exhibited in me; and I am sure that everyone will say, without any hesitation, that a fourth part of the labours I have performed, never would have been performed, *if I had not been a married man*. In the first place, they could not; for I should, all the early part of my life, have been rambling and roving about as most bachelors are. I should have had *no home* that I cared a straw about, and should have wasted the far greater part of my time. The great affair of home being *settled*, having the home secured, I had leisure to employ my mind on things which it delighted in. I got rid at once of all cares, all *anxieties*, and had only to provide for the very moderate wants of that home. But the children began to come. They sharpened my industry: they spurred me on. To be sure, I had other and strong motives: I wrote for fame, and was urged forward by ill-treatment, and by the desire to triumph over my enemies; but, after all, a very large part of my *nearly a hundred volumes* may be fairly ascribed to the wife and children.

I might have done *something*; but, perhaps not a *thousandth* part of what I have done; not even a thousandth part: for the chances are, that I, being fond of a military life, should have ended my days ten or twenty years ago, in consequence of wounds, or fatigue, or, more likely in consequence of the persecutions of some haughty and insolent fool, whom nature had formed to black my shoes, and whom a system of corruption had made my commander. *Love* came and rescued me from this state of horrible slavery; placed the whole of my time at my own disposal; made me as free as air; removed every restraint upon the operations of my mind, naturally disposed to communicate its thoughts to others; and gave me, for my leisure hours, a companion, who, though deprived of all opportunity of acquiring what is *called learning*, had so much good sense, so much useful knowledge, was so innocent, so just in all her ways, so pure in thought, word and deed, so disinterested, so generous, so devoted to me and her children, so free from all disguise, and, withal, so beautiful and so talkative, and in a voice so sweet, so cheering, that I must, seeing the health and the capacity which it had pleased God to give me, have been a *criminal*, if I had done much less than that which I have done; and I have always said, that if my country feel any gratitude for my labours, that gratitude is due to her full as much as to me.

*Care!* What *care* have I known! I have been buffetted about by this powerful and vindictive government; I have repeatedly had the fruit of my labour snatched away from me by it; but I had a partner that never frowned, that was never melancholy, that never was subdued in spirit, that never abated a smile, on these occasions, that fortified me, and sustained me by her courageous example, and that was just as busy and as zealous in taking care of the remnant as she had been in taking care of the whole; just as cheerful, and just as full of caresses, when brought down to a mean hired lodging, as when the mistress of a fine country house, with all its accompaniments; and, whether from her words or her looks, no one could gather that she regretted the change. What *cares* have I had, then? What have I had worthy of the name of *cares*?

And, how is it *now*? How is it when the *sixty-fourth year* has come? And how should I have been without this wife and these children? I *might* have amassed a tolerable heap of *money*; but what would that have done for me? It might have *bought* me plenty of *professions* of attachment; plenty of persons impatient for my exit from the world; but not one single grain of sorrow, for any anguish that might have attended my approaching end.

# YOUNG MEN, YOUNG WOMEN - AND BOOKS

When people have nothing useful to do, they may indulge their curiosity; but, merely to *read books*, is not to be industrious, is not to study, and is not the way to become learned. Perhaps there are none more lazy, or more truly ignorant, than your everlasting readers. A book is an admirable excuse for sitting still; and, a man who has constantly a newspaper, a magazine, a review, or some book or other in his hand, gets, at last, his head stuffed with such a jumble, that he knows not what to think about anything. An empty coxcomb, that wastes his time in dressing, strutting, or strolling about, and picking his teeth, is certainly a most despicable creature, but scarcely less so than a mere reader of books, who is generally conceited, thinks himself wiser than other men, in proportion to the number of leaves that he has turned over. In short, a young man should bestow his time upon no book, the contents of which he cannot apply to some useful purpose.

Books of travel, of biography, natural history, and particularly such as relate to agriculture and horticulture, are all proper, when leisure is afforded for them; and the two last are useful to a very great part of mankind; but unless the subjects treated of are of some interest to us in our affairs, no time should be wasted upon them, when there are so many duties demanded at our hands by our families and our country. A man may read books for ever, and be an ignorant creature at last, and even the more ignorant for his reading.

And, with regard to young women, everlasting book-reading is absolutely *a vice*. When they once get into the habit, they neglect all other matters, and, in some cases, even their very dress. Attending to the affairs of the house; to the washing, the baking, the brewing, the preservation and cooking of victuals, the management of the poultry and the garden; these are their proper occupations. It is said (with what truth I know not) of the *present queen* (wife of William IV) that she was an active excellent manager of her house. Impossible to bestow on her greater praise: and I trust that her example will have its due effect on the young women of the present day, who stand, but too generally, in need of that example.

# THE COURT MARTIAL

The object of my thus quitting the army, to which I was, perhaps, more attached than any man that ever lived in the world, was, to bring certain officers to justice for having, in various ways, *wronged both the public and the soldier*. With this object in view, I went strait to London, the moment I had obtained my liberty and secured my *personal safety*, which, as you will readily conceive, would not have been the case if I had not first got my discharge.

I must here go back a little, and give an account of the measures, which, while in the regiment, I had taken, preparatory to this prosecution; and, in order to give the reader a full view of all the circumstances; in order that he may be able to form a just opinion of what I was in the army, I will give him a short account of my progress.

I enlisted at Chatham in 1784; I joined the regiment, in Nova Scotia, in 1785; I was almost immediately made a corporal; in a few months afterwards I was made a sergeant; and, at the end of about a year and a half, I was made the sergeant-major.

As I advanced in experience, I felt less and less respect for those, whom I was compelled to obey. One suffers injustice from men, of great endowments of mind, with much less of heart-burning than from men, whom one cannot help despising; and, if my officers had been men of manifest superiority of mind, I should, perhaps, not have so soon conceived the project of bringing them, or some of them, at least, to shame and punishment for the divers flagrant breaches of the law, committed by them, and for their manifold, their endless, wrongs against the soldiers and against the public.

This project was conceived so early as the year 1787, when an affair happened, that first gave me a full insight into regimental justice. It was shortly this: that the quartermaster, who had the issuing of the men's provisions to them, *kept about a fourth part of it to himself*. This, the old sergeants told me, had been the case *for many years*; and, they were quite astonished and terrified at the idea of my complaining of it. This I did, however; but, the reception I met with convinced me, that I must never make another complaint, 'till I got safe to England, and safe out of the reach of that most curious of courts, a *court martial*.

From this time forward, I began to collect materials for an exposure, upon my return to England. I had ample opportunities for this, being the keeper of all the books, of every sort, in the regiment, and knowing the whole of its affairs better than any other man. But, the winter previous to our return to England, I thought it necessary to make extracts from books, lest the books themselves should be destroyed. And, here begins the history of the famous *court martial*. In order to be able to *prove* that these extracts were correct, it was necessary that I should have a *witness* as to their being *true copies*. This was a very ticklish point. One foolish step here, would have sent me down to the ranks with a pair of bloody shoulders. Yet, it was necessary to have the witness. I hesitated many months. At one time, I had given the thing up. I dreamt twenty times, I dare say, of my papers being discovered, and of my being tried and flogged half to death. At last, however, some fresh act of injustice towards us made me set all danger at defiance. I opened my project to a corporal, whose name was William Bestland, who wrote in the office under me, who was a very honest fellow, who was very much bound to me, for my goodness to him, and who was, with the sole exception of myself, the only sober man in the *whole regiment*.

To work we went, and during a long winter, while the rest were boozing and snoring, we gutted no small part of the regimental books, rolls, and other documents. Our way was this: to take a copy, sign it with our names, and clap the regimental seal to it, so that we might be able to swear to it, when produced in court. All these papers were put into a little box, which I myself had made for the purpose. When we came to Portsmouth, there was a talk of searching all the boxes, etc. which gave us great alarm; and induced us to take out all the papers, put them in a bag, and trust them to a custom-house officer, who conveyed them on shore, to his own house, whence I removed them in a few days after.

Thus prepared, I went to London, and, on the 14th of January, 1792, I wrote to the then Secretary at War, Sir George Yonge, stating my situation, my business with him, and my intentions; enclosing him a letter or petition, from myself to the king, stating the substance of all the complaints I had to make; and which letter I requested Sir George Yonge to lay before the king.

I waited from the 14th to the 24th of January, without receiving any answer at all, and then all I heard was, that he wished to see me at the War Office. At the War Office I was shown into an ante-chamber amongst numerous anxious-looking men, who, every time the door, which led to the great man, was opened, turned their eyes that way with a motion as regular and as uniform as if they had been drilled to it. These people eyed me from head to foot, and I never shall forget their look, when they saw, that I was admitted into paradise without being detained a single minute in purgatory.

Sir George Yonge *heard my story*; and that was apparently all he wanted of me. I was to hear from him again in *a day or two*; and, after waiting for *fifteen days*, without hearing from him, or anyone else, upon the subject, I wrote to him again, reminding him, that I had, from the first, told him, that I had no *other business in London*; that my stock of *money was necessarily scanty*; and, that to *detain me in London was to ruin me*. Indeed, I had, in the whole world, but about 200 guineas, which was a great deal for a person in my situation to have saved. Every week in London, especially as, by way of episode, I had now *married*, took, at least, a couple of guineas from my stock. I, therefore, began to be very impatient, and, indeed, to be very suspicious, that military justice in England was pretty nearly a-kin to military justice in Nova Scotia and New Brunswick.

The letter I now wrote was dated on the 10th of February, to which I got an answer on the 15th, though the answer might have been written in a moment.

I was, in this answer, informed, that it was the intention to try the accused upon *only part of the charges*, which I had preferred; and, from a new-modelled list of charges, sent me by the Judge Advocate [Sir Charles Gould], on the 23rd of February, it appeared, that, even of those charges that were suffered to remain, *the parts the most material were omitted.* But, this was not all. I had all along insisted, that, unless the court martial were held in *London*, I could not think of appearing at it; because, if held in a garrisoned place like Portsmouth, the thing must be a mere mockery. In spite of this, however, the Judge Advocate's letter of the 23rd of February informed me, that the court was to be held at Portsmouth, or Hilsea. I remonstrated against this, and demanded that my remonstrance should be laid before the king, which, on the 29th the Judge Advocate promised should be done by himself; but, on the 5th of March, the Judge Advocate informed me, that he had laid my remonstrance before ... *whom*, think you? Not *the king*, but the *accused parties*; who, of course, thought the court ought to assemble at Portsmouth or Hilsea, and, doubtless for the very reasons that led me to object to its being held there.

Plainly seeing what was going forward, I, on the 7th of March, made, *in a letter to Mr Pitt*, a representation of the whole case, giving him a history of the obstacles I had met with, which letter concluded thus: 'I have now, sir, done all a man can do in such a case. I have proceeded regularly, and, I may add, respectfully, from first to last: if I am allowed to serve my country by prosecuting men, who have injured it, I shall do it: if I am thwarted and pressed down by those, whose office it is to assist and support me, I cannot do it: in either case, I shall be satisfied with having done my duty, and shall leave the world to make a comparison between me and the men whom I have accused.'

This letter (which, by-the-by, the public robbers have not published) had the effect of changing the place of the court martial, which was now to be held in London; but, as to my other great ground of complaint, the leaving of the *regimental books unsecured*, it had no effect at all; and, it will be recollected, that, without those books, there could be, as to most of the weighty charges, no proof produced, without bringing forward Corporal Bestland, and the danger of doing that will be presently seen.

But, now, mark well as to these books; as to this great source of that sort of evidence, which was not to be brow-beaten, or stifled by the dangers of the lash. Mark well, these facts, and from them judge of what I had to expect in the way of justice.

On the 22nd *of January*, I wrote to Sir George Yonge for the express purpose of having the books secured; that is to say, taken out of the hands, and put out of the reach, of the parties accused. On the 24th *of January*, he told me, that HE HAD *taken care to give directions to have these documents secured*. On the 18th *of February*, in answer to a letter, in which I (upon information received from the regiment) complained of the documents not having been secured, he wrote to me, and I have now the letter before me, signed with his own hand, that he would write to the colonel of the regiment about the books, etc. 'Although,' says he, 'I cannot doubt but that the regimental books *have been* properly secured.' This was on the 18th *of February*, mind; and, now it appears, from the documents, which the public-robbers have put forth, that the first time any order for securing the books was given, was on the 15th *of March*, though the secretary *told* me he had done it on the 24th *of January*, and repeated his assertion in writing, on the 18th *of February*. There is quite enough in this fact alone to shew the public what sort of a chance I stood of obtaining justice.

Without these written documents nothing of importance could be proved, unless the non-commissioned officers and men of the regiment should happen to get the better of their dread of the lash; and, even then, they could only speak from memory. All, therefore, depended upon those written documents, as to the principal charges. Therefore, as the court martial was to assemble on the 24th of March, I went down to Portsmouth on the 20th, in order to know for certain what was become of the books; and, I found, as, indeed, I suspected was the case, that they had *never been secured at all*; that they had been left in the hands of the accused from the 14th of January to the very hour of trial; and that, in short, my request, as to this point, the positive condition as to this most important matter, had been totally disregarded. There remained then, nothing to rest upon with *safety* but our extracts, confirmed by the evidence of Bestland, the corporal, who had signed them along with me; and this I had solemnly engaged with him not to have recourse to, unless he was first out of the army; that is to say, out of the reach of the vindictive and bloody lash. He was a very little fellow: not more than about five feet high; and had been set down to be discharged when he went to England; but, there was a suspicion of his connexion with me,

N°6.

*The Life of WILLIAM·COBBETT._ written by himself.*

London. Publish'd Sept. 19. 1809. by H. Humphrey 27. S. James's Street.

Plate .6th

_ the Court Martial was assembled at Chelsea as I requested, and
Capt°. Powell and the other accused Persons were placed at the Bar; _
_when, blast-my-Eyes! I saw, the whole of that damn'd 51st Regiment
Drummers, Fifers and all, marching boldly into the Hall to bear Testi-
-mony against Me !! on this, I instantly ran to a boat which I had
Providentialy secured, and crossed the Thames. _
_ damn'd infernal-Ideots! did the Judge-Advocate and his Gang
of Publick Robbers think that I would stay to witness my own
Exposure and condemnation?

_ Vide . my own Memoirs
in the Political Register — 1809

*The Court Martial, at which Cobbett was conspicuous by his absence.
Underneath Gillray parodies Cobbett's explanation*

and, therefore, they resolved to keep him. It would have been cruel, and even perfidious, to have brought him forward under such circumstances; and, as there was no chance of doing anything without him, I resolved not to appear at the court martial, unless the *discharge* of Bestland was first granted. Accordingly, on the 20th of March, I wrote, from Fratton, a village near Portsmouth, to the Judge Advocate, stating over again all the obstacles that had been thrown in my way, complaining particularly that the books and documents had been left in possession of the accused, contrary to my urgent request and to the positive assurances of the Secretary at War, and concluding by demanding the discharge of a man, whom I should name, as the only condition upon which I would attend the court martial. I requested him to send me an answer by the next day at night, at my former lodging; and told him, that, unless such answer was received, he and those to whom my repeated applications had been made, might do what they pleased with their court martial; for, that I confidently trusted, that a few days would place me beyond the scope of their power.

No answer came, and, as I had learned, in the meanwhile, that there was a design to prosecute me for *sedition*, that was an additionalmotivetobequickinmymovements.AsIwasgoingdownto down to Portsmouth, I met several of the sergeants coming up, together with the music-master; and, as they had none of them been in America, I wondered what they could be going to London for: but, upon my return, I was told by a Captain Lane, who had been in the regiment, that they had been brought up to swear, that, at an entertainment given to them by me before my departure from the regiment, I had drunk *the destruction of the House of Brunswick*. This was false; but, I knew that that was no reason why it should not be *sworn* by such persons and in such a case. I had talked pretty freely, upon the occasion alluded to; but I had neither said, nor thought anything against the king, and, as to the *House of Brunswick*, I hardly knew what it meant. My head was filled with the corruptions and the baseness in the army. I knew nothing at all about politics. Nor would any threat of this sort have induced me to get out of the way for a moment; though it certainly would, if I had known my danger; for glorious 'Jacobinical' times were just then beginning. Of this, however, I knew nothing at all. I did not know what *the Suspension of the*

*Habeas Corpus Act* [1794] meant. When you have a mind to
do a thing, every trifle is an additional motive. Lane, who had
enlisted me, and who had always shown great kindness towards
me, told me they would send me to Botany Bay; and, I now
verily believe, that, if I had remained, I should have furnished
a pretty good example to those, who wished to correct military
abuses. I did not, however, leave England from this motive. I
could not obtain a chance of success, without exposing the back
of my poor faithful friend Bestland, which, had I not pledged
myself not to do, I would not have done. It was useless to appear,
unless I could have tolerable fair play; and, besides, it seemed
better to leave the whole set to do as they pleased, than to be
made a mortified witness of what it was quite evident they had
resolved to do.

*Botley, 14 June 1809*

# PHILADELPHIA
# JOURNALIST

## (1792–1800)

# PAUL HEDGEHOG PRESENTS
# PETER PORCUPINE

The celebrated Dean of St Patrick's somewhere observes that a man of talents no sooner emerges from obscurity, than all the blockheads are instantly up in arms against him. Fully persuaded of the truth of this observation, I should have been prepared for hostility, had I imagined myself a man of talents; but, knowing the contrary too well, I little expected that the harmless essays from my pen would have conjured up against me this numerous and stupid host. It is their misfortune, never to form a right conception of any person or thing, and therefore their abuse is not always a certain proof of merit in the object on which it is bestowed: their ignorance lessens the honour conferred by their envy, hatred and malice.

I have long been the butt of the silly aspersions of this grovelling tribe; but their spite never discovered itself in its deepest colours, till they saw me, as they imagined, 'issue from poverty to the appearance of better condition'. Then it was that their gall ran over, and jaundiced their whole countenances; then it was that the stupidest of all stupid gazettes, that lewd and common strumpet, the *Aurora*, became pregnant with the following *bastard*, as abundant in falsehood as any one that ever sprang from the loins of [Benjamin Franklin's] *Poor Richard*.

As the people of America may not be informed who PETER PORCUPINE is, the celebrated manufacturer of *lies*, and retailer of *filth*, I will give you some little account of this pestiferous animal. This wretch was obliged to *abscond* from his darling *Old England* to avoid being turned off into the other world before, what he supposed, his time. It may be well imagined, that in a land of liberty, and flowing with milk and honey, his *precipitate retreat* could not have been owing to any offence committed against the government very honourable to himself. Gnawed by the worm that never dies, his own wretchedness would ever prevent him from making any attempt in favour of human happiness. His usual occupation at home was that of a *garret-scribbler*, excepting a little *night-business* occasionally, to supply unavoidable exigencies: Grub Street did not answer his purposes, and being scented by certain tip-staffs for something more than scribbling, he took a *French leave* for France. His evil genius pursued him here, and *as his fingers were as long as ever*, he was obliged as suddenly to leave the republic, which has now drawn forth all his venom for her attempt to do him *justice*. On his arrival in this country, he figured some time as a *pedagogue*; but as this employment scarcely furnished him salt to his porridge, he having been literally without hardly bread to eat, and not a second shirt to his back, he resumed his old occupation of scribbling, having little chance of success in the other employments which drove him to this country. His talent at *lies* and *Billingsgate rhetoric*, introduced him to the notice of a certain foreign agent, who was known during the revolution by the name of *traitor*. This said agent has been seen to pay frequent visits to PETER. To atone for his transgressions in the mother country, as well as to get a little more bread to eat than he had been accustomed to, he enlisted in the cause of His Gracious Majesty. From the extreme of poverty and filth, he has suddenly sprouted into at least the appearance of better condition; for he has taken a house for the sale of his large poison, at the enormous rent of *twelve hundred dollars a year*, and has *paid a year's rent in advance*!! The public will now be enabled to account for the overflowings of his gall against the Republic of France, and all the republicans of this country, as well as his devotion to the cause of tyranny and of kings. From the frequency of visits paid him by the agent already mentioned, and his sudden change of condition, *secret service-money* must have been liberally employed; for his zeal to make atonement to his mother country seems proportioned to the magnitude of his offence, and the *guineas* advanced. As this *fugitive felon* has crept from his hole, his *quills* will now become harmless; for hitherto they have only excited apprehension, because the beast who shot them was concealed. I have a number of anecdotes respecting him, that I will soon trouble you with, for the amusement of the public. This statement will convince PETER, that I know him well, and that I have only disclosed a part of the truth.

PAUL HEDGEHOG

This *Paul Hedgehog* I know nothing of. I can hardly suppose that he is one of my cousins at New York: if he be, for the honour of our family, I hope that he is a bastard. But, let Paul be what he will, he is not the only one who has attempted to sink me in the opinion of a public that has ever honoured my essays with distinguished marks of approbation. I have been well informed, that it is currently reported, that Mr Thomas Bradford, the bookseller, 'put a coat upon my back', and that, when I was first favoured with his patronage, I had not a 'second shirt to my back'.

Were I to calculate upon the usual operations of truth and gratitude, I should look upon it as impossible that insinuations of this kind had ever been thrown out by Mr Bradford, or any of his family; but, nowadays, in this happy age of reason and liberty, we see such extraordinary things happen in the world, that to doubt, at least, does not argue an excess of credulity or incredulity.

Let the propagators of all these falsehoods be who they may, I am much obliged to them for giving me this opportunity of publishing the History of my Life and Adventures, a thing that I was determined to do, whenever a fair occasion offered, and which never could have been so well timed as at the moment when I am stepping into a situation where I may probably continue for the rest of my life.

I here remember well what I said in my *Observations on the Emigration of Dr Priestley*:

No man has a right to pry into his neighbour's private concerns; and the opinions of every man are his private concerns, while he keeps them so; that is to say, while they are confined to himself, his family, and particular friends; but, when he makes those opinions public; when he once attempts to make converts, whether it be in religion, politics, or anything else; when he once comes forward as a candidate for public admiration, esteem, or compassion, his opinions, his principles, his motives, every action of his life, public or private, become the fair subject of public discussion.

This is a principle I laid down in the first original page I ever wrote for the press. On this principle it is, that I think myself justified in the present publication, and that I am ready to approve of others for publishing whatever they may know concerning me. Let them write on, till their old pens are worn to the stump: let the devils sweat; let them fire their balls at my reputation, till the very press cries out murder. If ever they hear me whine or complain, I will give them leave to fritter my carcass, and trail my guts along the street, as the French *sans-culottes* did those of Thomas Mauduit.

# MRS COBBETT

I began my young marriage days in and near Philadelphia. At one of those times to which I have just alluded, in the middle of the burning hot month of July, I was greatly afraid of fatal consequences to my wife for want of sleep, she not having, after the great danger was over, had any sleep for more than forty-eight hours. All great cities, in hot countries, are, I believe, full of dogs; and they, in the very hot weather, keep up, during the night, a horrible barking and fighting and howling. Upon the particular occasion to which I am adverting, they made a noise so terrible and so unremitted, that it was next to impossible that even a person in full health and free from pain should obtain a minute's sleep. I was, about nine in the evening, sitting by the bed: 'I do think', said she, 'that I could go to sleep *now*, if it were not *for the dogs*.' Downstairs I went, and out I sallied, in my shirt and trousers, and without shoes and stockings; and, going to a heap of stones lying beside the road, set to work upon the dogs, going backward and forward, and keeping them at two or three hundred yards' distance from the house. I walked thus the whole night, barefooted, lest the noise of my shoes might possibly reach her ears; and I remember that the bricks of the causeway were, even in the night, so hot as to be disagreeable to my feet. My exertions produced the desired effect: a sleep of several hours was the consequence; and, at eight o'clock in the morning, off went I to a day's business, which was to end at six in the evening ...

Few men have been more frequently taken from home by business, or by necessity of some sort, than I have; and I can positively assert that, as to my return, I never once disappointed my wife in the whole course of our married life. If the time of return was contingent, I never failed to keep her informed *from day to day*; if the time was fixed, or when it became fixed, my arrival was as sure as my life. Going from London to Botley once with Mr Finnerty, whose name I can never pronounce without an expression of my regard for his memory, we stopped at Alton to dine with a friend, who, delighted with Finnerty's talk, as everybody else was, kept us till ten or eleven o'clock, and was proceeding to *the other bottle*, when I put in my protest, saying, 'We must go, my wife will be frightened.' 'Blood, man,' said Finnerty, 'you do not mean to go home tonight!' I told him I did; and then sent my son, who was with us, to order out the post-chaise. We had twenty-three miles to go, during which we debated the question whether Mrs Cobbett would be up to receive us, I contending for the affirmative, and he for the negative. She was up, and had a nice fire for us to sit down at. She had not committed the matter to a servant: her servants and children were all in bed; and she was up to perform the duty of receiving her husband and his friend. 'You did not expect him?' said Finnerty. 'To be sure I did,' said she; 'he never disappointed me in his life' . . .

# A CHEATING, SLY, ROGUISH
# GANG

---

*To Miss Rachel Smither,* 156 *Houndsditch*

MY DEAR FRIEND,

Since we have been in this country I have written to you half a dozen times, but have not had the good fortune to receive any answer. When I wrote to you before, I lived at Wilmington, a town about thirty miles from here, but since that I have found it to my advantage to remove to the capital. It is generally said, and often with much justice, that a rolling stone never gathers moss; this, however, has not been the case with me; for though my rambles in France and this country cost me above a hundred and ninety guineas, and though I was reduced to about eighteen at my arrival at Wilmington, I am now better off than ever, notwithstanding my expenses in my family have been enormous. But I must not take the merit of this entirely upon myself; my dear Nancy is entitled to her share of it; it perhaps is entirely owing to her care, industry and sweetness of temper that I owe all my success.

I told you before that we had a little boy; my wife was brought to bed of a second boy about the middle of last March, but it was still-born, though alive a few minutes before. She suffered a great deal. But now prepare your tender heart to pity us. On the 3rd of June our other dear little fellow was snatched from us. Oh, Miss Smither! I hope you will never experience a calamity like this. All I ever felt before was nothing – nothing at all, to this. The dearest, sweetest, beautifulest little fellow that ever was seen. We adored him. Everybody admired him. When we lived at

Wilmington people came on purpose to see him for his beauty. He was just beginning to prattle, and to chase the flies about the floor with a fan. I am sure I shall never perfectly recover his loss. I feel my spirits altered. A settled sadness seems to have taken possession of my mind; nor do I wish to be diverted from it. For my poor Nancy, I cannot paint to you her distress; for several days she would take no nourishment. We were even afraid for her – never was a child so adored. I had two of the ablest physicians in the place, but I was not to be blessed. I am happy, however, that my Nancy is re-established – thank God, our means enabled me to change houses directly, and we are come a little into the country for the summer, where I hope we may recover, at least, tranquillity.

Excuse me if my mind's being engaged with my own sorrows has led me too far without mentioning your good and kind father and sister. I hope you have all been happy since we saw you, and I pray God a continuation of your happiness.

This country is good for getting money, that is to say, if a person is industrious and enterprising. In every other respect the country is miserable. Exactly the contrary of what I expected it. The land is bad, rocky; houses wretched; roads impassable after the least rain. Fruit in quantity, but good for nothing. One apple or peach in England or France is worth a bushel of them here. The seasons are detestable. All is burning or freezing. There is no spring or autumn. The weather is so very inconstant that you are never sure for an hour, a single hour at a time. Last night we made a fire to sit by, and today it is scorching hot. The whole month of March was so hot that we could hardly bear our clothes, and three parts of the month of June there was a frost every night, and so cold in the daytime that we were obliged to wear great-coats. The people are worthy of the country – [a] cheating, sly, roguish gang. Strangers make fortunes here in spite of all this, particularly the English. The natives are by nature idle, and seek to live by cheating, while foreigners, being industrious, seek no other means than those dictated by integrity, and are sure to meet with encouragement even from the idle and roguish themselves; for, however roguish a man may be, he always loves to deal with an honest man. You have perhaps heard of the plague being at Philadelphia last year. It was no plague; it was a fever of the country, and is by no means extraordinary among the

Americans. In the fall of the year almost every person, in every place, has a spell of the fever that is called the fall-fever. It is often fatal, and the only way to avoid it is to quit the country. But this fever is not all. Every month has its particular malady. In July, for example, everybody almost, or at least one half of the people, are taken with vomitings for several days at a time; they often carry off the patient, and almost always children. In short, the country altogether is detestable.

The greatest part of my acquaintance in this country are French merchants from St Domingo and Martinico. To one of those islands I shall probably go in about eight or nine months; and in that case, if I live so long, I shall be in England in about three years. For I do not intend to stay much above a couple of years in the islands. Take care of my trunk and box, if you please, till you see me or hear from me. My Nancy's kind love to you all, and accept of mine at the same time. Doctor [Joseph] Priestley is just arrived here from England. He has attacked our English laws and Constitution in print, and declared his sentiments in favour of those butchers in France. He has, however, been attacked in his turn by an Englishman here. I will send you one of these pieces by another ship. Accept my love, and God bless you.

WM COBBETT

The English arms have been amazingly successful in the West Indies. The French have not an inch of land left of all their rich and fine possessions – the finest colonies in the world.

*Philadelphia, 6 July 1794*

# A BONE TO GNAW
# FOR THE DEMOCRATS

The proceedings of the United Irishmen, like those of the American self-created societies, contain general accusations against every branch of the government. An advantageous distribution of the words *liberty*, *tyranny*, *slavery*, etc., does wonders with the populace; but the intelligent reader looks deeper, general accusations do not satisfy; he seeks for instances of oppression, before he will believe that a government is oppressive. Let us extract, then, the instances of oppression complained of by the United Irishmen, from the bombastical rhapsody in which they are buried, and see to what they amount. They tell us that Butler, Bond, Rowan, and about four or five others, were detained some months in prison; and that Muir, Palmer, and Margarot, with two or three more, were transported; and all this (they say), for having done no more than what the mood of their country dictated. I am sure the reader is very well satisfied, that these men were all guilty of the crimes laid to their charge; but to avoid disputation with respect to this fact, I shall suppose them all innocent, and then the sum total of the tyranny against which the United Irishmen exclaim, will amount to eight or nine false imprisonments, and five or six unjust sentences of transportation. This is certainly a great deal too much; may the hand be withered that ever wields a pen in its justification! but, as the United Irishmen wished, as a mean of avoiding such acts of oppression in future, to overturn their monarchical government and establish a democratic one in its stead, it becomes incumbent on the reader, who would not be their dupe, to contrast the conduct of the government which they wanted to overturn with that of the one they intended to adopt. They have represented the British Government as being arrived at its last stage of tyranny, it will not then, I hope, be esteemed unfair, if I oppose to it the democratic Convention of France, when about the midway of its career.

It is not my intention to give a general character of this assembly; that would be superfluous: nor will I give way to that indignation which every man, who is not by nature a slave, must feel at the very mention of such a divan. General charges against any man, or set of men, as they are very seldom accurate, so they are little attended to, particularly when addressed to a reader, who is rather inclined towards the party accused. For this reason, I shall confine myself to a particular epoch, and even a particular spot. Lyons affords us the properest scene to be described on the present occasion; not because the dreadful deeds committed there surpass those at Nantz, and many other places; but because taking place within a short space of time, they admit with more facility the form of a compact relation.

In the perusal of this relation the candid reader will make me some allowances; my taste is far from the tragic; scenes such as these must lose half their terrors when drawn by a hand like mine: Melpomene alone should record the actions of the National Convention.

Some time after the death of Louis XVI, the city of Lyons was declared, by the Convention, in a state of revolt, it was attacked by a numerous army of democrats, and after having stood a siege of above two months was obliged to surrender. What followed this surrender, it is my intention to relate; but first, it is necessary to go back to the causes that led to the revolt; for though no earthly crime could justify the cruelties inflicted upon the brave and unfortunate Lyonnese, yet those cruelties do not appear in their deepest hue, till the pretended crimes of the sufferers are known.

By the new constitution of France [1791], the king could not be dethroned unless found at the head of an army marching against his country. This was to be regarded as the highest crime he could possibly commit, and even for this he could be punished no otherwise than by being dethroned. 'No crime whatever', says the constitution, 'shall be construed to affect his life.' This constitution every Frenchman had sworn, 'to obey, and to maintain with all his might.' When, therefore, it was proposed to the

Lyonnese, by the emissaries of the National Convention, to petition for the death of the king, they replied almost with one voice:

No, we have sworn, with all France, to maintain the new constitution with all our might; that constitution declares that no crime whatsoever shall affect the life of the king. For any thing we have yet seen or heard we believe him innocent of every crime that has been laid to his charge. The mode of his trial is unprecedented in the annals of injustice, the Convention being at once accuser, evidence, and judge. We believe him perfectly innocent; but whether he be or not, the constitution that we have, by a solemn oath, bound ourselves to maintain with all our might, declares that no crime whatever shall be construed to affect his life; that life, therefore, we cannot, we will not demand. The rest of the nation may sport with engagements which they have called the Almighty to witness, they may add the crime of assassination to that of perjury, they may stain themselves with the blood of their innocent and unfortunate prince, the Lyonnese never will.

Reader, you will hardly believe that this answer, so full of good sense, justice, piety, and honour, drew down on the gallant Lyonnese the most dreadful chastisement that ever was inflicted on any part of the human race. Read and be convinced.

No sooner was the determination of the Lyonnese made known to the Convention, than the latter began to concert schemes of vengeance, a numerous army was prepared, while the democratic agents of the Convention, who still had the executive authority at Lyons, spared no pains, so endeavouring to drive the city to what they termed open rebellion, and thus to furnish a pretext for its destruction. The doctrine of equality, so flattering to those who possess nothing, had gained them many converts among the lower classes of the people. To these was committed all authority, civil and military, and it is hardly necessary to say that they exercised every species of tyranny that envy, revenge, and popular fury could invent. All this was borne with a degree of resignation that has been justly regarded as astonishing in people who have since exhibited such unequivocal proofs of inherent valour. A sense of more immediate danger, however, roused them from their lethargy.

There was held, every night, a meeting of the leaders among

the partizans of the Convention. It consisted, in general, of men of desperate fortunes, bankrupts, quacks, the dregs of the law, apostate priests, and the like, not forgetting some who had been released from the galleys. In this infamous assembly, which took the name of Democratic Club, a plot, notwithstanding the precautions of the conspirators, was happily discovered; the President Challier, and two others, were tried and condemned to die, the democrats were driven from all the public offices, and the former magistrates reinstated.

This act of self-preservation was called a revolt against the republic, and in consequence of it, the Convention passed [in October 1793] decree upon decree, bearing death and destruction against the Lyonnese. Thus, those very men who had formed a constitution, which declares resistance against oppression to be a natural right, passed an act of proscription against a whole city, because they had dared to lift their hands to guard their throats against the knives of a band of assassins!

The city now began to arm for its defence; but being totally unprepared for a siege, having neither fortifications nor magazines, and being menaced on every side by myriads of ferocious enemies, the people were backward in declaring for hostility, knowing that in that case death or victory must be the consequence. There were, therefore, but about ten thousand men who had the courage to take up arms: but the desperate bravery of these amply made up for every want. During the space of sixty days they withstood an army of fifteen times their strength, plentifully provisioned, and provided with every instrument of destruction. Never, perhaps, were there such feats of valour performed as by this little army; thrice their numbers did they lay dead before their injured city.

The members deputed from the Convention to direct the attack, left nothing untried that might tend to the accomplishment of their object. They succeeded at last, in opening a communication with their partizans in the city, and in seducing many of the mob to espouse their interest. This was the more easy to effect, as the besieged were, by this time, upon the point of starving; the flesh of horses, dogs, and cats, had been for some days their only food, and even that began to grow extremely scarce. In this situation, without the least hopes of succour, some of those who wished well to their city, and who had not borne arms during the siege, undertook to capitulate with the enemy; but these, knowing the extremities to which they were driven, insisted upon executing the decrees of the Convention, which ordered them to put to death indiscriminately, all those who had taken up arms against its authority.

The besieged, then, seeing no hopes of a capitulation, seeing the city without another day's provision, and the total impossibility of succour from without (being completely invested on every side), had but one measure to adopt; to cut their way through their enemy, or fall in the attempt. A plan of retreat was therefore settled upon; the outposts were to be called in, and the whole were to assemble at the Vaise.

In the mean time, the deputies from the Convention, who were informed by their spies of all that was passing in the city, took care to have the road by which the retreating army was to pass, well lined with troops. The whole country round was under arms. Every person was ordered, on pain of death, not to let pass, or give shelter to, a single Lyonnese, man, woman, or child.

The out-posts were hardly called in, when their stations were taken possession of by the democratic army. Being so closely pressed, rendered the assembling more difficult; all was bustle, confusion, and terror. Not half of these who were under arms had time to join. A little corps was, however, at last formed. It consisted of between three and four thousand persons in all, headed by four field-pieces, and followed by six waggons, bearing the wreck of many a splendid fortune. Thus marched off the remains of these generous defenders of their city, bidding an eternal adieu to the scenes of their youth, the dwellings of their ancestors; resolving to die bravely, as they had lived, or find an asylum in a foreign land.

It was midnight when they began their retreat, lighted by the blaze of bombs and burning houses. Reader, cast your eyes on this devoted city. See children clinging to their fathers, distracted mothers to their sons; wives, holding in their arms what they held dearer than life, forgetting all but their husbands, marching by their side, and bracing death from ten thousand hands!

They had hardly begun their march, when a discharge of artillery bearing full upon them, threw them into some confusion. One of the waggons, in which were several old men and some children, was set on fire by a shell. Morning coming on, they perceived themselves beset on every side; they were charged by the cavalry, exposed to the fire of a numerous artillery, harassed at every turning, fired upon from every house, every bank and every hedge. Seeing therefore no hopes of escape they were determined to sell every drop of blood as dear as possible. They broke off into platoons, putting their wives and children in the centre of each, and took different directions, in order to divide the force of the enemy. But what were they to do against fifty times their number? The whole, about fifty persons excepted, were either killed or taken.

The victors showed such mercy as might be expected from them: not content with butchering their prisoners in cold blood, they took a pleasure in making them die by inches, and insulting them in the pangs of death. Placing several together, they killed one of them at a time to render death more terrible to the rest. Neither sex nor age had any weight with them: above two hundred women, thirty of whom had children at the breast, whom conjugal love had led to follow their husbands; more than fifty old men, whom filial piety had snatched from the assassin's stab, were all most savagely butchered. The death of Madame de Visague deserves particular notice. This young lady was about seventeen years of age, and very near her time of delivery: a party of the democrats found her behind a hedge, to which place she had drawn her husband, who was mortally wounded. When the cannibals discovered her, she was on her knees supporting his head with her arm: one of them fired upon her with a carabine, another quartered her with his hanger, while a third held up the expiring husband to be a spectator of their more than hellish cruelty.

Several wounded prisoners were collected together, and put into a ditch, with sentinels placed round them to prevent them from killing themselves, or one another; and thus were they made to linger, some of them two or three days, while their enemies testified their ferocious pleasure by all the insulting gesticulations of savages.

Such was the fury of the triumphant democrats, that the deputies from the Convention gave an order against burying the dead, till they had been cut in morsels. Tollet, the infamous Tollet, a democratic priest (that is to say, an apostate) of Trevoux, went, blood-hound like, in quest of a few unhappy wretches who had escaped the bloody 9th of October; and when, to perfidious promises, he had drawn them from their retreats, he delivered them up to the daggers of their assassins.

Of all the little army that attempted the retreat, only about forty-six escaped: six hundred and eighteen were brought back in chains; some of them died of their wounds, and all those who were not relieved from life this way, were dragged forth to an ignominious death.

During these dreadful scenes the deputies from the Convention, who were now absolute masters of the unfortunate city, were preparing others, if possible, still more dreadful. As a preliminary step, they reorganized the Democratic Society. To this infernal rendezvous the deputy *Javouges* repaired, and there broached his project in a speech, the substance of which was nearly as follows: After having represented *Challier* as a leader in the cause of liberty, as the hero of the republic, and the avenger of the people, he addressed himself to the assembly in nearly these terms:

Think of the slavery into which you are plunged by being the servants and workmen of others; the nobles, the priests, the proprietors, the rich of every description, have long been in a combination to rob the democrats, the real *sans-culottes* republicans, of their birthright; go, citizens; take what belongs to you, and what you should have enjoyed long ago. Nor must you stop here, while there exists an aristocracy in the buildings, half remains undone: down with those edifices raised for the profit or pleasure of the rich; down with them all; commerce and arts are useless to a warlike people, and destructive of that sublime equality which France is determined to spread over the whole globe.

He told this enslaved, this degraded populace, that it was the duty of every good citizen to discover all those whom he knew to be guilty of having, in thought, word, or deed, conspired against the republic. He exhorted them to fly to the offices (opened for receiving such accusations), and not to spare one lawyer, priest, or nobleman. He concluded this harangue, worthy of one of the damned, with declaring, that for a man to accuse his own father was an act of civism worthy a true republican, and that to neglect it was a crime that should be punished with death.

The deeds that followed this diabolic exhortation were such as might be expected. The bloody ruffians of democrats left not a house, not a hole unsearched: men and women were led forth from their houses with as little ceremony as cattle from their pens; the square where the guillotine stood was reddened with blood, like a slaughter-house, while the piercing cries of the surviving relations were drowned in the more vociferous howlings of *Vive la République!*

It is hard to stifle the voice of nature, to stagnate the involuntary movements of the soul; yet this was attempted, and in some degree effected, by the deputies of the Convention. Perceiving that these scenes of blood had spread a gloom over the countenances of the innocent inhabitants, and that even some of their soldiers seemed touched with compunction, they issued a mandate, declaring every one suspected of aristocracy, who should discover the least symptoms of pity, either by his words or his looks!

The preamble of this mandate makes the blood run cold: 'By the thunder of God! in the name of the representatives of the French people; on pain of death it is ordered,' etc. etc. Who would believe that this terrific mandate, forbidding men to weep, or look sorrowful, on pain of death, concluded with, *Vive la Liberté!* (Liberty for ever!)? Who would believe that the people, who suffered this mandate to be stuck up about their city like a playbill, *had sworn to live free*, or die?

However, in spite of all their menaces, they still found that remorse would sometimes follow the murder of a friend, or relation. Conscience is a troublesome guest to the villain who yet believes in an hereafter; the deputies, therefore, were resolved to banish this guest from the bosoms of their partizans, as it had already been banished from their own.

With this object in view they ordered a solemn *civic festival* in honour of Challier. His image was carried round the city, and placed in the churches. Those temples which had (many of them), for more than a thousand years, resounded with hosannas to the Supreme Being, were now profaned by the adorations paid to the image of a *parricide*.

All this was but a prelude to what was to follow the next day. It was Sunday, the day consecrated to the worship of our blessed Redeemer. A vast concourse of democrats, men and women, assembled at a signal agreed on, formed themselves into a sort of a mock procession, preceded by the image of Challier, and followed by a little detached troop, each bearing in its hand a chalice, or some other vase of the church. One of these sacrilegious wretches led an ass, covered with a priest's vestment and with a mitre on his head. He was loaded with crucifixes and other symbols of the Christian religion, and had the Old and New Testaments suspended to his tail. Arrived at the square called the Terreaux, they then threw the two *Testaments*, the crucifixes, etc. into a fire prepared for the purpose; made the ass drink out of the sacramental cup, and were proceeding to conclude their diabolical profanations with the massacre of all the prisoners, to appease the ghost of Challier, when a violent thunder-storm put an end to their meeting, and deferred the work of death for a few hours.

The pause was not long. The deputies, profiting by the infamous frenzy with which they had inspired the soldiery and the mob, and by the consternation of the respectable inhabitants, continued their butchery with redoubled fury. Those who led the unhappy sufferers to execution were no longer ordered to confine themselves to such as were entered on the list of proscription, but were permitted to take whoever *they thought worthy of death*! To have an enemy among the democrats, to be rich, or even thought rich, was a sufficient crime. The words *nobleman*, *priest*, *lawyer*, *merchant*, and even *honest man*, were so many terms of proscription. Three times was the place of the guillotine changed, at every place holes were dug to receive the blood, and yet it ran in the gutters! the executioners were tired, and the deputies, enraged to see that their work went on so slowly, represented to the mob that they were *too merciful*, that vengeance lingered in their hands, and that their enemies ought to perish *in mass*!

Accordingly, next day, the execution *in mass* began. The prisoners were led out, from a hundred to three hundred at a time, into the outskirts of the city, where they were fired upon or stabbed. One of these massacres deserves a particular notice. Two hundred and sixty-nine persons, taken indiscriminately among all classes and all ages, were led to *Brotteaux*, and there tied to trees. In this situation they were fired upon with grape-shot. Here the *cannoneers of Valenciennes*, who had not had the courage to defend their own walls, who owed their forfeited lives to the mercy of royalists, valiantly pointed their cannons against them, when they found them bound hand and foot! The coward is ever cruel. Numbers of these unfortunate prisoners had only their limbs broken by the artillery; these were dispatched with the sword or the musket. The greatest part of the bodies were thrown into the Rhone, some of them before they were quite dead; two men in particular had strength enough to swim to a sand-bank in the river. One would have thought, that thus saved as it were by miracle, the vengeance of their enemies would have pursued them no farther; but no sooner were they perceived, than a party of the *dragoons of Lorraine* crossed the arm of the river and stabbed them, and left them a prey to the fowls of the air. Reader, fix your eyes on this theatre of carnage. You barbarous, you ferocious monsters! You have found the heart to commit those bloody deeds, and shall no one have the heart to publish them in a country that boasts of an unbounded liberty of the press? Shall no one tell, with what pleasure you plunged your daggers into the defenceless breasts of those whose looks had often appalled your own coward hearts? Shall no one tell, with what heroic, what godlike constancy they met their fate? How they smiled at all your menaces and cannibal gesticulations? How they despised you in the very article of death? Strewed with every sweetest flower be the grave of *Mons. Chapuis de Maubourg*, and let his name be graven on every faithful heart! This gallant gentleman, who was counted one of the first engineers in Europe, fell into the hands of the democrats. They offered to spare his life, if he would serve in the armies of the Convention; they repeated this offer, with their carabines at his breast. 'No,' replied he, 'I have never fought but for my God and my king; despicable cowards! fire away!'

The murder *in mass* did not rob the guillotine of its prey: there the blood flowed without interruption. Death itself was not a refuge from democratic fury. The bodies of the prisoners who were dead of their wounds and of those who, not able to support the idea of ignominious death, had given themselves the fatal blow, were carried to the scaffold, and there beheaded, receiving thousands of kicks from the *sans-culottes*, because the blood would not run from them. Persons from their sick beds, old men, not able to walk, and even women found in child-bed, were carried to the murderous machine. The respectable Mons. Lauras was torn from his family of ten children and his wife big with the eleventh. This distracted matron ran with her children, and threw herself at the feet of the brutal deputy Collot d'Herbois. No mercy! Her conjugal tenderness, the cries of her children, everything calculated to soften the heart, presented themselves before him, but in vain. 'Take away,' said he, to the officious ruffians by whom he was surrounded, 'take away the she-rebel and her whelps.' Thus spurned from the presence of him who alone was able to save her beloved husband, she followed him to the place of execution. Her shrieks, when she saw him fall, joined to the wildness of her looks, but too plainly foretold her approaching end. She was seized with the pains of childbirth, and was carried home to her house; but, as if her tormentors had shown her too much lenity, the *sans-culotte* commissary soon after arrived, took possession of all the effects in the name of the sovereign people, drove her from her bed and her house, from the door of which she fell dead in the street.

Citizen Benjamin Franklin Bache's *Gazette* says, that 'it would be an easy matter to apologize for all the murders committed in France,' let him apologize for this. Not that I imagine he cannot do it according to the democratic creed, but it would be curious to hear his apology. Doctor Priestley also says, that all these things are for the good of the Unitarian religion, and therefore, says he, 'we must look upon them as a *blessing*'!

> Thus, *if eternal justice rule the ball*,
> *Thus shall their wives, and thus their children fall.*

About three hundred women hoped, by their united prayers and tears, to touch the hearts of the ferocious deputies; but all their efforts were as vain as those of Madame Lauras. They were threatened with a discharge of grape shot. Two of them, who, notwithstanding the menaces of the democrats, still had the courage to persist, were tied during six hours to the posts of the guillotine; their own husbands were executed before their eyes, and their blood sprinkled over them!

Mademoiselle Servan, a lovely young woman of about eighteen years of age, was executed, because she would not discover the retreat of her father! 'What!' said she nobly, to the democratic committee, 'what! betray my father! impious villains, how dare you suppose it?'

Madame Cochet, a lady equally famed for her beauty and her courage, was accused of having put the match to a cannon during the siege, and of having assisted in her husband's escape. She was condemned to suffer death; she declared herself with child, and the truth of this declaration was attested by two surgeons. In vain did she implore a respite, in vain did she plead the innocence of the child that was in her womb: her head was severed from her body amidst the death-howl of the democratic brigands.

Pause, here, reader, and imagine if you can, another crime worthy of being added to those already mentioned. Yes, there is one more, and hell would not have been satisfied if its ministers had left it uncommitted. *Libidinous brutality! Javouges*, one of the deputies from the Convention, opened the career. His example was followed by the soldiery and the mob in general. The wives and daughters of almost all the respectable inhabitants, particularly of such as had emigrated, or who were murdered or in prison, were put in a state of requisition, and were ordered on pain of death, to hold their bodies (I spare the reader the term made use of in the decree) in readiness for the embraces of the true republicans! Nor were they content with violation: the first ladies of the city were led to the tree of Liberty (of Liberty!) and there made to take the hands of chimney-sweepers and common felons! Detestable wretches! At the very name of democrat, humanity shudders, and modesty hides its head!

I will not insult the reader's feelings by desiring him to compare the pretended tyranny of the British Government with that I have here related; nor will I tell the United Irishmen, that even an Irish massacre is nothing compared to the exercise of the democratic laws of France; but I will ask them to produce me, if they can, an instance of such consummate tyranny in any government, or in any nation. Queen Mary of England, during a reign of five years, caused about five hundred innocent persons to be put to death; for this, posterity has, very justly too, branded her with the surname of bloody. What surname, then, shall be given to the assembly that caused more than that number to be executed in one day at Lyons? The massacre of St Bartholomew, an event that filled all Europe with consternation, the infamy and horrors of which have been dwelt on by so many eloquent writers of all religions, and that has held Charles IX up to the execration of ages, dwindles into child's play, when compared to the present murderous revolution, which a late writer in France emphatically calls 'a St Bartholomew of five years'. According to Mons. Bousset, there were about 30,000 persons murdered, in all France, in the massacre of St Bartholomew; there has been more than that number murdered in the single city of Lyons, and its neighbourhood; at Nantz there have been 27,000; at Paris, 150,000; in La Vendée, 300,000. In short, it appears that there have been two millions of persons, murdered in France, since it has called itself a republic, among whom are reckoned two hundred and fifty thousand women, two hundred and thirty thousand children (besides those murdered in the womb), and twenty-four thousand Christian priests!

And is there, can there be a faction in America so cruel, so bloody-minded, as to wish to see these scenes repeated in their own, or any other country? If there be, Great God! do thou mete to them, ten-fold, the measure they would mete to others; inflict on them every curse of which human nature is susceptible; hurl on them thy reddest thunderbolts; sweep the sanguinary race from the face of the creation!

If such, then, are the principles of those men called democrats, ought not every good man in this country to be very cautious how he gives them the least countenance? Ought he not to follow them in all their actions with an attentive eye, and let slip no opportunity of exposing their ambitious and destructive designs? For my part, I by no means desire to assume the dubious name of patriot; what I am doing, I conceive to be my duty; which consideration, as it will justify the undertaking, will in some measure apologize for the want of abilities that may appear in the execution.

Upon a view of the horrible revolution that at present agitates the world, we perceive that though the grand object of the democrats has been everywhere the same, yet their pretended motives have varied with their situation. In America, where the Federal Constitution had just been put in movement, and had begun to extend its beneficent effects, it was impossible to talk of *reformation*; at least it was impossible to make the people believe that it was necessary. The well-known wisdom and integrity and the eminent services of the President had engraven such an indelible attachment for his person on the hearts of *Americans*, that his reputation or his measures could be touched but with a very delicate hand. A plan of indirect operations was therefore fixed upon; and it must be allowed, that, by the help of a foreign agent, it was not badly combined. The outlines of this plan were to extol to the skies every act of the boxing legislators of France; to dazzle *those who have nothing* with the sublime system of 'equality'; to make occasional reflections on the resemblance between this government and that of Great Britain; to condemn the British laws (and consequently our own at the same time) as aristocratic, and from thence to insinuate that *'something yet remained to be done'*; and finally, to throw a veil over the insults and injuries received from France, represent all the actions of Great Britain in the most odious light, plunge us into a war with the latter, put us under the tutelage of the former, and recall the glorious times of violence and plunder. Thanks to government; thanks to the steady conduct of the executive power, this abominable plan has been disconcerted; the phalanx has been broken; but it is nevertheless prudent to pursue the scattered remains, draw them from their caballing assemblies, and stretch them on the rack of public contempt.

I do not know whether there were any of the United Irishmen, or their retainers, at the last St Patrick's feast, in this city; but I know that they drank to the memory of 'Brutus and Franklin (a pretty couple), to the Society of the United Irishmen, to the French, and to their speedy arrival in Ireland'. After this, I think it would be cruel to doubt of the patriotism of the United Irishmen, and their attachment to the British constitution.

In these toasting times it would have been something wonderful if the *sans-culottes* in America had neglected to celebrate the taking of Amsterdam by their brethren in France. I believe from my soul there have been more cannons fired here in the celebration of this conquest, than the French fired in achieving it. I think I have counted twenty-two grand civic festivals, fifty-one of an inferior order, and one hundred and ninety-three public dinners; at all which, I imagine, there might be nearly thirty thousand people; and as twenty thousand of them, or thereabouts, must have been married men, it is reasonable to suppose that eighteen or nineteen thousand women with their children were at home wanting bread, while their husbands were getting drunk at a civic feast.

There is in general such a sameness in those feasts, that it would be tiring the reader to describe them; and it would, besides, be anticipating what I intend to treat more at large, as soon as my materials for the purpose are collected. The grand civic festival at Reading (Massachusetts), however, deserves a particular mention, as it approaches nearer to a real French civic feast than anything I have yet heard of in this country.

The day was ushered in by the ringing of the bells, and a salute of fifteen discharges from a field-piece. The American flag waved in the wind, and the flag of France *over the British in inverted order*. At noon a large number of *respectable* citizens assembled at Citizen Rayner's, and partook of an elegant entertainment – after dinner Captain Emerson's military company in uniform assembled, and escorted the citizens (to the grog-shop, I suppose, you think?) to the *meeting-house*!! where an address, pertinent to the occasion, was delivered by the *Reverend Citizen Prentiss*, and united prayers and praises were offered to God, and several hymns and anthems were well sung; after which they returned in procession to Citizen Rayner's, when three farmers with their frocks and utensils, and with a tree on their shoulders, were escorted by the military company, formed in a hollow square, to the common, where the tree was planted in form, as an emblem of freedom, and the Marseillois hymn was sung by a choir within a circle round the tree. Major Bondman, by request, superintended the business of the day, and directed the manoeuvres.

These manoeuvres were very curious to be sure, particularly that of the Reverend Citizen Prentiss, putting up a long snuffling prayer for the successes of the French atheists! A pretty minister truly! There was nothing wanted to complete this feast but to burn the Bible, and massacre the honest inhabitants of the town. And are these the children of those men who fled from their native country to a desert, rather than deviate from what they conceived to be the true principles of the gospel? Are they such men as Prentiss, to whom the people of Massachusetts commit the education of their children and the care of their own souls? God forgive me if I go too far, but I think I would as soon commit my soul to the care of the devil.

Nor was the Reverend Citizen Prentiss the only one who took

upon him to mock heaven with thanksgivings for the successes of the French *sans-culottes*. From Boston they write: 'It was highly pleasing to republicans to hear some of our clergy yesterday returning thanks to the Supreme Being for the successes of the good *sans-culottes*.' Yes, reader, some of the clergy of Boston put up thanksgivings for what they imagined to be the successes of a set of impious wretches, who have in the most solemn manner abolished the religion these very clergymen profess, who have declared Christianity to be a farce, and its Founder an infamous impostor, and who have represented the doctrine of the immortality of the soul as a mere cheat, contrived by artful priests to enslave mankind. There is but too much reason to fear that many of those whose duty it is to stand on the watch-tower, whose duty it is to resist this pernicious doctrine, are among the first to object – let the clergymen in Boston remember –

> *That those whose impious hands are join'd*
> *From heaven the thunderbolt to wrest*
> *Shall, when their crimes are finished, find*
> *That death is not eternal rest.*

But they tell us that it is because the French are true republicans, that we ought to applaud them. What a sarcasm on republicanism! As if fire and sword, prisons and scaffolds, the destruction of cities, the abolition of all religious worship, the inculcation of a doctrine which leads to every crime, stifles remorse, and prevents a return to justice and humanity, were the characteristics of a true republic. If it be so, we ought to blush to call ourselves republicans.

Some of the democratic tribe have cried aloud against me, for speaking of the Dutch and French under the names of *Nick Frog* and the *Baboon*; but let them remember, that while they talk about *John Bull*, I must and will be permitted to keep up the allegory, particularly at a time when it is become more strikingly *à propos* than ever. '*Jupiter*', says the fable, 'sent the frogs a log of wood to reign over them; but a bull being let loose in the pasture, and having trod the guts of a few of them out, they set up a terrible outcry against the stupidity and negligence of King Log. Jupiter, tired at last with their everlasting croakings, and determined to punish them for their ingratitude to his anointed log, sent them a huge baboon that gobbled them up by hundreds at a meal.'

Patriot Paine, the heathen philosopher, has observed that republics never marry. There is more humour than truth in this observation; for though one would imagine that the name of *sister* which they give to each other would be an insuperable bar to such an union, yet experience proves the contrary; for the French Republic does not only marry, but is guilty of polygamy. She has already espoused the Republic of Batavia (commonly called Holland), and the poor little Geneva, and she is now swaggering about like a Jack wh—e with a couple of under punks at her heels. She wanted to make love to the cheek of John Bull, but John, beast as he is, had too much grace to be seduced by her. 'No,' said John, 'you heathenish cannibal, I will not touch you; you reek with blood; get from my sight, you stabbing strumpet!' John was half right: for she is indeed a cruel spouse; something like the brazen image formerly made use of in Hungary, that cracked the bones, and squeezed out the blood and guts of those who were condemned to its embraces.

How happy were we in escaping a marriage with a termagant like this! we were, indeed, within an inch of it. Brissot and his crew sent out one of their citizens [Genet] (who had been employed with so much success in negotiating the marriage with Geneva) to marry us by proxy, and the democrats were beginning to sing 'Come haste to the wedding', when the President, who had not burnt his Bible, saw that the laws of consanguinity did not allow of a marriage between two sisters, and therefore, like a good old father of his country, he peremptorily forbad the bans. Heavens bless him for it! if he had not done this, we might long ago have seen the *citizen inviting* the Congress, as Pichegru does the Dutch assembly, to send him five hundred oxen for breakfast. He had already begun to scamper about our streets with his *sans-culottes* dragoons (among whom, be it remembered, some of our democrats were base enough to enrol themselves), and he would by this time, perhaps, have ordered us, and not without reason, to call Philadelphia, Commune Afranchie.

The Convention, finding that we were not to be won by this boorish kind of courtship, began to send us billets-doux to soothe us into compliance. Among these, that which *invites* us to change our weights and measures is remarkable enough to merit a particular notice. A citizen somebody had been to measure the terrestrial *arc* contained between Dunkirk and Barcelona, from which operation it appeared that we ought (at the invitation of the French) to divide our *pound* into *ten ounces*, our *gallon* into *ten quarts*, our *day* into *ten hours*, our *quadrant* into a *hundred degrees*, etc. etc. etc., just like Hudibras,

> *For he by geometric scale*
> *Could take the size of pots of ale,*
> *And tell by sines and tangents straight,*
> *If bread and butter wanted weight.*

This communication was a sort of a present by way of breaking the ice; artful gallants begin with trifles – a handkerchief, a ring, any bauble marked with the lover's name, paves the way in affairs of love. If we had set about making the alterations, which we were invited to make, we should, undoubtedly, have been invited to divide our year according to the Anglican calendar, abolish Christianity and punish with death those who should have dared to worship *the ci-devant God*. I almost wonder that these generous *enlighteners* of the world, these generous encouragers of the arts and sciences, had not sent us, along with the models of weights and measures, models of their *lantern-posts* and *guillotines*. They talk about their *nautical discoveries*, why had they not sent us, then, a model of their *drowning-boats*, by which fifty women and children were sent to the bottom at a time? They might also have obliged us with an essay on the method of making bread, without taking the bran out of the flour; and how well pleased must the Congress have been with a treatise on legislative boxing! But, as the French have all the honour of these discoveries, so, I suppose, they mean to have all the profit too; and God punish the villain that would wish to rob them of it, I say.

The Convention, in this communication, resemble *Jack* in the *Tale of a Tub*: 'Flay, pull, tear all off,' say they, 'let not a single stitch of the livery of that d——d rogue, John Bull, remain.' The Congress, however, have thought proper to imitate the phlegmatic good nature of Brother Martin. 'Steady, boys, steady,' said they one to another; 'those fellows, there, are got keel uppermost, and they want to see us in the same plight.' I would have given a trifle for a view of the senators when they received this

*ten-ounces-to-the-pound* proposal; the gravity of a senator surpasses what I conceived of it, if they did not run a risk of bursting
their sides. The notice they have taken of it will, I hope, prevent
like *invitations* for the future; and convince the French that our
Congress is not an assembly

> *Where* quicks *and* quirks, *in dull debates,*
> *Dispute on* maximums *and* weights,
> *And cut the land in* squares,
> *Making king mob gulp down the cheat,*
> *And singling for* themselves the wheat,
> *Leave for the* herd *the* tares.

I do not know whether the French are irritated at our *sang
froid*, or at our consulting our interests with other nations, or
how it is, but certainly they begin to show their good-will to us
in a very odd manner. Their depredations on our commerce have
already surpassed those of the English. One captain writes, 'I
have been *robbed by them*; they have *broken open my trunks, and
took my all.*' Another says: 'They have called me a *damned
Anglo-American, beat me* and thrown me into prison.' Another
says: 'They have kept me here these four months; they do what
they please with my cargo; and *the Lord knows what will become
of me!*' Another *petitions* the *sans-culotte* general, and concludes
with, 'your petitioner shall ever *pray!*' And is this all? Do they
now talk of these things with the humility of slaves? No, execra-
tions! Have they emptied their galls on the English? Is there not
one curse, one poor spiteful curse, left for the *sans-culottes*? Ye
Gods! how men are sometimes ice and sometimes fire! When the
English took our vessels, what *patriot* bosom did not burn with
rage? There was nothing talked of but vengeance, war, and confiscation. Where is now all this 'republican ardour', where are all
those young men who 'burnt for an opportunity to defend the
*liberty*, rights, and property of their country'? Where are all those
courageous *captains* who entered into an association to oblige the
Government to declare war? Are they dead? do they sleep? or are
they gone with their chief, Barney, to fight, like Swisses, for the
French Convention? Last year, about this time, nothing was to
be heard but their malicious left-handed complaints; a rough
word or a wry look was thought sufficient to rouse the whole

Union to revenge the insults they received on the high seas. They now seem as insensible to every insult as the images at the head of their vessels; submit to their fate with Christian resignation, with, 'Lord have mercy upon us,' and 'your petitioners will ever pray!'

If any one wants to be convinced that the democratic outcry about the British depredations was intended to plunge us into war and misery, let him look at their conduct at the present moment. An Envoy Extraordinary [John Jay] was sent to England to demand restitution, which has not only been granted, but a long wished-for commercial treaty has also been negotiated. One would think that this would satisfy all parties; one would think that this would even shut the mouths of the democrats; but no; this is all wrong, and they are beginning to tear the treaty to pieces, before they know anything about it; they have condemned the whole, before they know any single article of it. They were eternally abusing Mr Pitt, because he kept aloof in the business; and, now he has complied, they say that no such thing should ever have been thought of. 'What!' say they, 'make a treaty with Great Britain!' And why not, wiseacres? Who would you make a treaty with, but those with whom you trade? You are afraid of giving umbrage to France, eh? Is this language worthy an independent nation? What is France to us, that our destiny is to be linked to hers? that we are not to thrive because she is a bankrupt? She has no articles of utility to sell us, nor will she have wherewith to pay us for what she buys. Great Britain, on the contrary, is a ready-money customer; what she furnishes us is, in general, of the first necessity, for which she gives us, besides, a long credit; hundreds and thousands of fortunes are made in this country upon the bare credit given by the merchants of Great Britain.

Think not, reader, whatever advantages we are about to derive from the treaty with Great Britain, that I wish to see such a marked partiality shown for that nation, as has hitherto appeared for the French; such meannesses may be overlooked in those despicable states that are content to roll as the satellites of others, in a Batavia or Geneva, but in us it never can. No; let us forget that it is owing to Great Britain that this country is not now an uninhabited desert; that the land we possess was purchased from the aborigines with the money of an Englishman; that his hand traced the streets on which we walk. Let us forget from whom we are descended, and persuade our children that we are the sons of the gods, or the accidental offspring of the elements; let us forget the scalping knives of the French, to which we were thirty years exposed; but let us never forget that we are not Frenchmen.

# REMARKS AGAINST PETER
# PORCUPINE

---

DEAR FATHER, when you used to set me off to work in the morning, dressed in my blue smock-frock and woollen spatter-dashes, with my bag of bread and cheese and bottle of small beer swung over my shoulder on the little crook that my old godfather Boxall gave me, little did you imagine that I should one day become so great a man as to have my picture stuck in the windows and have four whole books published about me in the course of one week.

Thus begins a letter which I wrote to my father yesterday morning, and which, if it reaches him, will make the old man drink an extraordinary pot of ale to my health. Heaven bless him! I think I see him now, by his old-fashioned fire-side, reading the letter to his neighbours. 'Ay, ay,' says he, '*Will* will stand his ground wherever he goes.' And so I will, father, in spite of all the hell of democracy.

When I had the honour to serve King George, I was elated enough at the putting on of my worsted shoulder-knot, and, afterwards, my silver-laced coat; what must my feelings be then, upon seeing half a dozen authors, all *doctors* or the devil knows what, writing about me at one time, and ten times that number of printers, bookbinders, and booksellers, bustling, running and flying about in all directions, to announce my fame to the impatient public? What must I feel upon seeing the newspapers filled from top to bottom, and the windows and corners of the houses placarded, with, *a Blue Shop for Peter Porcupine, a Pill for Peter Porcupine, Peter Porcupine detected, a Roaster for Peter Porcupine, a History of Peter Porcupine, a Picture of Peter Porcupine?* The public will certainly excuse me, if after all this, I should begin to think myself a person of some importance.

It is true, my heroic adversaries do all set out with telling their readers, that I am a contemptible wretch *not worth notice.* They should have said, not worth the notice *of any honest man,* and, as they would all naturally have excluded themselves by such an addition, they would have preserved consistency at least; but, to sit down hammering their brains for a fortnight or three weeks, and at last publish each of them a pamphlet about me and my performances, and then tell the public that *I am not worth notice,* is such a gross insult to common sense that nothing but democratic stupidity can be a sufficient excuse for.

At the very moment that I am writing, these sorry fellows are hugging themselves in the thought that they have silenced me, *cut me up,* as they call it. They think they see me prostrate, and they are swaggering over me, like a popish priest over a dead corpse. It would require other pens than theirs to silence me. I shall keep plodding on in my old way, as I used to do at plough; and I think it will not be looked upon as any very extraordinary trait of vanity to say, that the *Political Censor* will be read, when the very names of their bungling pamphlets will be forgotten.

I must now beg the reader to accompany me in some few remarks that I think it necessary to make on each of their productions, following the order in which they appeared.

### A ROASTER FOR PETER PORCUPINE

What can I say worse of this blustering performance, than that it bears all the internal evidence of being written by the blunderbuss author who disgusted the city with *Rub from Snub?*

### THE BLUE SHOP; or *Humorous* Observations, etc.

The inoffensive and unmeaning title of this pamphlet is fully expressive of the matter it is prefixed to, excepting that the word *humorous* was, perhaps, never before so unfortunately applied. Every one who has been taken in with this quarter-dollar's worth, whether a friend or an enemy of Peter Porcupine, curses it for

See Porcupine, in Colours just Portray'd, | Veild in darkness, acts the assassins part,
Urg'd by old Nick, to drive his dirty trade, | And triumphs much to stab you to the heart.

*Porcupine, a Print*

*The south-east corner of Third and Market Streets, Philadelphia*

the most senseless and vapid piece of stuff that ever issued from the press. The author, I hear, retorts, and swears the Americans are a set of stupid jack-asses, who know not what true humour is. 'Tis pity he had not perceived this before, he might then have accommodated his *humour* to their understandings. It is now too late to rail against their ignorance or want of taste, for, in spite of his railing and fretting, *James Quicksilver* will, by them, ever be looked upon as a most leaden-headed fellow.

PORCUPINE, A PRINT

This is a caricature, in which I am represented as urged on to write by my old master King George (under the form of a crowned lion), who, of course, comes accompanied with the devil. The *Jay*, with the treaty in his beak, is mounted on the lion's back, though, by the by, it has ever been said, by the democrats, that the lion rode the *Jay*. His Satanic Majesty holds me out a bag of money, as an encouragement to destroy the idol, liberty, to which he points. The American Eagle is represented as drooping his wings in consequence of my hostility, and America herself, on the same account, weeps over the bust of Franklin. This is almost the only part of the print of which I find fault; for, if by America the people of America be to be understood, I believe most of those who have read my essays will do me the justice to say, that I have endeavoured to make America laugh instead of weep. As to myself, I am the hero of the piece, I am brought forward to the front of the stage, where the artist makes me trample upon [Edmund] *Randolph's Defence* [his *Vindication* of his actions when recently, as Secretary of State, he had been accused of suggesting that the French distribute largesse among American politicians to secure their support], the *Rights of Man*, Old *Common Sense*, Maddison [James Madison, leader of the democrats], [Albert] *Gallatin*, [John] *Swanwick*, and *Peter Pindar*. How this blundering fellow came to place *Pindar* among the rest I cannot imagine. It discovers a total ignorance of that author's writings, and of my opinion concerning them. Can the American democrats approve, and can I disapprove, of a writer who says of Tom Paine –

> *Paine, in his thirst for reputation,*
> *Has written to deserve damnation?*

Can the democrats approve, and can I disapprove, of a writer who speaks of France and of Frenchmen in the following manner?

*Keel up lies* FRANCE! *long may she keep that posture!*
*Her knav'ry, folly, on the rocks have tost her;*
*Behold the thousands that surround the wreck!*
*Her cables parted, rudder gone,*
*Split all her sails, her mainmast down,*
*Chok'd all her pumps, crush'd in her deck;*
*Sport for the winds, the billows o'er her roll!*
*Now I am glad of it with all my soul.*

*To* BRITAIN *an insidious damn'd Iago—*
*Remember,* ENGLISHMEN, *old Cato's cry,*
*And keep that patriot model in your eye—*
*His constant cry,* 'Delenda est Carthago.'
*Love I the French? By heav'ns 'tis no such matter!*
*Who loves a Frenchman wars with simple nature.*

*The converse chaste of day, and eke of night,*
*The kiss-clad moments of supreme delight,*
*To love's pure passion only due;*
*The seraph smile that soft-ey'd* FRIENDSHIP *wears,*
*And sorrow's balm of sympathising tears,*
*Those iron-hearted fellows never knew.*

*Hear me, Dame Nature, on these men of* cork—
*Blush at a* FRENCHMAN's *heart, thy handy work;*
*A dunghill that luxuriant feeds*
*The gaudy and the rankest weeds:*
*Deception, grub-like, taints its very core,*
*Like flies in carrion* — *Prithee make no more.*

*Yes,* FRENCHMEN, *this is my unvarying creed,*
*Ye are not rational, indeed;*
*So low have fond conceit and folly sunk ye:*
*Only* a larger kind of monkey!

And yet this is the writer that the learned and sagacious democrats make me trample upon! I think my namesake Peter speaks here like a good honest Englishman, and though Mr Bache publishes his works, and boasts of being in correspondence with him,

I am very far from either trampling on those works or disliking their author.

Perhaps I ought to take some notice of the quarter whence this *caricature* and the *Blue Shop* issued, as it furnishes an instance, among thousands, of that degradation which the first movers in the French revolution have long been, and still are exhibiting to the world. These poor miserable catch-penny pictures and pamphlets are published by a man of the name of *Moreau* [St Méry, the emigré bookseller], who was one of those whom Tom Paine and his comrades Price and Priestley called, 'the great illuminated and illuminating National Assembly of France.' Goddess of Liberty! and dost thou permit this thy 'great illuminated and illuminating' knocker-down of Bastiles to wage a puny *underhand* war with one of King George's redcoats? Dost thou permit one of those aspiring 'legislators of the universe!' who commanded the folding doors of the *Louvre* to fly open at their approach, and who scorned to yield the precedence to princes and emperors, to dwindle down into a miserable *marchand d'estampes*? If these be thy tricks, Goddess of *French* Liberty, may the devil take Peter, if ever thy bloody cap and pike entice him to enlist under thy banners.

Mr Moreau, to his other misfortunes, adds that most calamitous one of thinking he can write. He is cursed with the scribbling itch, without knowing how to scratch himself with a good grace. As this is torment enough in itself, I do not wish to add to it by mentioning particular instances of his want of taste and talents. The greatest punishment I wish my enemies, is, that *Moreau* may be obliged to write all his lifetime, and that the rest may be obliged to read his productions.

THE HISTORY OF A PORCUPINE

This pamphlet is, I am told, copied, *verbatim*, from a chap-book, containing the lives of several men who were executed in Ireland some years ago, names and dates only are changed, to give the thing an air of plausibility. It is said to be published by two Scotch lads, lately arrived in the country, and who now live in some of the allies about Dock Street, no matter which. One of their acquaintances called on me some days after the publication appeared, and offered to furnish me with the book from which it is taken. This offer I declined accepting of. I shall only add here, as a caution to my readers, that these are the men who are seen hawking about a work in numbers, which they are pleased to call a *History of France*, and who are proposing to publish a *Monthly Magazine*.

## A PILL FOR PORCUPINE

It is a rule with book-makers, that a title should, as briefly as possible, express the nature of the work to which it is prefixed. According to this rule, *Pill* is a most excellent title to the performance now before me. A *Pill* is usually a compound of several nauseous, and sometimes poisonous, drugs, and such is the *Pill for Porcupine*.

Various have been the conjectures as to the author of this abusive piece. Be he who he may, he has certainly done me a favour in grouping me along with Messrs [Alexander] Hamilton, [Jeremy] Belknap, [Ebenezer] Morse, etc. I would cheerfully swallow my part of his pill, and even think it an honour to be poisoned, in such company as this.

Since the *sentimental* dastard, who has thus aimed a stab at the reputation of a woman, published his Pill, I have shown my marriage certificate to *Mr Abercrombie*, the minister of the church opposite me. All you who emigrate to the United States of America, to enjoy this unrestrained liberty of the press that they make such a fuss about, take care (if you mean to say a word in favour of your country) to bring your vouchers and certificates with you, or they'll stigmatize you for thieves; your wives will be called whores, and your children bastards! Blessed liberty of the press!

## THE IMPOSTOR DETECTED

This pamphlet ought, on every account, to come last: we have seen the rest rising above each other progressively; this of *Bradford's* crowns the whole, caps the climax of falsehood and villainy.

The former part of it bears the assumed name of *Tickletoby*, the latter, that of *Samuel F. Bradford*. It is evident, however, that both are by the same author; who he is, is not of much consequence: it is clear that he acted under the directions of Bradford, and Bradford must and shall answer for the whole.

What everyone recoils at the bare idea of, is Bradford's writing a pamphlet *against the works* of Peter Porcupine. Had he confined his attack to my private character and opinions, he would not have so completely exposed himself; but this, I suppose, his author would not consent to; I do not know any other way of accounting for his conduct.

Everyone perceives that the letter which Bradford inserts in *Tickletoby's* part of the pamphlet, is nothing but a poor and vain attempt to preserve consistency. However, to leave no room for dispute on this score, and to convict the shuffling Bradford on his own words, I am willing to allow him to be neuter with respect to *Tickletoby's* part, and will take him up on the contents of the letter which he signs. 'That I have made use,' says he, 'of the British corporal for a good purpose, I have little doubt – *Dirty water* will quench fire.'

Of his *making use* of me I shall speak by-and-by; at present I shall confine myself to the *dirty water*, which is the name he gives my writings. Now, how will he reconcile this with his zeal to spread them abroad, and with the aukward flattery he and his family used to bore my ears with? Had I believed the half of what they told me, I should have long ago expired in an extacy of self-conceit. When the *Observations on Priestley's Emigration* were published, Bradford and his wife took great care to inform me of the praises bestowed on them by several gentlemen, *Doctor Green* [Professor of Natural Philosophy at Princeton] in particular, and to point out to me the passages that gave the most pleasure. The *first Bone to Gnaw* gave universal satisfaction, they told me: it was read in all companies, by the young and by the old; and I remember that the sons told me, on this occasion, how delighted their uncle, the late worthy Attorney General, was with it; and that he said he should have loved me for ever, if I had not been so severe upon the French. Before the *New Year's Gift* appeared in public, Bradford told me he had read some pages of it to two of the *senators*, who were mightily pleased with it, and laughed very heartily. While the father was plying me with his *senators*, the sons played upon me from the *lower house*. Several of the members, *their intimate friends*, wanted to be blessed with a sight of me: one wanted to treat me to a supper, another wanted to shake hands with me, and a third wanted to embrace me. I shall name no names here; but I would advise the members of both houses to be cautious how they keep company with shop-boys and printers' devils.

I could mention a thousand instances of their base flattery, but it would look like praising myself in an indirect way. One more, however, I must not omit. Bradford, in endeavouring to prevail on me to continue the Congress Gallery, related a conversation that had taken place between him and Mr [Oliver] Wolcot, the present Secretary of the Treasury (and thereby hangs another tale which I will tell by-and-by), who assured him that some of the officers of government did intend to write an answer to *Randolph's Vindication*, but that my *New Year's Gift* had done its business so completely, that nothing further was necessary. He added, that they were all exceedingly delighted with my productions.

Again, if he thought my works *dirty water*, how came he to beg and pray for a continuation of them? When I gave his son William a final refusal, he urged, with *tears in his eyes* he urged, the loss his father's credit would sustain by it, and often repeated, that it was not for the sake of the *profit* but the *honour* of publishing my works, that made him so anxious to continue. My wife was present at this interview, and can, with me, make oath to the truth of what I have here asserted.

Nay, if my works were *dirty water*, why did he threaten to prosecute me for *not continuing them?* Dirty water is not a thing to go to law about. Did ever anybody hear of a man's prosecuting another, because he refused to bring him dirty water to throw on the public?

After all this praising, and flattering, and menacing, my poor labours are good for nothing. The writings which had given so much pleasure to Doctor Green, that the Attorney General would have loved me for ever for, that charmed all sexes and all ages, that made grave senators shake their sides with laughter, and congressmen want to treat and hug me; that were so highly approved of by the officers of government, that it was an *honour* to publish, and that I was threatened with a prosecution for not continuing; these writings are now become *dirty water*! Say rather, *sour grapes.*

I must, however, do the Bradfords the justice to say, that they very candidly told me, that everybody could perceive a falling off, *after the Congress Gallery*. How singular it was, that I should

I remember he concluded his advice, with telling me, that it was better to be led to church in a halter, to be tied to a girl that I did not like, than to be tied to the gang-way, or, as the sailors call it, married to *miss roper*. From the conclusion of this wholesome counsel, I perceived that the captain thought I had eloped on account of a bastard. I blushed, and that confirmed him in his opinion; but I declare to the reader, that I was no more guilty of such an offence, than Mr Swanwick, or any other gentleman who is constitutionally virtuous. No; thank heaven, I have none of the Franklintonian crimes to accuse myself of; my children do not hang their hats up in other men's houses; I am neither patriot nor philosopher.

I in vain attempted to convince Captain Berkley, that choice alone had led me to the sea; he sent me on shore, and I at last quitted Portsmouth; but not before I had applied to the port-admiral, Evans, to get my name enrolled among those who were destined for the service. I was, in some sort, obliged to acquaint the admiral with what had passed on board the *Pegasus*, in consequence of which, my request was refused, and I happily escaped, sorely against my will, from the most toilsome and perilous profession in the world.

I returned once more to the plough, but I was spoiled for a farmer. I had, before my Portsmouth adventure, never known any other ambition than that of surpassing my brothers in the different labours of the field; but it was quite otherwise now; I sighed for a sight of the world; the little island of Britain, seemed too small a compass for me. The things in which I had taken the most delight were neglected; the singing of the birds grew insipid, and even the heart-cheering cry of the hounds, after which I formerly used to fly from my work, bound o'er the fields, and dash through the brakes and coppices, was heard with the most torpid indifference. Still, however, I remained at home till the following spring, when I quitted it, perhaps, for ever.

It was on the 6th of May, 1783, that I, like Don Quixote, sallied forth to seek adventures. I was dressed in my holiday clothes, in order to accompany two or three lasses to Guildford fair. They were to assemble at a house, about three miles from my home, where I was to attend them; but, unfortunately for me, I had to cross the London turnpike road. The stage-coach had just turned the summit of a hill, and was rattling down begin to sink the instant I quitted them! Was this because they did no longer *amend my works* for me, or because they no longer pocketed the cash they produced! The Bradfords are booksellers dyed in grain. Heaven is with them worth nothing, unless they can get something by it.

With respect to the motives that gave rise to my pamphlets, I have already stated them, and as to their literary merit, though I have no great opinion of it, yet, after having heard them ascribed to Mr Bond, Mr Thornton (not the *language maker* but the secretary to the English ambassador), Dr [John] Andrews [Professor of Moral Philosophy in the University of Pennsylvania], the Rev. Mr Bisset, Mr Lewis, Mr [Theodore] Sedgewick, Dr [William] Smith, and, in short, to almost every gentleman of distinguished talents among the friends of the Federal Government, it would be mere grimace for me to pretend, that they have no merit at all. It is something singular, that the democrats never pitched upon any low fellow as the author; their suspicions always alighted among gentlemen of family, and gentlemen of learning. It is therefore too late to decry my performances as tasteless and illiterate, now it is discovered that the author was brought up at the plough tail, and was a few years ago a private soldier in the British army.

To return to my friend Bradford. Though I am ready to admit him as a neutral in all that is said by *Tickletoby*, I cannot do this with regard to what is ushered into the world as the performance of *Samuel F. Bradford*. This *hatter-turned-printer*, this sooty-fisted son of ink and urine, whose heart is as black and as foul as the liquid in which he dabbles, must have written, if he did write, at the special instance and request of his father; for, the Lampblack says, 'a father's wish is a law with me.'

After having premised this, making Bradford responsible for what is contained in his letter and his son's, I shall proceed to remark on such parts of both as I think worth my notice.

And first on the grand discovery of the letter to the *Aurora Man*. This is a letter which I wrote to the gazette, under the signature of A Correspondent, against the second part of the *Bone to Gnaw*. The letter, as now printed by Bradford, may, for ought I know, be a very correct copy. I remember the time and all the circumstances well. Bradford, who is as eager to get money into his hands as he is unwilling to let it out again, repeatedly asked me for a *Puff* to this pamphlet. This very son came to me for it as many as half a dozen times. I at last complied; not that I was unwilling to do it at first (for I had bored the cunning grandchild of the cunning almanack-maker several times before), but I could with difficulty spare time to write it.

*Puffs* are of several sorts. I believe the one now before us, is what is called a *Puff indirect*, which means, a piece written by an author, or by his desire, against his own performances, thereby to excite opposition, awaken the attention of the public, and so advance the renown or sale of his labours. A *Puff indirect* is, then, what I stand accused of, and as I have no argument at hand to prove the moral fitness of the thing, I must, as pleaders do in all knotty points, appeal to precedents. My authorities are very high, being no other than Addison, Phillips, and Pope.

No one that has read the *Spectator* (and who has not done that?) can have failed to observe, that he published many letters against his own writings, imitating the style and manner of his adversaries, and containing weak arguments, which he immediately overturns in his answer. Doctor Johnson tells us that, before the acting of PHILLIPS'S *Distressed Mother*, a whole *Spectator* was devoted to its praise, and on the first night, a select audience was called together to applaud it. The Epilogue to this play was written by Addison, who inserted a letter against it in the *Spectator*, for the sake of giving it a triumphant answer. But, Pope's famous puff is a case exactly in point.

He drew a comparison [says Dr Johnson] of Phillips's performance with his own, in which, with an unexampled and unequalled artifice of irony, though he has himself always the advantage, he gives the preference to Phillips. The design of aggrandizing himself he disguised with such dexterity, that, though Addison discovered it, Steele was deceived, and was afraid of displeasing Pope by publishing his paper.

Now, what censure does Lord Chief Justice Johnson (who, God knows, was far from being over lenient) pass on all this? None at all. He calls neither of these authors *an Imposter*: nor can I think he would have done so, had their puffs been written *at his request*, and for *his benefit*.

If a puff can ever be construed as an act of meanness, it must be, when its motive is self-interest. This cannot be attributed to me, as I could get nothing by promoting the sale of the work. I had a note of hand for it in my possession; which the number of copies sold could not augment the value of.

What impudence must a man be blessed with, who can usher to the world a puff, which he wished should be looked upon as something horridly villainous, when he himself requested it to be written, transcribed it himself, and carried it himself for publication? But here the Bradfords play a double game. 'It was not I *transcribed* it,' says old Goosy Tom; and 'a *father's wish* is a law with me,' returns the young Gosling. But, you hissing, web-footed animals, is it not between you? The puffing for fame belongs to me; but the transcribing and carrying to the press; all the interested part of the business, all the dirty work, lies among yourselves, and so I leave you to waddle and dabble about in it.

Having dismissed the *Puff*, we now come to the *breach of confidence* in publishing it. There are many transactions which we do not look upon as criminal, which, nevertheless, we do not wish to have made public. A lady, in love with a handsome young fellow, may make indirect advances, by the aid of a third person. This is certainly no crime; but should the confident preserve one of her letters, and afterwards publish it, I presume such confident would meet with general detestation. This is a parallel case so far; but when to this we add the aggravating circumstance of the confident being the original adviser of the correspondence, we are at a loss for words to express our abhorrence. Yet we must go still further with respect to Bradford. He has not only divulged what was communicated to him under this pledged secrecy, and at his pressing request, to serve him; but he has been guilty of this scandalous breach of confidence towards a man, to whom he owes, perhaps, that he is not now in jail for debt.

It is easy to perceive what drove him to this act of treachery. Revenge for the statement I had published concerning the *one shilling and seven-pence-halfpenny* pamphlet. He could not help fearing that people would resent this by avoiding his shop. He was right enough; for, though I am an Englishman, and of course, a sort of lawful prey to the democrats, yet they, even they, cannot help saying that he is an abominable sharper. To be revenged on me for this, he published the letter, and has thus done what all impotent vindictive men do, injured himself without injuring his adversary. I hinted that he had taken me in, and in return he betrays me: to the reputation of a sharper, he adds that of a villain.

After this, will any one say that I am to blame, if I expose this stupid, this mean, this shabby, this treacherous family? Do they deserve any quarter from me? Everyone says – no, Peter, no.

They say I lived in a garret when first they knew me. They found me sole tenant and occupier of a very good house, No 81 Callowhill. They say I was poor; and that lump of walking tallow streaked with lampblack, that calls itself *Samuel F. Bradford*, has the impudence to say that my wardrobe consisted of my old regimentals, etc. At the time the Bradfords first knew me I earned about 140 dollars per month, and which I continued to do for about two years and a half. I taught English to the most respectable Frenchmen in the city, who did not shuffle me off with notes as Bradford did. With such an income I leave the reader to guess whether I had any occasion to go shabbily dressed. It would look childish to retort here, but let the reader go and ask the women in Callowhill street about the rent in old Bradford's yellow breeches.

The Bradfords have seen others attack me upon my sudden *exaltation*, as they call it: upon my having a book-shop, and all this without any visible means of acquiring it: whence they wish to make people believe that I am paid by the British Government. It is excessively base in the Bradfords to endeavour to strengthen this opinion, because they know that I came by my money fairly and honestly. They were never out of my debt, from the moment they published the first pamphlet, which was in August 1794, till the latter end of May last. (At this time they owed me 18 dollars, which had been due for near six months, and which I was at last obliged to *take out in books*.) They used to put off the payment of their notes from time to time, and they always had at their tongues' end: 'we know you don't want money.' And these rascals have now the impudence to say that I was their needy hireling! 'Tis pity, as Tom Jones's Host says, but there should be a hell for such fellows.

It is hinted, and indeed said, in this vile pamphlet, that I have been encouraged by the American Government also. I promised the reader I would tell him a story about Bradford's patriotism, and I will now be as good as my word. In order to induce me, to continue the Congress Gallery, he informed me, that Mr

[Oliver] *Wolcot* had promised to procure him the printing of the Reports to Congress: 'So', added he, 'I will print off enough copies for the members, and so many besides as will be sufficient to place at the end of each of your numbers, and *Congress will pay for printing the whole!*' He told me he had asked Mr Wolcot for this job, which I looked upon as an indirect way of asking for a bribe, being assured that he built his hopes of succeeding, upon being the publisher of my works. Now, here's a dog for you, that goes and asks for a government job, presuming solely upon the merit of being the vender of what he, nine months afterwards, calls *dirty water*, and who adds to this an attempt to fix the character of government tool on another man. If I would have continued the Numbers, it is probable he might have printed the Reports: but this I would not do. I wanted no Reports tacked on to the end of my pamphlets: that would have been renewing the punishment of coupling the living to the dead.

Sooty Sam, the Gosling, tells the public that I used to call him a *sans-culotte* and his father a *rebel*. If this be true, I am sure I can call them nothing worse, and therefore I am by no means anxious to contradict him. But, pray, wise Mister Bradford of the 'political (and *bawdy*) book-store', is not this avowal of yours rather calculated to destroy what you say about my being *an artful and subtle hypocrite?* I take it, that my calling you *rebels* and *sans-culottes* to your faces is no proof of my hypocrisy; nor will the public think it any proof of your *putting a coat upon my back.* Men are generally mean when they are dependant; they do not, indeed they do not, call their patrons *sans-culottes* and *rebels*; nor do people suffer themselves to be so called, unless some weighty motive induces them to put up with it. This acknowledgment of Bradford's is conclusive: it shows at once on what footing we stood with relation to each other.

He says that I abused many of the most *respectable characters*, by calling them *speculators, landjobbers*, etc., who were continually seeking to *entrap and deceive foreigners*, etc. If I did call those men *speculators* and *landjobbers*, who are continually seeking to *entrap foreigners*; if I confined myself to such mild terms, I must have been in an extremely good humour. But, young Mister Lampblack, be candid for once and allow me that your father is a sharper. Oh! don't go to deny that now: what everybody says must be true.

'How grossly', says the son, 'did you frequently abuse the *People of America*, by asserting that, for the greater part, they were *aristocrats* and *royalists* in their hearts, and only wore the mask of hypocrisy to answer their own purposes.' If young Urine will but agree to leave out *People of America*, and supply its place with, *family of Goosy Tom*, I will own the sentence for mine; and I will tell the public into the bargain, how I came to make use of it. I entered Bradford's one day, and found him poring over an old book of *heraldry*. I looked at it, and we made some remarks on the orthography. In a few minutes afterwards he asked me if I knew anything of *the great Bradford family* in England. I replied, no. He then told me that he had just seen a list of new peers (*English* peers, reader!) among which was a *Lord Bradford*; and that he suspected that he was of a branch of their family! As the old women say, you might have knocked me down with a feather. I did not know which way to look. The blush that warmed my cheek for him then, renews itself as I write. He did not drop it here. He dunned my ears about it half a dozen times; and even went so far as to request me to make inquiries about it, when I wrote home. It was on this most ludicrous occasion, that I burst out, 'Ah, d—n you, I see you are all *aristocrats* and *royalists* in your hearts yet. Your republicanism is nothing but hypocrisy.' And I dare say the reader will think I was half right. I wonder what are the armorial signs of Bradford's family. The crest must be a *Goose*, of course. Instead of scollops and gueules, he may take a couple of printer's balls, a keg of lampblack and a jorden. His two great bears of sons (I except William) may serve as supporters, and his motto may be, *One shilling and seven-pence-halfpenny for a pamphlet*. All this will form a pretty good republican coat of arms.

Let it be remembered here too, that my calling the Bradfords *aristocrats* and hypocrites, does not prove me to be a *hypocrite*, a *needy hireling*, or a *coward*. As to this last term which young Lampblack has conferred on me, it is the blustering noise of a poor timid trembling cock, crowing upon his own dunghill. I hurl his *coward* back to his teeth, with the addition of *fool* and *scoundrel*. I think that is interest enough for one fortnight. The father has served the silly son, as the monkey served the cat, when he took her paw to rake the chestnuts out of the fire with.

They accuse me of being given to *scandal*. If I had published, or made use of, one hundredth part of the anecdotes they supplied me with, I should have set the whole city together by the ears. The governor's share alone would fill a volume. I'll just mention one or two, which will prove, that I am not the first old acquaintance that Bradford has betrayed. He told me of a judge, who, when he presented him an old account, refused to pay it, as it was *setting a bad example*. 'Ah, righteous judge! A Second Daniel!' He told me, that he went once to breakfast with Mr [Alexander] Dallas, now Secretary of the State of Pennsylvania, and that Dallas said to him: 'By G—d, Tom, we have *no sugar*, and I have not a farthing in the world.' 'So', says my Lord Bradford, 'I put my hand in my pocket, and tossed the girl a *quarter of a dollar*, and she went out and got some.' Another time, he said, Mr Dallas's hair-dresser was going to sue him for a few shillings, when he, like a generous friend, stepped in and put a stop to further proceedings, by *buying the debt* at a *great discount*. I forget whether he says he was repaid, or not.

These anecdotes he wanted me to make use of; but these, as well as all the others he furnished me with, appeared to me to be brought forth by private malice, and therefore I never made use of any of them. Though, I must confess, that, in one instance in particular, this was a very great act of self-denial.

From secretaries of state, judges and governors, let us come to Presidents. Don't start, reader, my bookseller knew nothing against General Washington, or he would have told it. No; we are now going to see a trait of Bradford's republicanism of another kind. *Marten's Law of Nations*, a work that I translated from the French for Bradford, is dedicated, *by him*, to the President of the United States. The dedication was written by me, notwithstanding the Bradfords were obliged to *amend* my writings. When a proof of it was taken off, old Bradford proposed a fulsome addition to it; 'give the old boy *a little more oil*,' said he. This greasing I refused to have any hand in, and notwithstanding I did not *know how to write*, and was a *needy hireling*, My lord and master, Bradford, did not think proper to make any alteration, though I could have no reasonable objection, as it was signed with his name.

While the old man was attempting to wheedle the President and the officers of the Federal Government, the son, *Samuel*, was wheedling the French Minister: the Bradfords love a double game dearly. He spent whole evenings with him, or at least he told me so. According to his account they were like two brothers. I cannot blame Mr Adet, who undoubtedly must have a curiosity to know all the secrets of Bradford's press. For my part, as soon as I heard of this intimacy, I looked upon myself as being as well known to the French Minister as I was to Bradford.

But, there is a tale connected with this, which must be told, because it will give the lie to all that young Lampblack has said about correcting and altering my works. His design is to make people believe that I was obliged to submit to his prunings. We shall see how this was in a moment. In the *New Year's Gift*, speaking of the French Minister, I make use of the following words: 'not that I doubt his veracity, though his not being a *Christian* might be a trifling objection, with some weak minded people.' The old Goosy wanted me to change the word *Christian* for *Protestant*, as he was a good friend, and might be useful to his son. He came himself with the proof sheet, to prevail on me to do this: but if the reader looks into the *New Year's Gift*, he will see that I did not yield.

Bradford never prevailed on me to leave out a single word in his life, except a passage in the *Congress Gallery*. 'Remember' (says the son in a triumphant manner) 'Remember what was erased from the *Congress Gallery*.' I do remember it, thou compost of die-stuff, lampblack and urine, I do remember it well; and since you have not told all about it, I will. The passage erased contained some remarks on the indecent and every way unbecoming expression of Mr Lewis, on the trial of [Robert] Randall [the land-speculator, for attempting to bribe congressmen], when he said, that gentleman would have served *his client* right, if they had *kicked him out of the room*. Bradford told me he had a *very particular reason* for wishing this left out, and as it was not a passage to which I attached much importance, left out it was: but, had I known that his *very particular reason* was, that he had engaged Mr Lewis as his counsellor in a suit which he had just then commenced against his deceased brother's widow and his own sisters, the passage should not have been left out, for him nor for Mr Lewis neither. I fear no lawyers. From this fact we may form a pretty correct idea of the *independence* of Bradford's press, when left to his own conducting.

Bradford pretends to detect me in a lie about my having *a*

*press.* I have two now at work for me, and the printers are always paid the instant their work is done. Can a Bradford say as much? He tells me something about my being *obliged* to pay my taxes. To be sure I am; but did any tax-gatherer ever dare clap his hand on any of my goods or chattels? No; but the land of Thomas Bradford; back-land which he got out of the old soldiers, who were fighting the last war while he was a sort of jailer; this land was sold last year *by the sheriff*, and that to pay the *taxes too.* You see, My Lord Bradford, that you have refreshed my memory to some purpose.

I think, the further we go the deeper my Lord Bradford gets in the mire. Let us stop the career, then. Let us dismiss him, his sons, his press and his shop, with a remark or two on one more passage of his son's letter. 'You' (meaning me) 'can declaim and *scandalize* with the greatest hero of *Billingsgate*, yet, in sober argument and *chastity* of manner, you are a mere *nincompoop*.' The reader must have observed, that Boileau, Roscommon and Pope, in their poetical rules, always convey the precept in an example; so we see here, that young Lampblack gives us an example of the very manner he decries. But, a word more about *chastity*: not quite in the same sense, though not so far from it as to render the transition very abrupt. *Chastity* from the pen of a Bradford! *Chastity* I say, from No 8 South Front Street! *Chastity* from the *bawdy-book shop*! I have no pretension to an overstock of modesty or squeamishness. I have served an apprenticeship in the army; yet have I often been shocked to see what the Bradfords sell. Not, perhaps, so much at the obscenity of the books, as at the conduct of the venders. I do not know a traffic so completely infamous as this. In London it is confined to the very scum of the Jews. It is ten times worse than the trade of a bawd: it is pimping for the eyes: it *creates* what the punk does but satisfy when created. These *literary panders* are the purveyors for the bawdy-house. However, as far as relates to the people in question, the sons are not to blame: 'a *father's wish* is a law with them.'

I shall conclude with observing, that though Bradford's publication was principally intended to do away the charge of having duped me in the one and seven-pence-halfpenny job, he has left it just as it was. His son, has, indeed, attempted to bewilder the reader by a comparison between the prices of the ensuing pamphlets; but what has this to do with the matter? His father took the *Observations*, was to publish them, and give me half the profits. Long after, many months after, every copy of the work was sold, I asked him for an account of it, which he brought me in *writing*, and in which my half of the profits was stated at *one shilling and seven-pence-halfpenny*, or, about *twenty-one cents*. Now, nothing posterior to this could possibly diminish the barefacedness of the transaction. I did not actually receive the *twenty-one cents*; I threw the paper from me with disdain; nor did I ever receive a farthing for the publication in question from that day to this.

I now take leave of the Bradfords, and of all those who have written against me. People's opinions must now be made up concerning them and me. Those who still believe the lies that have been vomited forth against me are either too stupid or too perverse to merit further attention. I will, therefore, never write another word in reply to anything that is published about myself. Bark away, hell-hounds, till you are suffocated in your own foam. Your labours are preserved, bound up together in a piece of bear-skin, with the hair on, and nailed up to a post in my shop, where whoever pleases may read them gratis.

# THIS MODERN JUDAS,
# TALLEYRAND

The following is taken from the *Boston Mercury*, and is said to be derived from an authentic source.

The Bishop of Autun, who resided some time in this country, under the name of Talleyrand Perigord, has informed the Directory of France, that they need not regard the United States any more than the State of Genoa, or Geneva; as our divisions have weakened us down to nothing in point of strength and exertion as a nation; and that there would probably soon be a revolution here, which would tend to throw us entirely into the French scale; as the partizans of France were increasing, and would soon turn out of the government all the Washingtonian Party, all of whom were in the British pay.

In this information he was joined by almost all the Americans who were before in France, or have since gone to that country.

In the meantime, the French party on this side of the Atlantic are continually exciting the French Government to acts of hostility against the United States; and are so desperately determined to destroy the British treaty, as to be willing, for the accomplishment of that purpose, to risk our independence, and even our national existence.

That the apostate Talleyrand was a spy in this country is evident from his being afterwards received with open arms by the very men who had proscribed him. But I have a word or two to say about this atheistical bishop. First he set up as a *merchant and dealer*, at New York, till he had acquired what knowledge he thought was to be come at among persons engaged in mercantile affairs; then he assumed the character of a *gentleman*, at the same time removing to Philadelphia, where he got access to persons of the first rank, all those who were connected with, or in the confidence of, the government. Some months after his arrival in this country, he left a message with a friend of his, requesting me to meet him at that friend's house. Several days passed away before the meeting took place: I had no business to call me that way, and therefore I did not go. At last this modern Judas and I got seated by the same fire-side. I expected that he wanted to expostulate with me on the severe treatment he had met with at my hands: I had called him an apostate, a hypocrite, and every other name of which he was deserving; I therefore leave the reader to imagine my astonishment, when I heard him begin with complimenting me on my *wit* and *learning*. He praised several of my pamphlets, the *New Year's Gift* [*to the Democrats*] in particular, and still spoke of them as mine. I did not acknowledge myself as the author, of course; but yet he would insist that I was; or, at any rate, they reflected, he said, *infinite honour* on the author, let him be who he might. Having carried this species of flattery as far as he judged it safe, he asked me, with a vast deal of apparent seriousness, whether I had received my education at *Oxford*, or at *Cambridge*! Hitherto I had kept my countenance pretty well; but this abominable stretch of hypocrisy, and the placid mien and silver accent with which it was pronounced, would have forced a laugh from a Quaker in the midst of meeting. I don't recollect what reply I made him; but this I recollect well, I gave him to understand that I was no trout, and consequently was not to be caught by tickling.

This information led him to something more solid. He began to talk about *business*. I was no *flour-merchant*, but I taught English; and, as luck would have it, this was the very commodity that Bishop Perigord wanted. If I had taught Thornton's or [Noah] Webster's language, or sold land or ashes, or pepper-pot, it would have been just the same to him. He knew the English language as well as I did; but he wanted to have dealings with me in some way or other.

I knew that, notwithstanding his being *proscribed* at Paris, he was extremely intimate with [Pierre] Adet [the French Minister to the United States]; and this circumstance led me to suspect his real business in the United States: I therefore did not care to take him as a scholar. I told him, that, being engaged in a translation for the press, I could not possibly quit home. This difficulty the lame fiend hopped over in a moment. He would very gladly come to my house. I cannot say but it would have been a great satisfaction to me to have seen the *ci-devant* Bishop of Autun, the guardian of the holy oil that anointed the heads of the descendants of St Louis, come trudging through the dirt to receive a lesson from me; but, on the other hand, I did not want a French spy to take a survey either of my desk or my house. My price for teaching was *six* dollars a month; he offered me *twenty*; but I refused; and before I left him, I gave him clearly to understand that I was not to be purchased.

I verily believe that, had I had any *flour* or *precious confessions* for sale, I might have disposed of them to good account; and even my pamphlets, though Bradford calls them *dirty water*, I think I could have sold to Bishop Judas for more than *one shilling and seven-pence-halfpenny* apiece.

There is no doubt of there being at this moment hundreds of honest missionaries among us, whose sole business is that of spies. They are flying about the country in every direction; not a corner of it will they leave unexplored. They are now much better acquainted with the sentiments of the people of the Union, and know more exactly those who are to be counted upon in case of a war, than either the Federal Government or State Governments.

# THE SCARE-CROW

In the spring of the year 1796, I took a house in Second Street, Philadelphia, for the purpose of carrying on the bookselling business, which I looked upon as being at once a means of getting money, and of propagating writings against the French. I went into my house in May, but the shop could not be gotten ready for some time; and from one delay and another, I was prevented from opening till the second week in July.

Till I took this house, I had remained almost entirely unknown, as a writer. A few persons did, indeed, know that I was the person, who had assumed the name of PETER PORCUPINE; but the fact was by no means a matter of notoriety. The moment, however, that I had taken a lease of a large house, the transaction became a topic of public conversation, and the eyes of the democrats and the French, who still lorded it over the city, and who owed me a mutual grudge, were fixed upon me.

I thought my situation somewhat perilous. Such truths as I had published, no man had dared to utter, in the United States, since the rebellion. I knew that these truths had mortally offended the leading men amongst the democrats, who could, at any time, muster a mob quite sufficient to destroy my house, and to murder me. I had not a friend, to whom I could look with any reasonable hope of receiving efficient support; and, as to the *law*, I had seen too much of republican justice, to expect anything but persecution from that quarter. In short, there were, in Philadelphia, about ten thousand persons, all of whom would have rejoiced to see me murdered; and there might, probably, be two thousand, who would have been very sorry for it; but not above fifty of whom would have stirred an inch to save me.

As the time approached for opening my shop, my friends grew more anxious for my safety. It was recommended to me, to be cautious how I exposed, at my window, anything that might provoke the people; and, above all, not to put up any *aristocratical portraits*, which would certainly cause my windows to be demolished.

I saw the danger; but also saw, that I must, at once, set all danger at defiance, or live in everlasting subjection to the prejudices and caprice of the democratical mob. I resolved on the former; and, as my shop was to open on a Monday morning, I employed myself all day on Sunday, in preparing an exhibition, that I thought would put the courage and the power of my enemies to the test. I put up in my windows, which were very large, all the portraits that I had in my possession of *kings*, *queens*, *princes*, and *nobles*. I had all the English ministry; several of the bishops and judges; the most famous admirals; and, in short, every picture that I thought likely to excite rage in the enemies of Great Britain.

Early on the Monday morning, I took down my shutters. Such a sight had not been seen in Philadelphia for twenty years. Never since the beginning of the rebellion, had anyone dared to hoist at his window the portrait of George III.

In order to make the test as perfect as possible, I had put up some of the *worthies of the Revolution*, and had found out fit companions for them. I had coupled *Franklin* and *Marat* together; and, in another place, [Thomas] *M'Kean* and [J.J.] *An*[c]*kerstrom* [who assassinated Gustavus III of Sweden]. The following tract records some amongst the consequences.

On the 19th instant [1796], Mr Elmslie, partner of Mr John Oldden, called on me with the infamous letter, which, without further preface, I shall lay before the reader.

*To Mr John Olden Merchant, Chestnut Street*

SIR,

A certain William Cobbett alias Peter Porcupine, I am informed is your tenant. This daring *scoundrell*, not satisfied with having repeatedly traduced the people of this country, vilified the most eminent and patriotic characters among us and *grosly* abused our allies the French, in his detestable productions, has now the astonishing effrontery to expose those very publications at his window for sale, as well as certain prints indicative of the prowess of our enemies the British and the disgrace of the French. Calculating largely upon the moderation or rather *pucellanimity* of our citizens, this puppy supposes he may even *insult* us with impunity. But he will e'er long find himself dreadfully mistaken. '*Tho* his miserable publications have not been hitherto considered worthy of notice, the late *manifestation* of his impudence and enmity to this country will not be passed over. With a view therefore of preventing your feeling the blow designed for him, I now address you. When the time of retribution arrives, it may not be convenient to discriminate between the innocent and the guilty. Your property therefore may suffer. For depend upon it brick walls will not skreen the rascal from punishment when once the business is undertaken. As a friend therefore I advise you to save your property by either compelling Mr Porcupine to leave your house or at all events oblige him to cease exposing his abominable productions or any of his courtley prints at his window for sale. In this way only you may avoid danger to your house and perhaps save the rotten *carcase* of your tenant for the present.

A HINT

16 *July* 1796

I have copied this loving epistle, word for word, and letter for letter, preserving the false orthography, as the manner of spelling may probably lead some of my readers to a discovery of the writer.

When Mr Vicesimus Knox [Headmaster of Tonbridge] (who is a sort of a democrat), publishes his next edition of *Elegant Epistles*, he will do well to give this a place amongst them; for, it is certainly a masterpiece in its way. It will be a good pattern for the use of future ruffians, who wish to awe a man into silence, when they are incapable of resisting him in print. But, the worst of it will be, the compiler will not have it in his power to say, that this was attended with success.

If I am right in my guess, the family of the author of this powder blunderbuss, makes a considerable figure in the *Tyburn*

*Chronicle*. His grandfather was hanged for house-breaking, and his *papa* came to the southern part of these states on his travels, by the direction of a righteous judge and twelve honest men.

So much for the author; now to his scrawl.

The cut-throat acts in character. He proceeds exactly in the manner of the Revolutionary Tribunal at Paris: that is, he arraigns, condemns and executes, all in the space of about five minutes. The first charge he brings against me is, that I have 'repeatedly traduced the people of this country'. I take notice of this, not because it is found in this base and cowardly letter, but because it has long been the theme of all those who wish to decry my performances, and because I am willing to let slip no opportunity of declaring my respect for a public, from whom those performances have ever, from the publication of my first essay, to the present moment, met with the most liberal encouragement.

Let any stupid member of the broken-up, backdoor clubs point out, if he can, one single sentence in the writings of Peter Porcupine, where the people of the United States are traduced. 'Tis true, I have not fallen into the beaten track of confounding the good with the bad, of lumping the enemies and the friends of public happiness together, and fawning on them indiscriminately. I have not said that they are all virtuous and wise, and that virtue and wisdom is to be found amongst them alone. No; I am no spaniel, nor will I be one. I address myself to the good sense of my readers, and to that alone: if they want a buffoon, or whining parasite, I am not their man.

But, I must do the people of this country the justice to say, that this is not their taste. They stand in no need of base flattery. Their love of truth has been fully exemplified in the rapid sale of my essays, while their contempt for the popular parasites has been unequivocally expressed in the fate of all the miserable attempts that have been made, to oppose their progress. I have received letters of thanks, and congratulation from every quarter of the Union, even from Richmond in Virginia: and not from *British Agents*, but from native Americans, real lovers of their country. I have received offers of service from persons of the first consequence, in their divers towns and countries, persons whom I never saw or heard of, previous to their communications. Let any fawning scribbler on liberty and equality produce such testimony of public approbation, if he can.

But, I have, it seems, 'vilified some of the most eminent and *patriotic* characters amongst us'. 'Tis pity, to be sure, that these *patriotic* characters should be vilified more than they have vilified themselves. What could I, or anybody else, say to vilify a man, for instance, a man who had made overtures to sell his country for 'a few thousands of dollars'; or another, who had done all in his power, 'to stop the wheels of government', by stirring men up to open rebellion against it? It is not I who have vilified the *eminent patriots*, it is citizen Joseph Fauchet [French Minister to the United States], the old Father Confessor on the banks of the Schuylkill, when he calls them, 'the pretended patriots of America', and when he says, they 'have already their prices'. Surely I might take upon me to repeat the expressions of the Minister of France, of our good and faithful allies, without being chargeable with vilifying the *eminent patriots*. And, if I have laughed at little Mr Swanwick, what have I done more than every man, every woman, and every child, in the United States, at least everyone that ever saw his person, listened to his harangues, or read his poetry? I wonder what I have done, that I must not laugh, that I must remain in a corner as demure as a cat, while everybody else are bursting their sides.

In France, the only country in Europe, (according to *Doctor Jaundice's* account of it), which is *not* in chains. Under that free and happy sky, the mild and humane rulers often issue decrees, forbidding people to weep or look sad, on pain of death, even at the moment they hear the last groans of their parents; but they have never yet carried their *douce humanité* so far as to forbid men to smile. They permit, nay, encourage, both men and women, to sing and laugh, and cut capers, at the very foot of the guillotine, while the pavement is running with human blood; and yet my cruel and inflexible persecutors will not suffer me to laugh, when I hear them bawling at a civic festival, or see them boxing with an old image that they had formerly adored.

Again, the cut-throat says, I have '*grosly* abused our allies the French'. This is false. By the treaty made between this country and the King of France, the French nation is, in my opinion, no more the ally of the United States, than the Chinese are. Louis XVI was, indeed, the ally, 'the *great* and *good* ally' (to make use of the words of Congress) of this country; and, I leave anyone who has read my works, to determine whether I have ever abused him or not. The Queen of France, the calumniated Antoinette, was the first foreigner, except some generous Englishmen, that advanced a shilling in the American cause: have I ever abused her memory? It was not I, though it was an Englishman, that cut off her head, and besprinkled her garments with blood, on a sign, hung over a public road. It was not I that guillotined her husband, in an automaton, every day, from nine in the morning to nine at night, for the diversion of the inhabitants of Philadelphia. I did not rejoice at the death of an innocent young prince, whose birth had been celebrated with uncommon pomp in this city, in the prosperous days of his father. I never reviled the gallant French officers and army who served in this country, and to whom America is really indebted; but, on the contrary, I have ever regretted their fate, and expressed my detestation of the barbarians who have dipped their hands in their blood.

The next charge is, I have 'the *astonishing effrontery* to expose for sale, certain prints, indicative of the prowess of the British, and the disgrace of the French'. Here the hang-in-chains writer alludes to a print, entitled, 'Earl Howe's Decisive Victory over the French Fleet, on 1 June, 1794'. This print has had a vast concourse of admirers. I had but two of them, one was sold instantly, and I have had more than five hundred applications for the other. What is very singular is, that one-third part of those who have wished to purchase this print were French republicans. The print is not sold, nor shall it be. I will keep it in my window, as long as any violence is talked of, and when that ceases, I will have it put in a gilt frame, and hung up in a conspicuous part of my house.

This offensive print is no more than a true representation of the action of the famous *first of June*, and if it be 'indicative of the disgrace of our allies', it is no fault of mine. If defeat is disgrace, they were certainly most shockingly disgraced on that day. But, I thought it had been long ago agreed on, that, though the fleet got a drubbing, and a pretty decent one too, the victory was, *in fact*, on the side of the French. I am sure Barrere told the French people so; and I am sure most of our newspapers told the people of America the same story. How many believed them, I will not pretend to say; but if it was a victory, *in fact*, I am treating people with a representation of it, that's all, and am by no means exposing what is 'indicative of British prowess'.

When William Penn was tracing out his beloved city of Philadelphia; if anyone had told him, that the time would come, when a man should be threatened with murder, for offering for sale, in one of the streets, a print 'indicative of British prowess', I much question, if the good man, though a Quaker, would not have said that it was a d—ned lie. Poor old fellow! he little dreamed what was to happen at the close of the 'enlightened eighteenth century'.

I could turn back to American publications, in which the prowess of Britons is the pleasing theme; in which the French are called, what I never called them, 'poor effeminate poltroons'. I could bring my readers back to the time, when they set the savages on to scalp the people of these states, and when the people of these States solicited the King of Great Britain to march an army against them. Has the American Revolution entirely changed the dispositions, affections, and even nature of the two rival nations? Did Great Britain lose every spark of courage, generosity, and virtue, when she lost America? That event certainly could not metamorphose the then inhabitants of the island, nor could it have any great effect on their children, or at least I presume so. The people of the United States have solemnly declared, in their Declaration of Independence, that the British nation are by nature, *just* and *magnanimous*; and will they now swallow their words at the command of the hirelings of the devastators of France?

To return to the print 'indicative of British prowess'; have I not as good a right to exhibit proof of this prowess at my window, as the democrats have to exhibit the proofs of theirs on the front of the church opposite it? The half-destroyed bust of George II remains as a monument of their valour, and why should I not be permitted to expose a print to perpetuate the valour of Earl Howe and his gallant fleet? These two pieces are, besides, necessary to the explanation of each other; for when a stranger asks, why the bust of the old king was so unmercifully mangled, the person he addresses himself to, shows him the naval victory of Lord Howe. 'There, sir,' says he, 'is the fatal cause.' If the impertinent querist goes on, and asks, how George II, who died upwards of thirty years ago (and whose bust remained untouched during the whole of the American war) could deserve this rough treatment on account of the drubbing given to the French fleet in 1794, we cut him short at once, by telling him, that he is a rank aristocrat, and totally unfit to live in a land of freedom.

Mr Oldden is told, that there is but one way left of saving his house, and that is, by obliging me to cease exposing my '*courtly* prints' at my window for sale. It would seem by this, that the cut-throats look upon me as Oldden's vassal; I shall convince them that I am not. To oblige me to desist from any branch of my lawful occupation would prove the toughest job that ever my landlord undertook, should he be silly enough to attempt it. As to obliging me to quit his house, there are no hopes there neither; for I have a lease of it, and a lease that I will hold in spite of all the *sans-culottes* in America.

But what does the cut-throat mean by '*courtly* prints'? I have Ankerstrom the regicide; that can be no courtly print at any rate. I have, indeed, the portraits of the late King and Queen of France; but as they are dead, one would imagine that they could create no alarm. Pour Louis little thought when he sent hither those portraits of himself and his queen, which now hang up in the Congress House, that the day would come, when a bookseller would be threatened with murder for exhibiting his likeness, in the capital of the Union. Others have exhibited him at their windows, stretched on the scaffold; they had a right so to do; every man to his taste, and I to mine. 'Tis true, I have the portraits of Mr Pitt and Lord Grenville, and several other noble personages; but then, I have Marat and [Louis-Michel] Lepel-letier, by way of rubbing off as I go. I have a Right Reverend Father in God in one corner of my window, and if I could procure the right irreverend Father in the Devil, Tom Paine, I would hoist him up in the other; for want of him I have Doctor Priestley, who, upon a shift, is very capable of supplying his place.

I have some groups, too, executed by order of the French Convention, which, I humbly presume, will not be called *courtly*. The taking the Bastile decorates one pane of my window, as it did the Birmingham clubroom; the French people on their marrow-bones acknowledging the existence of a God, by order of Robespierre, decorates another; and a third is ornamented with a representation of the glorious 'victory' obtained over the Swiss guards, on the 10th of August, 1792. I am promised a print of Poor Richard, in the arms of a brace of angels, who are carrying him off, God knows whither.

I am sure, now, all these things are republican enough; and if my sovereign lords will but please to take my whole collection into view, I cannot think that they will find me so criminal as I have been represented.

And then, there are my books and stationery, almost the whole of which is English. I have been looking round, and cannot for my life find any other American book than Adams's *Defence of the American Constitutions*, and Peter Porcupine's works. The latter of these my sovereigns have proscribed, and the former speaks about the *well-born*: so that, unless my gracious lords will condescend to permit me to sell these offensive things, I must shut up shop. But, if I must, I hope all the rest of the trade will be compelled to do the same. There is Mr Campbell has published Hume's *History of England*, a book as full as it can hold of kings' and queens' pictures, and *aristocracy* of all sorts and sizes; and contains, besides, a great number of instances of 'British prowess', and of 'the disgrace of our allies'. Mr Dobson too, and Mr Carey, have published books on *Royal* paper, and Mr Brown has dared to publish his gazette even on *Imperial*. These are crimes that I have never either committed or attempted. Is not this anti-republicanism to the last degree, and a downright insult on the citizens of the United States? Again, there is Mr Young, and several others that I could mention, who have the assurance to expose for sale, Walkden's *Royal British* ink-powder, stamped with the 'tyrant George's' arms. Shall all this go unpunished, and shall poor I be eat alive merely for exposing a print or two? Forbid it justice! Democratic justice forbid it!

Nor, should a strict inquisition take place, will the great Mr Franklin Bache himself come off blameless. He had informed the public, that he is in correspondence with *Peter Pindar*, and it is notorious that this Peter is not only an *aristocrat*, but a declared *royalist*. He has given Tom Paine the severest lashing he ever met with. And as to 'traducing the people of this country', does not Peter traduce them, when, in speaking of the United States, he says –

*Where sons of liberty their paeans sing,*
*And every scoundrel convict is a king.*

Is not this traducing the people? And yet Mr Bache publicly boasts of his intimacy with this fellow, and takes infinite pains to propagate his works! 'Birds of a feather will flock together,' says the old proverb, and it is no more than reasonable to suppose, that Mr Bache, whatever mask he may choose to wear, participates in the sentiments of his friend Pindar.

Nay, even Doctor Franklin was an aristocrat, and an abominable one too, as may be seen in the very last item of his last will and testament. 'I bequeath', says he, 'to my worthy friend George Washington, my gold-headed cane, surmounted with a *Liberty Cap*: if it were a *Sceptre* he is worthy of it!' Thus, you see, reader, after all the doctor's clamour against kings, he thought a Sceptre something better than a Liberty Cap. That the doctor was sincere here there is no doubt; men are generally so upon their deathbeds, howsoever profound their hypocrisy may have been through life. Poor Richard certainly deserves to be tumbled from his niche for this dying confession, and, I trust, 'when the day of retribution comes', as my cut-throat terms it, he will not be forgotten. 'Tis ridiculous, to be sure, to lay violent hands on a statue; but as this kind of heroism has made a very considerable figure in this 'Age of Reason', I do not see why old Lightning-Rod should escape any more than another.

Doctor Priestley, in his first American publication, congratulates himself on being *now* got into a country, where he can publish his sentiments, be they what they may, without any fear of persecution from either *church* or *state*. But he had forgot that there was the democratic gang, more intolerant than either. What will he say, when he sees the letter of my eavesdropping cut-throat? Will he not begin to repent of having so bitterly complained of the want of liberty of the press in England? One of his excuses for quitting his country was, that he had threatening letters sent to him. Perhaps my cut-throat thinks that all Englishmen are like the doctor; but he will find himself mistaken: all the stink pots of all the democrats in the western hemisphere shall never drive me from America, nor make me take coach in disguise, as the Birmingham philosopher did.

The democratic societies (for they were then in existence) might, perhaps, have informed Doctor Priestley, that he should be permitted to print whatever he pleased, and, if so, he might well venture to say that the press was free for him; but, unless he had received such previous intimation, his boast of enjoying the liberty of the press was made very much at hazard.

These people plead the liberty of the press, in the fullest extent of the word; they claim a right to print and publish whatever they please; they tell you that free discussion must lead to the truth, and a thousand other arguments they have always ready at their fingers ends to oppose to every kind of restraint. They have calumniated the best of governments and the best of men; they revile all that is good and all that is sacred, and that too in language the most brutal and obscene; and, if they are accused of indecency, or called on for proofs of what they advance, they take shelter in their sanctuary, *the liberty of the press*. But, on the other hand, if anyone has courage enough to oppose them, and is so happy as to do it with success; if the mildest of their expressions are retorted, they instantly threaten their opponents with violence and even murder. Their doctrine is, that the press is free for them, and them alone. This is democratic liberty of the press; just such as is enjoyed in that free and happy country whose revolutionary career the people of this country are called upon to imitate.

Much has been said and sung about the Sedition Bills of Mr Pitt, and the restraint on the liberty of the press in England; but, whatever that restraint may be, it is by law. The law says, that there are such restraints, and, therefore, he who trespasses deserves punishment. The laws of this country say, that the press is free, and we well know what invidious comparisons are continually made between this country and England, in that respect; but, if men are to be murdered, or have their houses burnt for exercising this much talked of liberty, it is time to cease giving it a place among the advantages that the United States enjoy over the 'mother country', as it is sometimes called in derision. When a foreigner arrives in Great Britain, he looks at the written law; there he sees how far he is permitted to carry the use of the press; and, so long as he keeps within the bounds prescribed, his person and property is safe. There is no subaltern power, whose consent he has to obtain, before he dares publish a book, or expose a print for sale. His house is not threatened with destruction, because his window exhibits what is indicative of the prowess of his nation, and of the disgrace of their enemies; at any rate, he is not threatened with murder, for having stepped forward in defence of the laws and the government of the country.

When I first took up the pen, I found a good deal of difficulty (as the public will see, one of these days) to get access to the press at all, not because the manuscript I offered contained anything libellous or immoral, but because it was not adapted to what was supposed to be the taste of the public. In fact, the press was at the time, generally speaking, as far as related to what is usually termed politics, in the hands of a daring and corrupt faction, who, by deceiving some, and intimidating others, had blocked up every avenue to true information. My publications were looked upon as so many acts of rebellion against this despotic combination, and, therefore, every possible trick was essayed to discredit them and their author; all these tricks have, however, proved vain.

My object, and my only object, in writing, was to contribute my mite towards the support of a government under which I enjoyed peace and plenty. This object I have pursued as steadily as my small share of leisure would allow me; and that I have not laboured in vain, the present conduct of the democratic faction most amply proves. The cut-throat's letter, which I now lay before the public, shows to what a state of desperation they are driven. They at first made some pitiful attempts to answer me; those sunk out of sight, and were forgotten for ever. They then vomited forth calumnies against the author; calumnies so totally void of all truth and even probability, that even their own herd did not believe a word they contained.

Among other abominable falsehoods contained in the *Aurora* concerning me, is my having refused to pay my taxes in this country. To which I answer, that, the small portion of taxes that I have had to pay, has been paid without hesitation. No man, either in a private or public capacity, ever called on me twice for payment of the same sum. The taxes for the property I now rent I have paid up to January next. I owe nobody, neither the State nor the people of the State, a farthing; let the members of the *ci-devant* democratic society say as much if they can.

Next they published a blasphemous book under my assumed name: this failed also, and the city of New York has witnessed their shameful defeat as well as Philadelphia. At last, smarting all over with the lashes I had given them, and fearing a continuation, they have had recourse to the poor sneaking trick of a threatening letter. A trick of robbers, who have not courage enough to venture their necks. I have often been congratulated on my triumph over this once towering, but fallen and despicable faction, and I now possess undeniable proof that the triumph is complete.

It is in vain that the cut-throat would persuade us, that the democrats do not think my 'miserable productions worthy of notice'; the very scrawl of this their stupid secretary proves that they have dreaded them, and that they yet dread them. If they despised my 'miserable productions', why not laugh at them, as I do at theirs? Why not suffer them to rot on the shelf, like the *Political Progress of Britain*, or be kicked about the street like the *Aurora*? Threatening Mr Oldden with the destruction of his house, unless he could prevail on me to cease publishing, is curious enough in itself; but it is much more curious, when accompanied with the observation, that my publications are *miserable* and *unworthy of notice*.

Of all the stupid inventions that ever entered the brains of this bungling clan, the cut-throat letter to Mr Oldden is the most ridiculous. Had they studied for years, they could not have found out anything that would have pleased me so well. It will for ever silence their clamours about the liberty of the press; it will prove to the people most fully, the truth of what I have always told them; that is, that these 'pretended patriots', these advocates for liberty and equality, would, if they had become masters, have been a divan of cruel and savage tyrants. That they know nothing of liberty but the name, and that they make use of that name merely to have the power of abolishing the thing. It will prove to all the world, that they have long dreaded me, that they still dread me, and that I despise them.

I shall conclude with this unequivocal declaration; that, as to the past, I would not retract a sentence, nor a single expression of what I have written, if the most bloody of the most bloody democrats had his foot upon my breast, and his long knife at my throat; and that, for the future, I will continue to publish and expose for sale whatever I please, and that I will never cease to oppose in some way or other, the enemies of the country in which I live, so long as one of them shall have the impudence to shew his head. Hitherto I have given acids only, I will now drench them with vinegar mixed with gall.

# THE SCOURGE THAT HANGS
# OVER ME

*To Edward Thornton, Secretary to the British Legation to
the United States. [On leave in England]*

DEAR SIR,

Here am I, sent into exile by the Yellow Fever, which has
depopulated the city, and which has found its way once more
into my own house. My clerk, Mr [Ezra] Serjeant, is very ill with
it, but we have some hopes of his recovery. This circumstance
will account for the vapidness of my papers, a file of which I
have taken the liberty to send you, accompanied with a new
pamphlet by Mr [Robert] Harper [*Observations on the Dispute
between the United States and France, 1797*]. The pamphlet is not
worth a farthing. It is a mere *softener* for the people, to make
them satisfied with the taxes imposed on them. The absurdity of
the calculations it contains you will at once perceive; but it is a
trick well enough for a republican pen. You know, the great
object is to prevent the people from looking back to *old times*.
The precious *word* (for it is no more) *Independence* is ever held
up as the cheap purchase of every thing that we are accustomed
to look upon as of any value. The little pamphlet called the
*Cannibals' Progress* [June 1798], I send you to let you see how I
am working against the French. I have published twenty-five
thousand of this work, and about as many more have issued, by
my permission, from the German and other presses in the States.
It has been, and long will be, a mighty engine. The little boys
and the poor people buy it, and it is read in every family. Of our

politics you will have a much better account than it is in my power to give you.

In answer to your obliging favour of the 7th of June, I have first to observe, that you have had much more trouble with my little affairs than I wished to give you, or than I could have expected you to take. I dare say Marshall [the bookseller, later of Simpkin, Marshall] is a rascal. He wrote me by the packet, and told me he had had some *difference* with the society [distributing Hannah More's tracts]. My answer I enclose, that you may see how I have stung him. Be so good, sir, as to put the number of his house in the address, and drop the letter in the penny post. As I expect to hear from Miss Hannah More by the next packet, I shall defer, 'till then, giving any bookseller an order on the subject. I am sorry, sir, you should have had so much trouble, and will spare you the pain of any further conversations with the covetous dogs. I daresay Marshall wished to turn the whole work to his own private advantage; or to suppress it altogether. Such is the abominable spirit that governs the bookselling tribe in general. My friend and fellow labourer, Mr [John] Wright [bookseller and publisher of the *Anti-Jacobin*], I am sure is a noble exception. I am glad to hear you speak so highly of his merits.

You make me very happy, sir, in telling me that I am highly esteemed in England; that is the place where I wish to be esteemed. Whether I shall escape the scourge that continually hangs over us here, I know not; but, if I do, a few years will most certainly see me once more in dear Old England, far distant from yellow fevers and universal suffrage. If Mrs Cobbett's health continues to decline, which I am afraid will be the case, it is impossible for me much longer to resist her solicitations, which grow more and more earnest every day.

My *materials* augment daily both in quantity and in excellence of quality. I much wish, my fingers itch, to write a pamphlet on the subject of the *mode of election here*, [*The Trial of Republicanism*, 1799] and its *pretty* consequences, addressed to some famous *reformist* on your side of the water; but, I am afraid, it would not do at present; and I imagine that it will come out to full as much advantage, after the parties in England have got rid of the apprehensions which are common to them all, and the opposition have time again to bring forth their stalking-horse, *Reform*.

I have now on the table before me the beginning of a pamphlet, containing observations on those parts of the rascally *New Annual Register*, which relate to the disputes between America, Great Britain, and France. If I do not make [George] Robinson and his crew blush, the hide of a *sectarian* is thicker than an oak plank and more impenetrable. You are, without doubt, aware of the deep mischief that these rancourous caitiffs are engaged in? I look upon them as the most implacable and most dangerous adversaries that the government of Great Britain has to contend with. Your Tookes, Foxes, and Th[e]lwals, advance to the assault and are blown to attoms; but Robinson's gang proceed by sap. They begin to shelter themselves at the very foot of the glacis, and never show their dastard heads till their damnable work is accomplished. I have the vanity to think, that I can unearth them; or, at least, give them a most disagreeable annoyance. They are extremely careful what they say about affairs which are pretty well understood at home, but they were less cautious respecting America: they trusted to the ignorance of their readers, and laid aside their sophistry and misrepresentation for direct falshood. I am in hopes I shall get this pamphlet out here in two months' time, or less. I intend to send Wright a copy in manuscript.

I trust that this will find you well, and that we shall, 'ere long, have the pleasure to see you in America; though, indeed, it is almost a sin to wish a person to quit England for such an infernal climate.

I am, sir,
With the greatest respect,
your most humble
and most obdt serv
WM COBBETT

*Bustleton, 27 August 1798*

# FAREWELL TO AMERICA

I sailed from New York, on my return to England, on the 1st of June, 1800, having ordered a farewell advertisement to be inserted in the public papers the day before. Soon after I began to publish the *Porcupine* in London, an American wrote to me, complaining of my indiscriminating attacks on his countrymen; to this complaint I published the following answer:

SIR,
   I shall preface my answer to your remonstrance with an extract from my *farewell address to your countrymen*, which address it is probable you may not have seen.
   You will, doubtless, be astonished, that after having had such a smack of the sweets of *liberty*, I should think of rising thus abruptly from the feast; but this astonishment will cease, when you consider, that, under a general term, things diametrically opposite in their natures are frequently included, and that flavours are not more various than tastes. Thus, for instance, nourishment of every species is called *food*, and we all like food; but while one is partial to roast beef and plum pudding, another is distractedly fond of flummery and mash; so is it with respect to *liberty*, of which, out of its infinite variety of sorts, yours unfortunately happens to be precisely that sort which I do not like.
   When people care not two straws for each other, ceremony at parting is mere grimace; and as I have long felt the most perfect indifference with regard to a vast majority of those whom I now address, I shall spare myself the trouble of a ceremonious farewell. Let me not, however, depart from you with indiscriminating contempt. If no man ever had so many and such malignant foes,

no one ever had more friends, and those more kind, more sincere, and more faithful. If I have been unjustly vilified by some, others have extolled me far beyond my merits; if the savages of the city have scared my children in the cradle, those children have, for their father's sake, been soothed and caressed by the affectionate, the gentle, the generous inhabitants of the country, under whose roofs I have spent some of the happiest hours of my life.

*Thus* and *thus*, Americans, will I ever speak of you. In a very little time, I shall be beyond the reach of your friendship, or your malice; beyond the hearing of your commendations or your curses; but being out of your power will alter neither my sentiments nor my work. As I have never spoken any thing but truth to you, so I will never speak any thing but truth of you: the heart of a Briton revolts at an emulation in baseness; and though you have, as a nation, treated me most ungratefully and unjustly, I scorn to repay you with ingratitude and injustice. To my friends, who are also the real friends of America, I wish that peace and happiness which virtue ought to ensure, but which, I greatly fear, they will not find; and as to my enemies, I can wish them no severer scourge than that which they are preparing for themselves and their country. With this I depart for my native land, where neither the moth of *Democracy*, nor the rust of *Federalism* doth corrupt, and where thieves do not, with impunity, break through and steal five thousand dollars at a time.

# THE WAR OF 1812

## (1812-15)

# THE WAR WITH THE UNITED STATES

This war, which was spoken of by a hireling of *The Times* news-paper and others, with such ineffable contempt, has now assumed a very formidable mien; and those who were so eager for the war, begin to revile each other with regard to the conducting of it.

There are, at this time, three political factions in the country; the one that is in possession of the distribution of the public money; the Whig faction; and the faction of the Wellesleys and Cannings. The two latter would join if they could; but, each aims at the possession of the power of giving places and pensions, and, in short, at being the ministry.

These two, therefore, cannot agree wholly; but, they both attack, though upon different occasions and different grounds, those who are in possession of the paradise of Whitehall.

Amongst other objects of attack is that of *negligence as to the American War*. The *Chronicle* and *The Times* are equally bitter against the ministers upon this subject; they revile them for hav-ing plunged the country into a war with America without pro-viding a sufficient maritime force to cope with that new enemy. A *sufficient force!* Why, *The Times* newspaper spoke of the navy of the United States as a thing not worthy of the name; it laughed at 'Mr Madison and *his navy*'; it predicted that a few months would add that navy to our own; it, in short, spoke of it in a tone of contempt which I should in vain attempt to describe.

And yet, it now blames the ministers for not having provided a sufficient force to cope with that contemptible navy; that navy which was an object of the most cruel ridicule.

The defeat and capture of the *Guerriere*, the *Frolic*, and the

*Macedonian* must, of course, be matter of astonishment to those, who listened to the language of these presumptuous and foolish men; but, in what respect are the ministers to blame for it any more than they were for the evacuation of Madrid, and for all the consequences of the unexpected retreat of our army in the Peninsula? The ministers had a great abundance of ships, of all sizes, on the American station; and what were they to do more? I recollect, and so must the reader, that, at the time of the encounter between *Commodore Rodgers* and *Captain Bingham*, the words in the mouths of all these writers were: 'Let one of our FRIGATES meet with Rodgers, and *we ask no more.*' This wish; this challenge, was repeated a thousand times over; the public cannot have forgotten the fact; nay, the sentiment was universal. Upon what ground, then, are the ministers now to be blamed? Are they to be blamed, because, upon trial, it has been found, that our frigates are not a match for those of America? Are they to be blamed, because they did not entertain a meaner opinion of our frigates, compared with those of America, than any other man in England entertained, or, at least, dared to say that he entertained?

We are told, by the writers in the interest of the two OUT factions, that the republican frigates are bigger, longer, have heavier guns, and the like, than our frigates have.

'The varlet's a *tall man,*' said Bobadil when he had been cudgelled.

But are these new discoveries? Were the facts not all well known before to all these writers, when they so boldly challenged out the American frigates to combat with ours? When Rodgers attacked Bingham, the size of his ship was well known and particularly described; and, yet, no one then called for heavier ships to be sent out to the American coast.

Why, then, are the ministers to be blamed for not sending out heavier ships?

Besides, they have heavier ships upon the station, and it cannot be their fault if those ships do not fall in with the American frigates. What are they to do with our frigates? If ours are unable to face the American frigates, what are, I ask, the ministers to do with them? Are they not to suffer them to go on a cruise, lest they should fall in with a *tall* Yankee? In short, it is another of the tricks of faction to blame the ministers for these misadventures of the navy; and, the attempts made by the ministerial

*James Madison, brilliant spokesman for the Federalists*

prints to account for our defeat upon the ground of our *inferiority of force* is another of the means made use of to deceive the people, and to encourage them in the continuation of the war.

When, until now, did we think of disparity of force? When, until now, did we dream of an English ship surrendering to a ship, the superiority of the force of which it required *a minute calculation* to show? When, until now, did an English captain hesitate to attack a ship of a few guns more than his own?

Instead of all the *calculations* that we have seen in the newspapers; instead of those swelled out accounts of the vast force of the American frigates, we should be plainly told, that we have *now* an enemy to cope with equal to ourselves as far as his numbers will go.

Amongst all the *calculations* and computations, however, that we have heard, I have not perceived it any where taken into account, that we have *experience*, which the Americans have not. Where did Isaac Hull gain his naval experience: and where Mr Decatur? There are two Decaturs, the father and son. They were my neighbours, in the country, in Pennsylvania. They were farmers more than seamen, though the elder went occasionally to sea as commander of a merchant ship. If it be the father who has taken the *Macedonian*, he must be upwards of three-score years of age; and, if it be the son, I am sure it is the first battle he ever was in; for, twelve years ago, he was but a mere lad. The father was a man of great probity and of excellent sense; and, I have no doubt that the son is the same; but, I'll engage, that both have had more experience in raising Indian corn than in naval tactics.

Something, therefore, in our estimates, should be allowed for our superiority in point of *experience*. We have no officer of the navy, who has not passed a great part of his life on actual service; we have scarcely one who has not been in numerous battles; and, in the unfortunate case above spoken of, one of the captains appears to have been of long standing even in that rank.

When we are speaking of the naval preparations of Napoleon, we always dwell upon the difficulty of his forming naval *officers*: but here we see, in the case of America, that that is attended with no difficulties at all; we here see gallant and consummate commanders start up in a trice, and, in a moment, is dissolved the charm which bound us in ignorance as to this important species of information.

The truth is, I believe, that, amongst the first qualities of a naval commander, are *sobriety*, *vigilance*, and *consideration for his crew*; and these qualities are within the reach of every man. The American Government, too, has *a wide range for choice*; with it no intrigues, commonly called *interest*, is likely to prevail; because the possession of the powers of the state depend solely upon the *will of the people*, and the government, having *such* support, is not reduced to the necessity of seeking support from any individuals; and, of course, is not exposed to the danger of being compelled to employ as commanders, or as officers of any rank, persons not recommended by their own good qualities.

This is a very great advantage possessed by the American Government; an advantage to which, perhaps, it owes those successes, which we so sorely lament, and which seem to be very likely to form an era in the naval history of the world.

In my preface to the republication of Mr Chancellor Livingstone's *Treatise on Merino Sheep*, I showed how necessarily it would follow from the introduction of flock-keeping in America, that she would become independent of us to woollens. Nevertheless, and in spite of all the facts which have, from time to time, been published relative to the manufacturing of cloths in that country, there are still men to treat with *ridicule*, ay, even with *ridicule*, the idea of America being able to make her own coats and blankets. I remember, that, while I was in Newgate for two years, for writing about the flogging of the local militia, at the town of Ely, in England, under the superintendence of German troops, there came a gentleman, who was, I believe, a dealer in wool, to ask my opinion relative to the future commerce with America. After having spent about a quarter of an hour in a detail of facts, which, in my mind, contained *proof unquestionable*, that the woollen trade with America was for ever *at an end*, he began a sentence upon the surprising increase of the manufactures in America, which he concluded in words to this effect: 'I dare say, that, in less than *half a century*, we shall not ship a bale of cloth to that country.' This put me in mind of the effect that the Botley parson's sermons used to have upon me; and I lost no time in changing the subject of conversation.

I am not one of those who shall regret this independence of America, which I do not think will prove any injury to England in the end; but I could have wished the change to have been *less abrupt*, and effected without war, and without the animosities and the sufferings inseparable from war. To me it appears as absurd as it is unnatural, that the American farmer should not have his coat untaxed at the custom house in England. I can see no sense and no reason in it. Nor do I see why the people of England, or any portion of them, should make coats or knives, or any thing else for the use of other countries, except merely in such quantities as may be necessary to exchange for wine and oil, and some few other things which really are useful to man. The use of commerce is to effect an exchange of the products of one climate for those of another; but governments have turned it into the means of *taxation*, and, in many cases, that appears to be its only object. An exchange of *English coals* for *French wine*, the former at 30s. a chaldron at Paris, and the latter at 6d. a bottle in London; that would, indeed, be a commerce to be contemplated with pleasure. But a commerce, carried on under a code of prohibitions and penalties, such as those now everywhere in existence, is not to be desired. It is an instrument of taxation, and an endless source of war, and it is nothing more.

Those, however, who are of a different opinion, may look upon the war with America as one of the surest means of destroying, or, at least, diminishing for ever, the best branch of what they admire; but, while I blame the ministers for the war, I must say, that the merchants and manufacturers (I mean the powerful ones) have no right to blame them. The ministers, in their measures towards America, have done no more than pursue *that same system*, of which those merchants and manufacturers have a thousand times, and in the strongest terms, expressed their approbation. At the outset of this long and destructive war, who stood forward so readily in support of it as this class of persons? The war-whoop has invariably originated with them. They indulged the selfish hope of seeing themselves in possession of all the trade and all the riches of the world. The English newspapers contain a record of their love of war, of war against anybody, so long as it promised *gain to them*. They have, over and over again, called the war which began in an invasion of France by the Duke of Brunswick, 'a just and *necessary* war'; but, of late, they appear to have been taught by their *poor-books* and the list of *Bankrupts*, that the war is not quite so *necessary*, however *just* they may still think it. *They* have, I repeat it, no right to complain against the ministers, who have not deviated from the system of Pitt and Grenville, and who, with regard to America, are only acting upon the very same principles, and pursuing the very same objects, that have been acted upon and pursued from the year 1792 to the present day; and the manufacturers are tasting, as is most meet, of the fruit of the tree of their own planting and protecting.

# DISPUTE WITH THE AMERICANS

My article 'American War' was devoted principally to the task of endeavouring to convince the Prince Regent and the public, that it was neither dangerous nor dishonourable to yield to the terms upon which we might have had, and may yet have, peace with America: and, to my great mortification, though, I must confess, not much to my surprise, I now see, from the contents of the last *Gazette*, wherein is His Royal Highness's *Declaration*, that all my endeavours have been of no avail, and that war, long, expensive and sanguinary war, will now take place with an enemy, who, above all others, is capable of inflicting deep wounds upon this already-crippled, or, at least, exhausted nation.

From the first publication of the Letters which passed between Lord Wellesley and Mr Pinckney, soon after the French had announced their intention to repeal the Berlin and Milan Decrees; from the very day of that publication, which took place soon after I was imprisoned in Newgate for two years (with a fine to THE KING, which I have since paid, of a thousand pounds) for having written and published upon the subject of flogging certain English militia men, at the town of Ely, in England, who had been first reduced to submission by German troops; from the very day of that publication I began to fear the present sad result of the dispute which had then assumed a new and more serious character than it had ever before worn. With that fear in my mind, I bent all my feeble powers towards preventing such result. I have failed: opinions and counsels the direct opposite of mine have prevailed; and time will show who was right and who wrong.

Upon former occasions the real grounds of war have, but too often, been lost sight of in the multitude and confusion of subsequent events; the government has had the address to enlist the passions of men on its side, and the voice of reason has been stifled.

But, *here*, as I was from the first resolved it should be, there is a clear, a distinct, an undisguisable ground before our eyes; we know well what we are at war for: we know, and must bear in mind, that we are at war for the purpose of *enforcing our practice of stopping American vessels upon the high seas, and taking out of them all such persons as our naval officers may deem to be British seamen.* This is now become the clearly defined subject of the war with America.

The DECLARATION, does not contain any *new* matter: it is a summary of what our ministers have before alleged and asserted in their correspondence with the American Government and its divers agents. But, there are some few passages of it which require to be particularly noticed.

The question relating to the Orders in Council has been before so amply discussed, in my several Letters and articles upon the subject, that I will not encumber my present remarks with any thing relating thereunto; but, will confine myself to what relates to the impressment of persons out of American ships on the high seas.

Upon this point the DECLARATION says:

His Royal Highness can never admit, that in the exercise of the *undoubted* and hitherto *undisputed right of searching neutral merchant vessels in time of war*, the impressment of British seamen, when found therein, can be deemed *any violation of a neutral flag.* Neither can he admit, that the taking such seamen from on board such vessels, can be considered by any neutral state as a hostile measure, or a justifiable cause of war. There is no right more clearly established, than the right which a sovereign has to the allegiance of his subjects, more especially in time of war. Their allegiance is no optional duty, which they can decline, and resume at pleasure. It is a call which they are bound to obey: *it began with their birth, and can only terminate with their existence.* If a similarity of language and manners may make the exercise of this right more liable to *partial mistakes*, and *occasional abuse*, when practised towards the vessels of the United States, the same circumstances make it also a right, with the exercise of which, in regard to such vessels it is more difficult to dispense.

The doctrine of *allegiance*, as here laid down, I admit, with some exceptions; but, as to the right of impressing British seamen, on the high seas, out of neutral ships, I deny it to be founded on *any* principle or maxim laid down by *any* writer on public law. Indeed, the DECLARATION does not say that it is: it says, that the right of SEARCHING neutral vessels in time of war is '*undoubted* and has *hitherto been undisputed*'. This is not correct; for, not only has even *this* right been doubted, not only are there two opinions about it in the books on public law, but the writers on public law are, for the most part, *against* the said right as *we practise it*, and they contend, that we have no right to seize enemy's goods on board of merchant ships which are neutral. Nay, the contest has given rise to military resistance on the part of our now-ally, Russia, Denmark, and Sweden; and, what is still more, Great Britain ceased, upon their *threats*, to exercise this, even *this*, right of seizing *enemy's goods* on board of neutral ships of war.

But, this right; this right of SEARCHING neutral ships; what has it to do with the *impressment of persons* on board of such ships? That is what the Americans object to, and are at war against. They are not at war against our right of *search*, even in our own interpretation of that right. What they object to is, the stopping of their vessels on the high seas, and taking *people* out of them by force; a practice which, I repeat it, is sanctioned by no principle or maxim of any writer on public law, nor by any usage heretofore known in the world.

The DECLARATION does not assert, as Lord Castlereagh did, in his letter to Mr Russell, that this practice is sanctioned by any former usage: but, it *declares* the right from the *right of search*. It says, that, *in exercising* 'the right of search', that is to say, the right to search for articles *contraband of war*, and for *enemy's goods*, we have a right to impress British seamen, if we find them. So that, this is the new shape of the defence of the practice: we do not now assert that we have a right to stop American vessels upon the high seas *for the purpose* of impressing our seamen; but, having stopped them for the purpose of exercising our old '*right of search*', we have a right to avail ourselves of the opportunity to take out persons whom our own officers, at their discretion, may judge to be British seamen.

This is not even *plausible*, in my opinion: for, what right can we have to impress, if we have no right to stop for the purpose of impressing? I may enter another's house to search for a stolen coat, and, if I find there my hat, I may seize it as well as my coat, having due authority for the first; but, be it observed, that to steal the hat was as criminal as to steal the coat; and, if I had known, or suspected, that the hat was there, I might have had my search-warrant for the former as well as for the latter.

The law of nations calls the high seas the common right of nations. A ship there is a parcel of the state to which she belongs, and the sovereign rights of the state travel with her. The sole exception is, as has been before stated, that belligerents have a right to search neutrals for *goods of the enemy*, and for *warlike stores and troops*, carrying for the enemy's use; because, as far as neutrals are engaged in such a service, they are deemed to be *in the service of the enemy*.

In all other respects a neutral ship carries with her, on the high seas, the rights of sovereignty appertaining to the state to which she belongs.

Now, it is well known, that no nation has a right to enter the territory of another to exercise any authority whatever, much less that of seizing persons and carrying them away by force; and, indeed, is it not fresh in everyone's memory, what complaints were made against the French for entering the territory of the Elector of Baden, and seizing the Duke of Enghein?

If we have a right to enter American ships on the high seas, and take out of them, by force of arms, British seamen, what should hinder us from having the same right as to any of the sea-ports of America? Nay, why should we not go and seize our numerous manufacturers, who have been (contrary to our laws) carried to America, and who are filling America with cloths and cutlery? Their alleging, that they went thither to avoid the effect of prosecutions for libel or for some other of our state crimes, would be no bar to our claim upon them; and, in short, they could never be safe to the last moment of their lives.

It is said, that the seamen on board of American ships are *deserters*. Be it so. We may be sorry that they do desert; but it is no crime in the Americans that our sailors go into America. Is it not well known that numerous deserters from the Austrian and Prussian armies have at all times deserted into the neighbouring states; and is it not equally well known, that the neighbouring state has invariably possessed the undisputed right of giving them protection, and of enlisting them in its service?

Why, therefore, should we deem it a crime in America, whose abundance of lands and provisions, whose high price of labour, and whose happiness to the lower orders of mankind, hold out their arms to the whole world?

And here I cannot help introducing a remark upon the proposition, made by Lord Castlereagh to Mr Russell, that the American Government should stipulate to *deliver up* all British seamen in the service of Americans. Mr Russell is said to have expressed himself as having been *shocked* at this proposition, which has afforded an abundant theme of abuse of him by our hireling writers. But, I have no scruple to say, that I firmly believe, that it is a proposition that never was before made to any independent state; even to the most petty state of Germany. There was a plan, some years ago, in agitation amongst the states of Europe, for putting in force a mutual surrender of each other's subjects, whereupon the Abbé Raynal remarks, that, if it had gone into effect, each of the several states might have taken the motto of *Dante* over the entrance to his *infernal regions*: 'He who enters here leaves even *hope* behind.' He represents it as the utmost stretch of tyranny; a point, he says, which the world ought to perish rather than reach. And, therefore, though Lord Castlereagh's proposition did not go this length; though it was confined to British *seamen*, we have no reason to abuse Mr Russell for his expression.

It will be said, may be, that Mr Russell was ordered to stipulate for the surrender, on our part, of all American seamen. Ay; but the difference is, that Mr Russell proposed the surrender of those only who had been *impressed by us*; whereas we wanted to stipulate for the surrender of those British seamen who had gone into America of *their own free will*. We wanted to have surrendered to us, men who were employed in American *merchant* ships: they wanted us to surrender men, whom we had seized in their ships and forced into our *men-of-war*.

But, is it possible, that any one can find anything to object to in a request, that, as a *preliminary*, we should give up the Americans, whom we had impressed into our service? What is the state of those men, now on board of our ships of war? What is their state? Has the reader reflected upon this? They must be useless on board of ship; they must not act; they must do no seaman's duty; or, they must, according to our own doctrine, lately exemplified at Horsemonger Lane, be TRAITORS, worthy of being hanged, ripped up, and cut in quarters.

His Royal Highness's DECLARATION says, that allegiance to his father and his successors begins with a man's birth and ends but with his death. And, is it not the same with American citizens? Do they not owe similar allegiance to their country? Or is it about to be pretended, that none but kings can claim this sort of allegiance?

I do not think that any one, even of the writers in *The Times* and *Courier*, will have the impudence to set up this doctrine; but, this they must do before they can make out any good ground of charge against the Americans for having demanded, as a preliminary, the surrender of the impressed American seamen.

Captain Dacres, in accounting for the loss of his frigate, expressly states, that he had *many Americans on board*, whom he permitted to be spectators, from a reluctance to compel them to fight against their country. And, can the reader believe, that this was the only instance in which native Americans were unwillingly serving on board of British ships of war? What, then, again, I ask, must be the state of those Americans? And, what are we to think of those writers who abuse Mr Russell for proposing to us their surrender as a step preliminary to any further arrangement?

The DECLARATION complains, that America demanded the abandonment of the practice of impressment as a *preliminary* to her passing a law to prevent British seamen from being received on board her ships.

The hireling writers have treated this demand as something too insolent to be for a moment listened to. The DECLARATION does not treat it in this lofty style; but it speaks of it in pretty strong terms, as thus:

The proposal of an armistice, and of a simultaneous repeal of the restrictive measures on both sides, subsequently made by the commanding officer of his Majesty's naval forces on the American coast, were received in the same hostile spirit by the Government of the United States. The suspension of the practice of impressment was insisted upon in the correspondence which passed on that occasion, as a *necessary preliminary* to a cessation of hostilities. Negotiation, it was stated, might take place without any suspension of the exercise of this right, and also without any armistice being concluded: but Great Britain was required *previously* to agree, without any knowledge of the adequacy of the system which could be substituted, to negotiate upon the basis of *accepting the legislative regulations of a foreign state*, as the sole *equivalent* for the exercise of *a right*, which *she has felt to be essential to the support of her maritime power*.

Well, and what then? *A right* it is called again; but, if America *deemed* it to be a right, as she has uniformly done, what wonder was there that she made the proposition? Great Britain might *feel*, though I should have chosen the word *deem*, as smacking less of the boarding-school Miss's style; Great Britain might *feel*, if feel she must, that the practice complained of was essential to the support of her maritime power; but did it hence follow, that America, and that impressed Americans, should like the practice the better for that? We have so long called ourselves the *deliverers* of the world, that we, at last, have fallen into the habit of squaring up all our ideas to that appellation: and seem surprised that there should be any nation in the world inclined to wish for the diminution of our power.

The Americans, however, clearly appear to see the thing in a different light. They, in their home-spun way, call us any thing but deliverers; and, it must be confessed, that, whatever may be our general propensity, we do not seem to have been in haste to *deliver* impressed American seamen.

That one nation ought not to yield *a right*, depending for compensation solely upon the legislative provisions of a foreign state is very true; but, if the right be doubtful; if it be unsupported by any law, principle, maxim, or custom, then the case is different; and then, indeed, the offer of a legislative provision is a proof of a sincere desire to accommodate.

If my view of the matter be right, and I verily believe it is, this is the light in which that offer ought to be viewed; and I most deeply lament that it was not thus viewed by the ministers.

These lamentations, however, are now useless. The sound of war is gone forth: statement and reasoning are exhausted; the sword is to decide whether England is, or is not, to impress, at the discretion of her naval officers, persons on board American merchant ships on the high seas.

There is one passage more in the DECLARATION, upon which I cannot refrain from submitting a remark or two. After stating, that America has made only *feeble remonstrances* against the injuries she has received from *France*, the DECLARATION, this '*memorable* document', as the *Courier* calls it, concludes thus:

This disposition of the Government of the United States – this *complete subserviency to the Ruler of France* – this hostile temper towards Great Britain – are evident in almost every page of the official correspondence of the American with the French Government.

Against this course of conduct, the real cause of the present war, the Prince Regent solemnly protests. Whilst contending against France, in defence not only of the liberties of Great Britain, BUT OF THE WORLD, his Royal Highness was entitled to look for a far different result. From their *common origin* – from their *common interest* – from their *professed principles of freedom* and independence, the United States were the last power in which Great Britain could have expected to find a *willing instrument*, and *abettor of French tyranny*.

Disappointed in this just expectation, the Prince Regent will still pursue the policy which the British Government has so long, and invariably maintained in *repelling injustice*, and in supporting the general rights of nations; and, under the *favour of* PROVIDENCE, relying on the justice of his cause, and the tried loyalty and firmness of the British nation, his Royal Highness confidently looks forward to a successful issue to the contest, in which he has thus been compelled most reluctantly to engage.

The last paragraph is in the old style, and will hardly fail to remind Mr Madison of the documents of this kind issued about *six-and-thirty years ago*. However, the style is none the worse for being old; though one cannot but recollect the occasion upon which it was formerly used.

I regret, however, to find, in this solemn document, a distinct charge against the American Government of *subserviency to the Ruler of France*; because, after a very attentive perusal of all the correspondence between the American and French Governments,

I do not find anything, which in my opinion, justifies the charge. The truth is, that 'the *Ruler of France*' *gave way* in the most material point to the remonstrances of America; and, I have never yet read a Message of Mr Madison, at the opening of a session of Congress, in which he did not complain of the conduct of France. The Americans abhor an alliance with France; and, if they form such an alliance, it will have been occasioned by this war with us.

This charge of subserviency to Buonaparte has a thousand times been preferred against Mr Madison, but never, that I have seen, once *proved*. It is, indeed, the charge which we have been in the habit of preferring against all those powers, who have been at war with us: Spain, Holland, Prussia, Denmark, Sweden, and though last not least, Russia, as will be seen by a reference to Mr Canning's answer to the propositions from Tilsit.

'Subserviency to the Ruler of France!' We stop the American merchantmen upon the high seas; we take out many of their own native seamen; we force them on board of our men-of-war; we send them away to the East Indies, the West Indies, or the Mediterranean; we expose them to all the hardships of such a life and all the dangers of battle, in a war in which they have no concern: all this we do, for we do not deny it; and when, *after* MANY YEARS *of remonstrances*, the American Government arms and sends forth its soldiers and sailors to compel us to desist, we accuse the government of *subserviency to the Ruler of France*, who, whatever else he may have done, has not, that I have ever heard, given the Americans reason to complain of impressments from on board their ships. Many unjust acts he appears to have committed towards the Americans; but he has wisely abstained from impressments, which, as I have all along said, was the *only ground* upon which the people of America could have been prevailed upon to enter heartily into a war with any power: it is a popular ground: the war is in the cause of the people: accordingly, we find the motto to the war is: *Liberty of the seas and seamen's rights*.

I therefore regret exceedingly that the DECLARATION styles America 'a *willing instrument* and *abettor* of French tyranny'. It is a heavy charge; it is one that will stick close to the memory of those who support the war; it will tend to inflame, rather than allay, the angry passions; and, of course, it will tend to kill all hopes of a speedy reconciliation.

As to what the DECLARATION is pleased to say about the *common origin* of the two nations, if of any weight, it might be urged, I suppose, with full as much propriety by the Americans *against our impressments*, as it is now urged against their resistance. I remember that it was urged with great force in favour of American submission to be taxed by an English parliament; but, as the result showed, with as little effect as it possibly can be upon this occasion.

There is one thing in this *calling cousin*, as the saying is, that I do not much like. The calling cousin always *proceeds from us*. The Americans never *remind us*, that we are of the same origin with them. This is a bad sign on our side. It is we, and not they, who tell the world of the relationship. In short, it is well enough for a newspaper to remind them of their origin; but I would not have done it in a solemn declaration; especially, when I was accusing them of being the willing instrument and abettor of our enemy.

*Common interest.* That, indeed, was a point to dwell on; but, then, it was necessary to produce something, at least, in support of the proposition. The Americans will *query the fact*; and, indeed, they will flatly deny it. They will say, for they have said, that it is not for *their interest*, that we should have more power than we now have over the sea; and, that they have much more to dread from a great naval power, than from an overgrown power on the continent of Europe. They are in no fear of the Emperor Napoleon, whose fleets they are now a match for; but they are in some fear of us; and, therefore, they do not wish to see us stronger.

It is in vain to tell them, that we are fighting in defence of the *liberties of the world*. They understand this matter full as well as we do, and, perhaps, a little better. I should like to see this proposition attempted to be *proved*. I should like to hear my Lord Castlereagh, beginning with the Declaration against the Republicans of France, continue on the history of our hostilities to the present day, taking in those of India by way of episode, and concluding with the war for the *right of impressment*, make it out, *how* we have been and are *defending the liberties of the world*.

I dare say that his lordship could make it out clearly enough. I do not pretend to question the fact or his ability; but it would be at once instructive and entertaining to hear how he would do it.

'From their *professed* principles of *freedom*.' From these the DECLARATION says, that His Royal Highness expected the United States would have been the last power to become a willing instrument of *French tyranny*. Very true: of *French tyranny*: but, that did not hinder him from expecting them to be the enemy of *impressing men from on board their ships*; and, it should have been shown how this disposition proved them to be a willing instrument to French tyranny, or of any tyranny at all.

It is useless to revile; it is useless to fly off to other matter. We impress men on board of American ships upon the high seas; we take out (no matter whether by mistake or otherwise) American seamen as well as English; we force them to fight on board our ships; we punish them if they disobey. And, when they, after years of complaints and remonstrances, take up arms in the way of resistance, we tell them that they show themselves the willing instruments and abettors of French tyranny.

I wish sincerely that this passage had been omitted. There are other parts of the DECLARATION that I do not like; but this part appears to me likely to excite a great deal of ill-will; of lasting, of rooted, ill-will.

I do not like the word *professed*, as applied to the American *principles of freedom*. The meaning of that word, as here applied, cannot be equivocal, and assuredly would have been better left out, especially as we never see, in any of the American documents, any expressions of the kind applied to us and to our government.

But, to take another view of the matter, *why* should His Royal Highness expect the Americans to be disinclined towards France, because they profess principles of freedom? *Why* should he, on *this account*, expect that they would lean to *our side* in the war?

Does the DECLARATION mean to say, that the Government of France is more tyrannical than was that monarchy, for the restoration of which a league was made in Europe in the years 1792 and 1793? From its tone, the DECLARATION may be construed to mean, that *our* government is *more free* than that of France, and that, therefore, we might have expected the Americans, who profess principles of freedom, to be on *our side* in a contest against *French tyranny*.

Hem! Mum!

Well, well! We will say nothing about the matter; but, it must be clear to every one, that the Americans may have their *own opinion* upon the subject; and, they may *express it too*, until we can get at them with an *ex-officio*. They may have their own opinion upon the matter; and their opinion may possibly differ from ours. They are, to be sure, at a great distance; but, they are a *reading* and an *observing* and a *calculating* people; and, I'll engage, that there is not a farmer in the back States who is not able to give a pretty good account of the blessings of *English Liberty*.

Besides, leaving this quite out of the question; supposing that the Americans should think us freemen and the French slaves, why should that circumstance prevent them from leaning to the side of France? What examples of the effect of such morality amongst nations have the Regent's ministers to produce? How often have we seen close alliances between free and despotic states against states either free or despotic? How often have we been on the side of despots against free states? England was once in offensive alliance with France against Holland; Holland and France against England; and, it ought never to be forgotten, that England, not many years ago, favoured the invasion of Holland and the subjugation of the States-General by a Prussian army. Have *we* not formed alliances with Prussia, Austria, Russia, Spain, Naples, and all the petty princes of Germany, against the *Republic* of France? Nay, have we refused, in that war, the co-operation of Turkey and *Algiers*? And, as for the old Papa of Rome, 'the Whore of Babylon', as our teachers call him, his alliance has been accounted holy by us, and his person an object of our peculiar care and protection.

Why, then, are we to expect, that America is to refrain from consulting her interests, if they be favoured by a leaning towards France? Why is she to be shut out from the liberty of forming connections with a despotism, supposing a despotism now to exist in France?

The truth is, that, in this respect, as in private life, it is interest alone that guides and that must guide; and, in my mind, it is not more reasonable to expect America to lean on our side on account of the nature of the government of our enemy, than it would be to expect a Presbyterian to sell his sugar to a Churchman, because the only man that bade him a higher price was a Catholic.

Here I should stop; but, an article, upon the same subject, in the *Morning Chronicle* of the 13th instant, calls for observation.

Upon the falsehoods and impudence of *The Times* and the *Courier*, that is to say, the principal prints on the side of the Wellesley party and that of the ministers, I have remarked often enough. I was anxious to hear what the Whigs had to say, and here we have it. Mr Ponsonby and Mr Brougham had pledged themselves to support the war, if America was not satisfied with the repeal of the Orders in Council; and here we have the grounds of that support. On this account the article is interesting, and, of course, worthy of an attentive perusal.

Notwithstanding the tedious length of the papers on both sides, the question between the Court of London and the Government of the United States is simply *the right of impressment of seamen on board trading ships* – and this is, in truth, the sole cause of the war. If we were to examine the value of this cause to the two parties, it cannot be denied but that to *the Americans it is exceedingly slight*, and to the British *highly material*. The Americans cannot regard it as an *insult*, because *it is a right which has been at all times asserted and acquiesced in by sovereign states respectively*. Then, viewed as an *injury*, what is it? That they shall go to war to prevent British subjects who have forfeited their allegiance, abandoned their country, and left their families probably starving, from being impressed on board their merchant vessels – that is to say; they claim the right to afford an asylum and employ the *refuse* of the British navy – men without principle, for it is only the profligate that are likely to become the objects of their protection. In this view, then, the point is of little consequence to the Americans, but it is interesting to the British to assert the power inherent in every state to reclaim its subjects; and the time may come when the principle would be equally important to America herself.

But, say the American ministers, it is not so much the right itself, as the violent and insulting mode of exercising it that we complain of; for we have upon reflection agreed in the principle of international law, that free bottoms do not make free goods, and therefore we have no objection to the search of our merchant ships for contraband of war; but, in that case, whenever warlike stores, etc. are found on board an American vessel, she is detained and carried into a port, for adjudication by a competent court. Whether the adjudication be always impartial or not is another affair, but in this respect nations are on an equal footing, and these Admiralty Courts, well or ill-conducted, are recognized by all maritime nations. But with respect to the impressment of seamen, the act is violent because summary, and because it is subject to no revisal – to no adjudication – and because the individual seized has no means of redress. By this sort of reasoning there is a tacit admission on the part of America, that it is not to the act itself which they object so much as to the manner of the act; and accordingly we see various suggestions made by Americans, for entering into an amicable discussion on the means of getting over the outrageous way in which the right is exercised, and of giving security to both nations against the abuse in question. On the other side, Lord Castlereagh declares the readiness of the British Government to receive and discuss any proposition on this subject coming from the American Government; though he would not enter into a negotiation, in preliminary to which should be the concession of this right, and so far we think he was clearly right.

But is it not monstrous that two people of common origin, and of almost inseparable interests, should remain at war on a point upon which there is so little difference between them? Surely without any sacrifice of etiquette on either side, the expedients might be canvassed, by which this mighty cause of war might be removed. Let each party promulgate their thoughts on the subject, and if there be an honest disposition to peace, it must follow.

The argument on both sides is short, and may be put in a few words. The agreement ought to be so drawn as to make it most dangerous to the captain of an American ship to employ a British seaman on board; and, on the other side, to make it equally dangerous for a British captain to seize and carry off an American seaman, under pretext of his being a British subject. Or, in other words, it ought to be made their interest to abstain from those two causes of national offence. Various modes have been suggested for this purpose. The most effectual undoubtedly would be to ordain by a treaty, that the subjects of each power, if found on board the merchants' vessels of the other, *should be considered in the nature of contraband of war*, inasmuch as their natural sovereign was thereby deprived of their service in war, and that that should be a cause to detain the vessel for adjudication. By this the American captain or his owners would most seriously suffer by having British seamen on board; and, on the other hand, the British captain would equally suffer, if he had all the risk and loss to incur of an improper detention. Against this, however, the arguments are strong. The American captain may have been imposed upon by the similarity of language, etc; and when brought into one of our ports, where there is a competent court to adjudge the point, a real American seaman might find it impossible to adduce proofs of his nativity. Besides, in both events, the penalty would be inordinate.

Another suggestion has been made, that the British naval officer impressing a seaman on board an American vessel, and *vice versa*, should be bound to make a certificate in duplicate (or what the French call a *procès verbal*), to the fact, one copy of which he should deliver to the American captain, and transmit the other to the Admiralty to be filed; and that the seaman seized should have his action for damages in the Courts of Law, the certificate to be produced by the Admiralty as proof of the trespass, if the person can prove himself to be a native of the country that he pretended to be. We confess we think that this ought to satisfy both governments, for this would make officers cautious in exercising the right which at the same time cannot be safely surrendered.

This is poor, paltry trash. But, it contains one assertion, which I declare to be *false*. It is here asserted, that 'the right of impressment of seamen on board of trading ships, is a right which has, *at all times been asserted, and acquiesced in by sovereign states respectively*'. – I give this an unqualified denial. I say, that it is a right, which *no nation* has before asserted, and that *no nation* ever acquiesced in.

Let the *Morning Chronicle* name the nation that has ever done either: let him cite the instance of such a practice as we insist upon: let him name the writer, every English writer, on public law, who has made even an attempt to maintain such a doctrine; nay, let him name the writer, who has laid down any principle, or maxim, from which such a right can possibly be deduced. And, if he can do none of these, what assurance, what a desperate devotion to faction, must it be to enable a man to make such an assertion! The assertion of the 'value of the cause' being slight to America, in comparison to what it is to us, has no better foundation. The *value*! what is of value, what is of any value at all, if the *liberty* and *lives* of the *people* of America are of no value? And when we know, when no man will deny, when official records of the fact exist, that hundreds of native Americans have been impressed and sent to serve on board our ships of war: when this is notorious; when it neither will nor can be denied, what is of value to America if this cause be not of value? As to the proposition for making English seamen *contraband of war*, it is so impudent, it is so shameful, it is even so horrid, that I will do no more than just name it, that it may not escape the reader's indignation. Indeed, there needs no more than the reading of this one article to convince the Americans, that all the factions in England are, in effect, of one mind upon the subject of this war; and, I am afraid, that this conviction will produce consequences, which we shall have sorely to lament, though I shall, for my own part, always have the satisfaction to reflect, that every thing which it was in my power to do, has been done, to prevent those consequences.

# THE RAID ON WASHINGTON D.C.

The expedition against the *city of Washington* [August 1814] or, rather, the result of it, has produced, in this country, the effect which might naturally have been expected: 'The Yankees are done for! Their *metropolis* has been *taken*! They ran away at the sight of our troops! Mr Madison and his government have decamped! The States are left without rulers!' The 'ill-organized association', says *The Times* newspaper, 'is on the eve of dissolution, and the world is speedily to be delivered of the *mischievous example of the existence of a government founded on democratic rebellion.*' Thus says *The Times*, and thus says a vast majority of this taxed nation. This was to be expected. The *name of metropolis* was enough. The people here were sure to look upon it as the *London* of America; and, of course, to conclude that America was subdued, or very nearly subdued. This is, too, the notion held forth by the newspapers; and, in fact, it universally prevails. Now, the truth is, that the city of Washington is no city at all, except in name. It was *begun to be built* only about sixteen years ago. The Congress has not met at it above ten or twelve years. It was built by a sort of lottery, the shares of which fell, at one time, to less than ten per cent of their cost. The lottery was drawn; the prizes were not paid. I do not, indeed, know what may have been done since I left the country; but at that time it was the general opinion that it never would be a place of any consideration, though the law compelled the Congress to meet there. 'Wherever the king is there is the court;' but the Republican Government of America, though they may have had the puerile pride of erecting a Capitol and a President's palace, could not make a city, which supplies a numerous population, and great wealth.

But our officers, naval as well as military, appear to have perceived what would hit the taste of war-loving Johnny Bull. Johnny, who has no doubt of his having *conquered France*, would, of course, be delighted at the prospect of conquering America, towards which he would necessarily look on the capture of Washington as an almost last step; and, indeed, I heard some people, usually very sensible, say, upon the receipt of the news, 'Thank God, we shall now have peace, and have the *income tax taken off.*' What, in the eye of common sense, is the event of which we have made such a boasting? We have, with an enormously superior naval force, ascended a very capacious bay in America, to the distance of about sixty miles. We have landed an army; we have repulsed the militia of superior numbers; (as *we* say;) we have entered a straggling town of wooden buildings, which our own newspapers had told us the Americans themselves had acknowledged to be defenceless; we have set fire to several buildings and some ships; we have, thank God, burnt the President's palace, and a building on a ridiculously grand scale, called the *Capitol*, where the legislature of the Union held its sittings; we have then *retreated*, and regained our ships with such haste, that we have been compelled to leave our dead, and many of our *wounded officers*, as well as men, *to the mercy of the enemy*, whom our newspapers call unprincipled, cowardly, and cruel. This is what the *Morning Chronicle* calls one of the most *gallant dashes* of the war. *This is styled success. This is a victory to boast of.* This is to induce the Americans to go down upon their knees, and solicit peace on any terms! Why did our army not *remain* at Washington? When the French got to Berlin, Vienna, Naples, Hanover, Madrid, Amsterdam, they remained in them as long as they pleased. When they got to Moscow even, they remained for some weeks. But we – we capture the *metropolis* of America, and we decamp instantly. We set off in such haste, that we leave behind us many of those who have been *wounded* in the enterprise.

Oh, reader! how has Napoleon been abused for leaving behind *him* his sick and wounded, when he retreated from Russia! and yet we can extol the bravery and wisdom of those who, in our own service, do the same thing! Far am I, however, from blaming Mr Ross for leaving his wounded behind him, for, in the first place, he was sure that he left them in the hands of a very humane people; and, in the next place, by delaying his departure,

*The taking of the City of Washington by the British Forces under Major General Ross, 24 August 1814*

A  General Ross and the British Army
B  Cannon taken from the Americans
C  The City of Washington
D  The American Flotilla destroyed
E  The Dock Yard and Arsenal burnt
F  The Rope Walk

G  The River Potomac
H  The Great bridge destroyed
I  The War Office
K  The President's Palace on Fire
L  The Senate House
M  The Treasury

he might have added a very long list to his killed and wounded. But it is impossible to find out any apology for Mr Ross, upon this occasion, without furnishing an apology for the so-much-reprobated conduct of Napoleon. Mr Ross assigns the best possible reason for his wonderful expeditious retreat to the ships, namely, he was afraid that if he delayed this movement, the *militia might collect in such numbers as to intercept him.* The *militia.* What, that same sort of troops whom he had just overthrown, as it were, by merely showing his redcoats? How were they to *collect* in such haste? Whence were they so speedily to come? I owe you, Mr Ross, for this acknowledgment, though, perhaps, made involuntarily; because it proves clearly that you were fully convinced that you were not among a people on whose cowardice and whose want of patriotism you could place a moment's reliance; because it clearly proves, in short, that if we succeed in this way we have a people, an *armed people*, to subdue.

There is one fact stated in the report of the enterprise, to which our news writers pay no attention; but which is of very great importance. After the American troops had gone off, and left ours to enter the city, General Ross, our commander, had his *horse shot under him*, as he was going along at the head of his men, by a gun fired from *the window of a private house.* There can be no doubt that the ball was intended for the rider. This might have given him, and, I dare say, did give him, a tolerable lively idea of what sort of people he was got amongst, and it ought to convince wise Johnny Bull, that to follow the advice of *The Times* newspaper, and send a large force into the heart of the country, there to take up a 'commanding position', is much easier upon paper than it is upon land. *The Times* and *Courier* are nettled that our commanders did not *date their despatches* from the Capitol. I dare say that they had an inclination that way; but then, the militia might have collected! In short, they had not time to do it with safety. That was the reason why they did not do it! and, for my part, I think the reason quite satisfactory. The episode to the 'brilliant dash', seems to have been marked with nearly all the characteristics of the 'brilliant dash' itself. Sir Peter Parker, with his ship's company and marines, go in search of a parcel of militia *in a wood.* The reader may not, perhaps, be aware, that there is no sort of resemblance between the American and the English militia. These militia in America receive *no pay*, no *clothing*, no *arms*, from the government. Every man goes out in his own ordinary array, and carries his own arms and accoutrements. Ninety-nine times out of a hundred he finds his own powder and ball. In short, it was a body of the people, voluntarily assembled, and acknowledging no *superior* not of their *own electing*: this was the sort of force against whom Sir Peter Parker marched. They were, as *usual*, greatly *superior in numbers*; and, as *usual*, they were *defeated*, and *ran away*. But, in the end, Sir Peter lost his life, and his second in command succeeded ... in *what*? Why, in bringing off to the ship *almost all* our wounded!

As to the destruction of the public buildings at the city of Washington, it will give great pleasure to all those who really love *republican* governments. There are *palaces* enough elsewhere. America wants none; and it will, I dare say, be very long before she will see another. There are very good buildings in Baltimore, Philadelphia, and many other elegant and populous cities. There wants no grandeur; there wants no capitol, no palace, no metropolis, no court. All these bring taxes and standing armies; and the Americans want neither. There was, the other day, an article in *The Times* newspaper which struck me as a remarkable instance of the force of habit, and as a clear proof that a man may accustom himself to slavish ideas, till he, in good earnest, regards as a reproach every mark of freedom. The article to which I allude, was a commentary on a paper published by a person to whom the defence of New York was committed, and who, in a very pressing manner, *invites, exhorts, requests*, and *beseeches* persons capable of bearing arms, to come forth and augment his force, etc. etc. Upon this, the editor of *The Times* observes, that this officer cuts a most *sorry* and *lamentable* figure; and he jests most wearily upon the *tone* of the poor gentleman, 'who,' says he, '*invites, exhorts, requests, beseeches:* anything but COMMANDS.' Well, and what of that? Are the *people* less happy because no one assumes a *commanding* tone towards them? Is their situation less enviable for that? Is their character less dignified because they will not suffer themselves to be *commanded* in any way whatever? They do not like to be *commanded* by anybody; and why should we quarrel with them on that account?

This editor, and many others, seem astonished that Mr Madison should have been two years at war without being prepared for

*defence*. But what do they mean by *defence?* Three hundred –
nay, twenty hundred thousand men, would not be sufficient to
guard every point, where a few men can be landed for a few
hours, on a coast (including bays and mouths of rivers) of *three
or four thousand miles in extent*. Such adventures as Admiral
Cochrane gives an account of, might, with such a navy as ours,
be performed on such an extent of coast in spite of two or three
millions of regular soldiers. The *defence* of *America*, and, indeed,
of any country, does not mean the preventing of the bombard-
ment of a village, or the burning of a city, or the carrying off of
*'stock'*. It means the preventing of that country from being subdued, or, so much crippled as to make a disgraceful peace. And
this defence, in America, must be *left to the people themselves*. Mr
Madison could raise no regular armies. The people do not give
him the means to do it. They know very well that, for want of
a regular army, they are liable to have some towns knocked down
or sacked; but they prefer this to the putting of a standing army
in the hands of any man in their country. We, indeed, are of
a taste widely different. We have field marshals, hundreds of
generals, and colonels, and majors, and captains, and barrack-
masters and commissaries, and cadets, and so on. We have military depots, academies, colleges, and so on, to a long list. We
have, besides, great numbers of foreign officers, some of whom
have had *commands* in England itself, and of counties of England.
We have also great numbers of foreign soldiers in our pay. This
is our taste. We like to have these people. But, then, we *very
cheerfully* pay for all these fine things. We are willing to purchase
our safety in this way. Now, as I never heard that the Americans
have quarrelled with us on this account, why should we quarrel
with them for their *taste?* They prefer a few towns sacked or
beaten down now and then, to the paying for a standing army,
for barracks, depots, military colleges. Their taste may be bad.
They may prove themselves very stupid in not liking to see their
streets crowded with beautiful, tall, straight gentlemen, with
pretty hair and caps, with furs, and whiskers, with cloaks, and
glittering swords, and boots, that shine like japan mugs. But
*stupidity is not a crime*; and if they do not like these things we, who
have so much more refinement amongst us, and so much more
elevation of mind, should view them with pity rather than with
scorn; should speak of them with compassion, rather than with

reproach. We might as reasonably reproach them (and the French too, by the by) for not having a taste for *tythes*. We like these too. Mr Burke said so many years ago. We like to give our clergy a tenth part of our crops. But, then, have we not our churches and cathedrals, our prayers and sermons, our bells and singing, our Lord's supper, our baptism, confirmation, churching of women, absolution of the sick, and burial of the dead? We have all these things, and a great many more, in return for the tenth of our crops; and the Americans (poor fellows!) have none of them. Yet we ought not to *reproach* them on this account. It is, doubtless, bad taste in them; but, as I said before, bad taste is not *criminal*.

Another thing I wish to point out to the attention of the reader. He frequently sees, in our newspapers, *extracts from American papers*, all tending to degrade the government and decry its measures. Out of the three or four hundred newspapers, published in America, there are, probably, ten or twelve who proceed in this tone. These are carefully sent hither by consuls, or other persons residing there. From these only, extracts are published *here*: and, be it observed, that if we possessed the papers on the other side of the question, we should *be exposed to utter ruin* if we were to publish such extracts from them as it would be necessary to publish in order to give the public a fair view of the state of men's minds in America. But the hireling prints here do one thing for us: they, by their extracts, prove to us *how great is freedom* in America. *The Times* tells us, that one paper in America expresses its opinion that the president himself had a famous escape from Washington: and that another *expresses its regret that he was not taken by the enemy*. Now, reader, imagine, for a moment, the case of an enemy landed in England, and some writer expressing *his regret that the said enemy had not captured the king*! You tremble for the unfortunate creature. I see you tremble. Your teeth chatter in your head; I hear them chatter: and well they may. How many loyal men do I hear exclaim: 'Send the traitor to the gallows. Rip out his bowels and throw them in his face! Cut off his head! Quarter his vile carcass, and put the quarters at the king's disposal.' Yet we hear the American writers wishing that their chief magistrate had been taken by the enemy; and we do not find that anything is either said or done to them. Their publications are suffered to take their free course.

If they be true, and speak sense and reason, they will gain adherents, as they ought. If false, or foolish, they will only gain the writer's hatred or contempt, which, I dare say, has been the case in the instance before us. But, reader, let us not, with this fact full in our eyes, be induced to believe that the Americans have nothing to fight for: or that any man who loves freedom can wish to see a change in the government; or, at least, in the *sort* of government which exists in that country. As to Mr Madison, against whom our hired men rail so much, he cannot be much to blame for anything relating to the war. It was the *Congress;* the representatives of the people; the *real* not the *sham* representatives of the people – who *declared* war. In fact, it was the people themselves, who were resolved no longer to endure that which they had so long, and so loudly complained of. A war in America *must* be the people's war. The defence of the country *must* be left to the people. Not only as to the fighting, but as to the time, place, and everything else belonging to the war. The people know very well the extent of their danger. They are well apprized of every thing. They were aware beforehand that what has taken place would take place; and though many individuals must and will suffer, that will excite no general discontent against the government. Of one thing I am very certain; and that is, that we are carrying on precisely that sort of warfare which all the real friends of republican government would wish to see us carry on. It is a sort of warfare (especially when the *ground* of the war is considered) which cannot fail to *unite* the parties, into which the people have been divided; nor do I think it at all improbable, that we may cause Mr Madison to be president four years longer than he would have been without our war against his country, and our threat to *depose* him. For many men will naturally say that, though they would have liked to see him, following the example of Washington and Jefferson, decline a third term as President; yet, seeing that his so doing might be interpreted as a mark of submission to us, he ought again to be elected.

The favourite idea in England appears to be, that we ought to send out a great *overwhelming* force, get possession of some place in the heart of the country, and there compel the government to surrender up the republic on our own terms. I suppose that our commanders knew better than to *attempt* anything of the kind. I suppose that our government knew better than to order them, or to authorize them to make any such attempt. And yet, what are we to do by such a mode of warfare as we are now carrying on? Suppose we were to get possession of New York, and some other maritime towns, what should we gain but an enormous expense to keep those places? Cooped up in them, how ridiculous should we look! No: we shall never beat that people, unless the *people themselves join us*; and as this has not been the case yet in any one instance, what reason have we to expect but that it never will be the case, in spite of all the allurements held out to that people in the prospect of participating in the support of the army, the navy, the church, the law, the nobility and the financial system of the former *'mother* country'? But we must not, in this larger view of the American war, overlook particular events, and especially that just announced to us from *Fort Erie*.

In my last I noticed the bloody battle of Chippewa. After that battle, it appears that the contest was renewed (our army having been *reinforced*) in the front of Fort Erie, into which the Yankees had retired, and where our gallant countrymen and their associates seemed to have been resolutely bent to fulfil our wishes, and to give them 'a *drubbing*'. Alas! the 'drubbing' fell upon our own gallant army, who amounted to only about two thousand men, and who were compelled to retreat with all possible speed, leaving 905 either dead, wounded, or prisoners! The American general, Gaines, says, that he destroyed our people *at the point of the bayonet*. Our general says that the angle of a bastion was blown up with two hundred of our men on it. This last might be, and yet the case would not be much altered in our favour. Such a conflict as this I never before read. It surpasses that of Chippewa; and that surpassed, in point of proportionate destruction, anything in modern warfare. And it ought to be observed, that a great part of that army of Yankees were *militia*; some of them *volunteers*; and not a man of them who would suffer anyone to say that he had him under his *command*! It is, then, a fact beyond all dispute, that the Yankees will *sometimes* fight; and as there is no such thing as ascertaining beforehand the precise time when the fighting fit will come on them, they being such an irregular sort of people, and subject to no kind of discipline, I think it is the height of prudence in our commanders on the Atlantic coast not to venture too far at a time from our ships.

Upon hearing of the *battle of Erie*, (for it cost as many men as

several of the *battles* of Wellington), I was, I must confess, eager
to hear what *The Times* writer would be able to say upon the
subject. I had half a mind to hope that he would begin to repent
of the part he had acted in the stirring up of this war, but on
reflection, I concluded that, like the reprobates mentioned in the
good book, repentance was not in his power. This conclusion was
right, as the reader will now see.

'The *unfortunate event* which cast a partial shade over the
success of our Canadian army, is at length communicated to us
in an authentic shape. We extract from the papers received yesterday from that part of the world, a copy of Sir George Prevost's
general order, dated Montreal, 25 August, which states the loss
sustained at the attack on Fort Erie, on the 13th prevailing, at
802 killed, wounded, and missing. Compared with the whole
number of General Drummond's force, this loss is no doubt very
considerable; but we are glad to see no hint given that the event
is likely to occasion our troops to fall back. The misadventure
must, no doubt, be ranked amongst *those chances of war* to which
the *bravest armies*, and *best-laid plans*, are subject. It was
preceded by a brilliant achievement, executed four days before
by Captain Dobbs, of the Royal Navy, who, with a party of
seamen and marines, most gallantly boarded and took two armed
schooners, anchored close to Fort Erie. The consequence of this
capture being to deprive the enemy's position of a great part of
its defence, General Drummond resolved to follow it up by a
general attack on Fort Erie and the American entrenchments. In
this daring attempt he had *nearly* attained *complete success*. The
spirit of our brave soldiers *surmounted every obstacle*. They had
actually entered the fort, and had already turned part of its guns
against the enemy's last point of refuge, when suddenly a tremendous explosion took place, which not only destroyed many valuable lives, but necessarily involved all our operations in confusion
and left no alternative but a precipitate retreat to our first
approaches. It is *evident*, therefore, that General Gaines's boast
of having repulsed our men at the *point of the bayonet* is idle
gasconade. The *lamentable* result was, in all probability, occasioned by *accident*; but if the American general had any share in
it, it was one which reflected more credit on his *policy* than on
his *bravery*. To spring a mine on an assailing enemy may be, in
such circumstances, an allowable mode of destruction; but whilst

*humanity* is pained by contemplating such an event, there is no counter feeling of admiration for the *heroism* of those by whom the dreadful deed was executed!'

Oh! you vile hypocrite! humanity on your lips! on those same lips from which have proceeded so many urgent exhortations to exterminate the Americans; and who, in this very same number of your sanguinary paper, *commend* Sir Thomas Hardy for having bombarded, and, as you then thought, burnt to ashes the dwellings of the people of the village of Stonington! *Humanity!* This cant may do in a country where cant is so much in vogue; but be you assured that it will only excite contempt in the breast of the enemy. You can discover 'no heroism', can you, in the defenders of Fort Erie, who had lost their waterside defence before the battle began? The *three* officers of Colonel Scott's regiment, who came out of battle alive and *not wounded*, would, like Job's servants, tell you a different story; unless indeed like Bobadil, they were (which I am sure they would not do) to attribute their beating to the *planets*, instead of the American bayonets. For my part, I believe General Gaines's in preference to General Drummond's report. Not because I question the veracity of the latter, but because I know that he might be misinformed, and that General Gaines *could not be* misinformed as to the fact. But, as I said before, this fact of the blowing up of the angle of a bastion does not materially affect the merits of the case; and, unless the American people be very different in their natures from all other people, the event must have created a wonderful sensation in the country; and I am sure, that, in the eyes of any man in England whose reason is not totally deadened by prejudice, it must have excited a dread that, if we pursue that project of subjugation so strongly recommended by the writers here, we are now embarked in a war of extraordinary bloodshed, of no ordinary duration, and of an expense that will keep on all our present taxes, and occasion constant, annual loans.

### To the Prince Regent

SIR,

During the years 1811 and 1812, while I was imprisoned in a felon's jail, for having written and caused to be printed and published, an article on the subject of flogging of English local

*Cobbett in Newgate Prison*

militiamen, at the town of Ely, in England, and about the attendance of German troops at the ceremony; while I was expiating
this offence by two years imprisonment in a felon's jail, and by
paying, at the close of the period, *a thousand pounds fine* to you,
acting in the name and behalf of your father, who, during my
imprisonment, became afflicted with his present malady; during
this long period of seclusion from my home and from the wholesome air, I addressed to you several *letters on the dispute with
America*: in which letters I endeavoured to convince you that the
dispute, if it terminated in war, might lead to very fatal consequences to this country. I, in these letters, stated clearly the
grounds of the dispute; I traced the causes of our ill-blood with
America to their origin; I pointed out how the dispute might be
put an end to without a war; I endeavoured to show you the
probable fatal consequences of a war with that nation of freemen,
taking up arms *voluntarily*, and upon conviction of the goodness
of their cause. I spent whole days and nights in endeavours to
warn you against believing the reports of the venal wretches who
were labouring to persuade this nation that we had only to go to
war with Mr Madison in order to effect *a breaking up of the
American Union*: and I was the more anxious on this point, as it
was the general opinion that, unless the states could be induced
to *divide*, we never should long be able to cope with them in a
war within their territory.

As the vanity naturally belonging to an author makes me conclude that you read these letters with great attention, I will not
here go into any detail on their contents. But if we now look at
the state of the war in the gross, without any particular feature
being taken into view, does it not appear that we should have
been fortunate if my advice had been followed? We should never
then have heard of the affairs of the *Java*, the *Guerriere*, the
*Macedonia*, the *Avon*, and many others; nor should we have ever
heard of the battles of Lake Ontario and Lake Champlain ... It
is stated, in the newspapers, that you in your speech, said that
this war originated in the 'MOST UNPROVOKED AGGRESSION
on the part of the Government of the United States.' It is to be
lamented, that you did not take this opportunity of contradicting,
in a pointed manner, the assertion contained in Mr Madison's
late message; because he, most explicitly asserts, that *we were the
aggressors*. He says:

Having forborne to declare war until to other aggressions had been added *the capture of nearly one thousand American vessels*, and the *impressment of thousands of sea-faring citizens*, and until a final declaration had been made by the Government of Great Britain, that her hostile orders against our commerce would not be revoked, but on conditions as impossible as unjust, whilst it was known that these orders would not otherwise cease but with a war, which had lasted nearly twenty years, and which, according to appearance at that time, might last as many more – having manifested on every occasion and in every proper mode, a sincere desire to meet the enemy on the ground of justice, our resolution to defend our beloved country, and to oppose to the enemy's persevering hostility all our energy, with an undiminished disposition towards peace and friendship on honourable terms, must carry with it the good wishes of the impartial world, and the best hopes of support from an omnipotent and kind Providence.

Now, Sir, what I could have wished to see was a *contradiction* of this assertion with regard to these *thousand vessels* and these *thousands of impressed American citizens*. You may be well assured, that this message will be read with deep and general interest on the Continent of Europe. This message and your speech are before the world. Not before this nation only, but before all the nations in the world. Every man will form his own judgment upon them. It is not reasonable to suppose that Mr Madison's assertion will be disbelieved, unless it be *proved* to be false. It may do *here* for our public prints to call him, as they do, '*liar, fool, traitor, usurper, coward*,' and the like. This may satisfy those who inhabit the country through which runs the Serpentine River; but it will have no weight, or, at least, no weight *against* Mr Madison, in other countries. His assertion, therefore, relative to the *thousand vessels* and the *thousands of impressed sea-faring citizens* I could wish very much to see contradicted and disproved in some official and authentic way; for, until that be done, I am afraid, that we may lay our account with his being believed by a great majority of the world. And, if he be believed; if the world do believe, that we really did *capture a thousand Republican vessels*; that we really did impress *thousands of sea-faring citizens* before the Congress declared war, I am afraid that it must be doubted whether the declaration of war was wholly an *unprovoked* aggression on the part of America. I am aware, that there will be no doubt upon the subject in this country, which never was engaged in any war so popular as this. I believe, that, if the whole nation, paupers and all, were put to the vote, that there would appear for the war nine hundred and ninety-nine out of every thousand. The press worked up the people to the war pitch, where it keeps them. There are prevalent these notions: 1st, that the Republic *joined* Napoleon in the war against us; 2nd, that we are now able to *punish* her for this; 3rd, that she went to war for the purpose of robbing us of *maritime rights* essential to our *very existence*; 4th, that she may *now, now, now!* be crippled for ever; 5th, that we ought, at least, to continue the war, 'till we have *effaced*, by victories over the Republican ships, the recollection of the affairs of the *Java*, the *Guerriere*, the *Macedonia*, the *Avon*, and of those on the Lakes. Then the events in the Chesapeake, and the description of them, have caused the nation to look upon the Republicans as cowards. This is very inconsistent with the before-mentioned notion; but it prevails. So, that, here are all sorts of ingredients necessary to make a war popular, and popular it is beyond every thing that ever was popular. It is quite useless for any one to attempt to remove any of these notions, which have taken fast hold, and which it will require some years of war to shake. *Jonathan*, therefore, has no ground for reliance on any *opposition* in this country. The opposition in Parliament will only be as to the *mode* of prosecuting the war. If they censure, the burden of their censure will be, not against the *war*, but against those who have *not done enough* against the enemy. The war, therefore, has popularity to recommend it. This I allow, and, in so doing, I have the mortification to confess, that all my labours against the war have proved wholly useless. Still I think myself bound to endeavour, as occasion may offer, to give my reason against its further continuance.

I was happy to see, in the newspaper report of your speech, that you have '*a sincere desire* to bring this war to a conclusion on *just and honourable terms;*' and as Mr Madison expresses the same desire, let me hope, that the conclusion of the war may soon take place, without waiting till more sea battles have effaced the recollection of those which have already taken place. But, Sir, what a pity it is that the war did not end with the war in Europe. What a pity it is that Mr Madison has to complain of *delays* on our part to give effect to our own proposition for a direct negotiation, after we had refused the offer of the mediation of our own ally the Emperor of Russia! And what a pity it is, that the American people have, in our public prints, seen so much abuse of their Chief Magistrate, and so many threats to *reconquer* their country! ... Perhaps you do not know, that the *present* injuries, which we are able to inflict on America, are the greatest of blessings in the eyes of some of her statesmen. They have always wished for something that would separate her as widely as possible from Great Britain. Whether wisely or not is another matter. They have always wished it; and, if they can see this accomplished by the destruction of twenty or thirty towns on the coast, they will think the acquisition wonderfully cheap.

'When to marry or to fight,' as some are, 'both parties are equally eager; they soon get together.' Both parties are in earnest and eager in this case; and they will soon reach one another, though the distance between them is so great. The battle will be a famous one. A great *kingdom*, the mistress of the sea and dictatress of Europe, on the one side; and the *last of Republics* on the other. Not only the question of maritime rights is now to be decided; but the question of the nature of Governments. The world is now going to see, whether a Republic, without a standing army, with half a dozen frigates, and with a Chief Magistrate with a salary of about *five thousand pounds a year*, be able to contend, single-handed, against a kingdom with a thousand ships of war, an army of two hundred men, and with a Royal Family, whose civil list amounts to more than a million pounds a year. Nothing was ever so interesting as this spectacle. May the end be favourable to the honour and happiness of this country and mankind in general!

W. COBBETT

# TALL MEN MAKE GOOD SOLDIERS

Abundance of *good* food is the cause, to be sure, of the superior
size and strength of the people of that country.

Nor is this, in any point of view, an unimportant matter. A
tall man is, whether as labourer, carpenter, bricklayer, soldier, or
almost anything else, *worth more* than a short man: he can look
over a higher thing; he can reach higher and wider; he can move
on from place to place faster; in mowing grass or corn he takes
a wider swarth, in pitching he wants a shorter prong; in making
buildings he does not so soon want a ladder or a scaffold; in
fighting he keeps his body farther from the point of his sword.
To be sure, a man *may* be tall and *weak*: but this is the exception
and not the rule: *height* and *weight* and *strength*, in men as in
speechless animals, generally go together. Aye, and in enterprise
and courage too, the powers of the body have a great deal to do.
Doubtless there are, have been, and always will be, great numbers
of small and enterprizing and brave men; but it is *not in nature*,
that *generally speaking*, those who are conscious of their inferiority
in point of bodily strength, should possess the boldness of those
who have a contrary description.

To what but this difference in the *size* and *strength* of the
opposing combatants are we to ascribe the ever-to-be-blushed-at
events of our last war against the United States! The *hearts* of
our seamen and soldiers were as good as those of the Yankees:
on both sides they had sprung from the same stock: on both sides
equally well supplied with all the materials of war: if on either
side, the superior skill was on ours: French, Dutch, Spaniards,
all had confessed our superior prowess: yet, when, with our whole
undivided strength, and to that strength adding the flush and

pride of victory and conquest, crowned even in the capital of France; when, with all these tremendous advantages, and with all the nations of the earth looking on, we came foot to foot and yard-arm to yard-arm with the Americans, the result was such as an English pen refuses to describe. What, then, was the *great cause* of this result, which filled us with shame and the world with astonishment? Not the want of *courage* in our men. There were, indeed, *some moral causes at work*; but the main cause was, the great superiority of size and of bodily strength on the part of the enemy's soldiers and sailors. It was *so many men* on each side; but it was men of a different size and strength; and, on the side of the foe men accustomed to daring enterprise from a consciousness of that strength.

Why are abstinence and fasting enjoined by the Catholic Church? Why, to make men *humble*, *meek*, and *tame*; and they have this effect too: this is visible in whole nations as well as in individuals. So that good food, and plenty of it, is not more necessary to the forming of a stout and able body than to the forming of an active and enterprizing spirit. Poor food, short allowance, while they check the growth of the child's body, check also the daring of the mind; and, therefore, the starving or pinching system ought to be avoided by all means. Children should eat *often*, and as much as they like at a time. They will, if at full heap, never take, of *plain food*, more than it is good for them to take. They may, indeed, be stuffed with *cakes* and *sweet things* till they be ill, and indeed, until they bring on dangerous disorders: but, of *meat plainly* and *well cooked*, and of *bread*, they will never swallow.

With regard to ARITHMETIC, it is a branch of learning absolutely necessary to every one, who has any pecuniary transactions beyond those arising out of the expenditure of his week's wages. All the books on this subject that I had ever seen, were so bad, so destitute of every thing calculated to lead the mind into a knowledge of the matter, so void of principles, and so evidently tending to puzzle and disgust the learner, by their sententious, and crabbed, and quaint, and almost hieroglyphical definitions, that I, at one time, had the intention of writing a little work on the subject myself. It was put off, from one cause or another; but a little work on the subject has been, partly at my suggestion, written and published by Mr Thomas Smith of

Liverpool, and is sold by Mr Sherwood, in London. The author has great ability, and a perfect knowledge of his subject. It is a book of principles; and any young person of common capacity, will learn more from it in a week, than from all the other books, that I ever saw on the subject, in a twelvemonth.

While the foregoing studies are proceeding, though they very well afford a relief to each other, HISTORY may serve as a relaxation, particularly during the study of grammar, which is an undertaking requiring patience and time. Of all history, that of our own country is of the most importance; because, for a want of a thorough knowledge of what *has been*, we are, in many cases, at a loss to account for *what is*, and still more at a loss to be able to show what *ought to be*. The difference between history and romance is this; that that which is narrated in the latter, leaves in the mind nothing which it can apply to present or future circumstances and events; while the former, when it is what it ought to be, leaves the mind stored with arguments for experience, applicable, at all times, to the actual affairs of life. The history of a country ought to show the origin and progress of its institutions, political, civil, and ecclesiastical; it ought to show the effects of those institutions upon the state of the people; it ought to delineate the measures of the government at the several epochs; and, having clearly described the state of the people at the several periods, it ought to show the cause of their freedom, good morals and happiness; or of their misery, immorality, and slavery; and this, too, by the production of indubitable facts, and of inferences so manifestly fair, as to leave not the smallest doubt upon the mind.

Do the histories of England which we have, answer this description? They are very little better than romances. Their contents are generally confined to narrations relating to battles, negociations, intrigues, contests between rival sovereignties, rival nobles, and to the character of kings, queens, mistresses, bishops, ministers, and the like; from scarcely any of which can the reader draw any knowledge which is at all applicable to the circumstances of the present day.

# RETURN TO AMERICA
## (1817-1819)

# RURAL RIDES IN AMERICA

The situation of Long Island is this: It is about a hundred and thirty miles long, and, on an average, about eight miles broad. It extends in length from the Bay of the City of New York to within a short distance of the State of Rhode Island. One side of it is against the sea, the other side looks across an arm of the sea into a part of the State of New York (to which Long Island belongs) and into a part of the State of Connecticut. At the end nearest the city of New York it is separated from the site of that city, by a channel so narrow as to be crossed by a steam-boat in a few minutes; and this boat, with another near it, impelled by a team of horses, which works in the boat, form the mode of conveyance from the Island to the city, for horses, waggons, and every thing else.

The Island is divided into three counties; King's County, Queen's County, and the County of Suffolk. King's County takes off the end next New York city, for about thirteen miles up the island; Queen's County cuts off another slice about thirty miles further up; and all the rest is the County of Suffolk. These counties are divided into townships. And, the municipal government of Justices of the Peace, Sheriffs, Constables, etc., is in nearly the English way, with such differences as I shall notice in the *second part* of this work.

There is a *ridge of hills*, which runs from one end of the island to the other. The two sides are flats, or, rather, very easy and imperceptible slopes towards the sea. There are no rivers, or rivulets except here and there a little run into a bottom which lets in the sea-water for a mile or two as it were to meet the springs. *Dryness* is, therefore, a great characteristic of this island. At the place where I live, which is in Queen's County, and very nearly the middle of the island, crosswise, we have no water, except in a well seventy feet deep, and from the clouds; yet, we never experience a want of water. A large rainwater cistern to take the run from the house, and a duck-pond to take that from the barn, afford an ample supply; and I can truly say, that as to the article of water, I never was situated to please me so well in my life before. The rains come about once in fifteen days; they come in abundance for about twenty-four hours: and then all is fair and all is dry again immediately: yet here and there, especially *on the hills*, there are *ponds*, as they call them here; but in England, they would be called *lakes*, from their extent as well as from their depth. These, with the various trees which surround them, are very beautiful indeed.

The *farms* are so many plots originally scooped out of woods; though in King's and Queen's Counties the land is generally pretty much deprived of the woods, which, as in every other part of America that I have seen, are beautiful beyond all description. The walnut of two or three sorts, the plane, the hickory, chestnut, tulip tree, cedar, sassafras, wild cherry (sometimes sixty feet high); more than fifty sorts of oaks; and many other trees, but especially the flowering locust, or acacia, which, in my opinion, surpasses all other *trees*, and some of which, in this island, are of very great height and girt. The orchards constitute a feature of great beauty. Every farm has its orchard, in general of cherries as well as of apples and pears.

There is one great draw-back to all these beauties, namely, the *fences*; and, indeed, there is another with us South-of-England people; namely, the general (for there are many exceptions) slovenliness about the homesteads, and particularly about the *dwellings of labourers*. Mr BIRKBECK complains of this; and, indeed, what a contrast with the homesteads and cottages, which he left behind him near that exemplary spot, Guildford in Surrey! Both blots are, however, easily accounted for.

The *dwellings and gardens, and little outhouses of labourers*, which form so striking a feature of beauty in England, and especially in Kent, Sussex, Surrey, and Hampshire, and which constitute a sort of fairy-land, when compared with those of the labourers in France, are what I, for my part, must feel the want of seeing upon Long Island. Instead of the neat and warm little cottage, the yard, cow-stable, pig-sty, hen-house, all in miniature, and the garden, nicely laid out and the paths bordered with flowers, while the cottage door is crowned with a garland of roses or honeysuckle; instead of these, we here see the labourer content with a shell of boards, while all around him is as barren as the sea-beach; though the natural earth would send melons, the finest in the world, creeping round his door, and though there is no English shrub, or flower, which will not grow and flourish here. This want of attention in such cases is hereditary from the first settlers. They found land so plenty, that they treated small spots with contempt. Besides, the *example* of neatness was wanting. There were no gentlemen's gardens, kept as clean as drawing-rooms, with grass as even as a carpet. From endeavouring to imitate perfection, men arrive at mediocrity; and, those who never have seen, or heard of perfection, in these matters, will naturally be slovens.

Yet, notwithstanding these *blots*, as I deem them, the face of the country, in summer, is very fine. From December to *May*, there is not *a speck of green*. No green-grass and turnips, and wheat, and rye, and rape, as in England. The frost comes and sweeps all vegetation and verdant existence from the face of the earth. The wheat and rye *live*; but, they lose all their verdure. Yet the state of things in *June*, is, as to crops, and fruits, much about what it is in England; for, when things do begin to grow, they grow indeed; and the general harvest for *grain* (what we call *corn*) is a full month *earlier* than in the south of England!

The question eagerly put to me by every one in Philadelphia is, 'Don't you think the city *greatly improved?*' They seem to me to confound *augmentation* with *improvement*. It always was a fine city, since I first knew it; and it is very greatly augmented. It has, I believe, nearly doubled its extent and number of houses since the year 1799. But, after being, for so long a time, familiar with London, every other place appears little. After *living* within a few hundred yards of Westminster Hall and the Abbey Church, and the Bridge, and looking from my own windows into St James's Park, all other buildings and spots appear mean and insignificant. I went to day to see the house I formerly occupied. How small! It is always thus: the words *large* and *small* are carried about with us in our minds, and we forget real *dimensions*. The idea, *such as it was received*, remains during our absence from the object. When I returned to England, in 1800, after an absence from the country part of it, of sixteen years, the trees, the hedges, even the parks and woods, seemed so *small*! It made me laugh to hear little gutters, that I could jump over, called *Rivers*! The Thames was but a *Creek*! But, when, in about a month after my arrival in London, I went to *Farnham*, the place of my birth, what was my surprise! Everything was become so pitifully *small*! I had to cross, in my post-chaise, the long and dreary heath of Bagshot. Then, at the end of it, to mount a hill, called Hungry Hill; and from that hill I knew that I should look down into the beautiful and fertile vale of Farnham. My heart fluttered with impatience mixed with a sort of fear, to see all the scenes of my childhood; for I had learnt before, the death of my father and mother. There is a hill, not far from the town, called *Crooksbury Hill*, which rises up out of a flat, in the form of a *cone*, and is planted with Scotch fir trees. Here I used to take the eggs and young ones of crows and magpies. This hill was a famous object in the neighbourhood. It served as a superlative degree of height. *As high as Crooksbury Hill* meant, with us, the utmost degree of height. Therefore, the first object that my eyes sought was this hill. *I could not believe my eyes!* Literally speaking, I for a moment, thought the famous hill removed, and a little heap put in its stead; for I had seen in New Brunswick, a single rock, or hill of solid rock, ten times as big, and four or five times as high! The post-boy, going down hill, and not a bad road, whisked me, in a few minutes to the Bush Inn, from the garden of which I could see the prodigious *sand hill*, where I had begun my gardening works. What a *nothing*! But now came rushing into my mind, all at once, my pretty little garden, my little blue smock-frock, my little nailed shoes, my pretty pigeons that I used to feed out of my hands, the last kind words and tears of my gentle and tender-hearted and affectionate mother! I hastened back into the room. If I had looked a moment longer, I should have dropped. When I came to reflect, *what a change*! I looked down at my dress. What a change! What scenes I had gone through! How altered my state! I had dined the day before at a secretary of state's in company with Mr *Pitt*, and had been waited upon by men in gaudy liveries! I had had nobody to assist me in the world. No teachers of any sort. Nobody to shelter me from the consequence of bad, and no one to counsel me to good, behaviour. I felt proud. The distinctions of rank, birth, and wealth, all became nothing in my eyes; and from that moment (less than a month after my arrival in England) I resolved never to bend before them.

The Philadelphians are *cleanly*, a quality which they owe chiefly to the Quakers. But, after being long and recently familiar with the towns in Surrey and Hampshire, and especially with Guildford, Alton, and Southampton, no other towns appear clean and neat, not even Bath or Salisbury, which last is much about upon a par, in point of cleanliness, with Philadelphia; and, Salisbury is deemed a very cleanly place. Blandford and Dorchester are clean; but, I have never yet seen any thing like the towns in Surrey and Hampshire. If a Frenchman, born and bred, could be taken up and carried blindfold to Guildford, I wonder what his sensations would be, when he came to have the use of his sight! Every thing near Guildford seems to have received an influence from the town. Hedges, gates, stiles, gardens, houses inside and out, and the dresses of the people. The market day at Guildford is a perfect *show* of cleanliness. Not even a carter without a clean smock-frock and closely-shaven and clean-washed face. Well may Mr Birkbeck, who came from this very spot, think the people *dirty* in the western country! I'll engage he finds more dirt upon the necks and faces of one family of his present neighbours, than he left behind him upon the skins of all the people in the three parishes of Guildford. However, he would not have found this to be the case in Pennsylvania, especially in those parts where the Quakers abound; and, I am told, that, in the New England States, the people are as cleanly and as neat as they are in England. The sweetest flowers, when they become putrid, stink the most; and, a nasty woman is the nastiest thing in nature.

Lancaster is a pretty place. No *fine* buildings; but no *mean* ones. Nothing *splendid* and nothing *beggarly*. The people of this town seem to have had the prayer of HAGAR granted them: 'Give me, O Lord, neither *poverty* nor *riches*.' Here are none of those poor, wretched habitations, which sicken the sight at the *outskirts* of cities and towns in England; those abodes of the poor creatures, who have been reduced to beggary by the cruel extortions of the rich and powerful. And, this remark applies to *all* the towns of America that I have ever seen. This is a fine part of America. *Big barns*, and modest dwelling houses. Barns of *stone, a hundred feet* long and *forty wide*, with two floors, and raised roads to go into them, so that the waggons go into the *first floor upstairs*. Below are stables, stalls, pens, and all sorts of conveniences. Upstairs are rooms for threshed corn and grain; for tackle, for meal, for all sorts of things. In the front (south) of the barn is the cattle-yard. These are very fine buildings. And, then, all about them looks so comfortable, and gives such manifest proofs of ease, plenty, and happiness! Such is the country of WILLIAM PENN'S settling! It is a curious thing to observe the *farmhouses* in this country. They consist almost without exception, of a considerably large and a very neat house, with sash windows, and of a *small house*, which seems to have been *tacked on* to the large one; and, the proportion they bear to each other, in point of dimensions, is, as nearly as possible, the proportion of size between a *Cow* and *her Calf*, the latter a month old. But, as to the *cause*, the process has been the opposite of this instance of the works of nature, for, it is *the large house which has grown out of the small one*. The father, or grandfather, while he was toiling for his children, lived in the small house, constructed chiefly by himself, and consisting of rude materials. The means, accumulated in the small house, enabled a son to rear the large one; and, though, when *pride* enters the door, the small house is sometimes demolished, few sons in America have the folly or want of feeling to commit such acts of filial ingratitude, and of real self-abasement. For, what inheritance so valuable and so honourable can a son enjoy as the proofs of his father's industry and virtue? The progress of wealth and ease and enjoyment, evinced by this regular increase of the size of the farmer's dwellings, is a spectacle, at once pleasing, in a very high degree, in itself; and, in the same degree, it speaks the praise of the system of government, under which it has taken place. What a contrast with the farmhouses in England! There the *little* farmhouses are falling into ruins, or, are actually become cattle-sheds, or, at best, *cottages*, as they are called, to contain a miserable labourer, who ought to have been a farmer, as his grandfather was. Five or six farms are there *now* levelled into one, in defiance of *the law*; for, there is a law to prevent it. The *farmer* has, indeed, a *fine house*; but, what

*William Penn*

*American Quakers going to a meeting in summer*

a life do his labourers lead! The cause of this sad change is to be found in the crushing taxes; and the cause of them, in the Borough usurpation, which has robbed the people of their best right, and, indeed, without which right, they can enjoy no other. They talk of the *augmented population* of England; and, when it suits the purposes of the tyrants, they boast of this *fact*, as they are pleased to call it, as a proof of the fostering nature of their government; though, just now, they are preaching up the vile and foolish doctrine of PARSON MALTHUS, who thinks, that there are *too many* people, and that they ought (those who *labour*, at least) to be *restrained from breeding so fast*. But as to the fact, I do not believe it. There can be nothing in the shape of *proof*; for no actual enumeration was ever taken till the year 1800.

They are *roasting an ox on the Delaware*. The fooleries of England are copied here, and every where in this country, with wonderful avidity; and, I wish I could say, that some of the vices of our *higher orders*, as they have the impudence to call themselves, were not also imitated. However, I look principally at the mass of farmers; the sensible and happy farmers of America.

The people (those who have been lazy) are chopping away with axes the ice, which has grown out of the snows and rains, before their doors, during the winter. The hogs (best of scavengers) are very busy in the streets seeking out the bones and bits of meat, which have been flung out and frozen down amidst water and snow, during the two foregoing months. I mean including the present month [February]. At New York (and, I think, at Philadelphia also) they have *corporation* laws to prevent hogs from being in the streets. For *what reason*, I know not, except putrid meat be pleasant to the smell of the inhabitants. But, corporations are seldom the wisest of law-makers. It is argued, that, if there were no hogs in the streets, people would not throw out their orts of flesh and vegetables. Indeed! What would they do with those orts, then? Make their hired servants eat them? The very proposition would leave them to cook and wash for themselves. Where, then, are they to fling these effects of superabundance? Just before I left New York for Philadelphia, I saw a sow very comfortably dining upon a full quarter part of what appeared to have been a *fine leg of mutton*. How many a family in England would, if within reach, have seized this meat from the sow! And, are the tyrants, who have brought my industrious countrymen to that horrid state of misery, *never* to be called to account? Are they *always* to carry it as they now do? Every object almost, that strikes my view, sends my mind and heart back to England. In viewing the ease and happiness of this people, the contrast fills my soul with indignation, and makes it more and more the object of my life to assist in the destruction of the diabolical usurpation, which has trampled on king as well as people.

At BIBERY. Here I am amongst the thick of the Quakers, whose houses and families pleased me so much formerly, and which pleasure is all now revived. Here all is easy, plenty, and *cheerfulness*. These people are never *giggling*, and never in *low-spirits*. Their minds, like their dress, are simple and strong. Their kindness is shown more in acts than in words. Let others say what they will, I have uniformly found those whom I have intimately known of this sect, sincere and upright men; and I verily believe, that all those charges of hypocrisy and craft, that we hear against Quakers, arise from a feeling of *envy*; envy inspired by seeing them possessed of such abundance of all those things, which are the fair fruits of care, industry, economy, sobriety, and order, and which are justly forbidden to the drunkard, the glutton, the prodigal, and the lazy. As the day of my coming to Mr TOWN-SHEND'S has been announced beforehand, several of the young men, who were babies when I used to be there formerly, came to see 'BILLY COBBETT,' of whom they had heard and read so much. When I saw them and heard them, '*What a contrast*', said I to myself, with the senseless, gaudy, upstart, hectoring, insolent, and cruel Yeomanry Cavalry in England, who, while they grind their labourers into the revolt of starvation, gallantly sally forth with their sabres, to chop them down at the command of the Secretary of State; and, who, the next moment, creep and fawn like spaniels before their Boroughmonger Landlords! At Mr TOWNSHEND'S I saw a man, in his service, lately from YORKSHIRE, but an Irishman by birth. He wished to have an opportunity to see me. He had read many of my 'little books'. I shook him by the hand, told him he had now got a good house over his head and a kind employer, and advised him *not to move for one year*, and to save his wages during that year.

On to TRENTON. I am at the stage-tavern, where I have just dined upon cold ham, cold veal, butter and cheese, and a peach-pye; nice clean room, well furnished, waiter clean and attentive, plenty of milk; and charge, *a quarter of a dollar*! I thought that Mrs JOSLIN at Princeton (as I went on to Phila-delphia), Mrs BENLER at Harrisburgh, Mr SLAYMAKER at Lan-caster, and Mrs M'ALLISTER, were low enough in all con-science; but, really, this charge of Mrs ANDERSON beats all. I had not the face to pay the waiter a quarter of a dollar; but gave him half a dollar, and told him to keep the change. He is a black man. He thanked me. But, they never *ask* for anything. But, my vehicle is come, and now I bid adieu to Trenton, which I should have liked better, if I had not seen so many young fellows loung-ing about the streets, and leaning against door-posts, with quids of tobacco in their mouths, or segars stuck between their lips, and with dirty hands and faces. Mr Birkbeck's complaint, on this score, is perfectly just.

*Brunswick, New Jersey.* Here I am, after a ride of about thirty miles, since two o'clock, in what is called a Jersey-waggon, through such *mud* as I never saw before. Up to the stock of the wheel; and yet a pair of very little horses have dragged us through it in the space of *five hours*. The best horses and driver, and the worst roads I ever set my eyes on. This part of Jersey is a sad spectacle, after leaving the brightest of all the bright parts of Pennsylvania. My driver, who is a tavern-keeper himself, would have been a very pleasant companion, if he had not drunk so much spirits on the road. This is the *great misfortune* of America! As we were going up a hill very slowly, I could perceive him looking very hard at my cheek for some time. At last, he said: 'I am wondering, sir, to see you look so *fresh* and so *young*, con-sidering what you have gone through in the world;' though I cannot imagine *how* he had learnt who I was. 'I'll tell you', said I, 'how I have contrived the thing. I rise early, go to bed early, eat sparingly, never drink anything stronger than small beer, shave once a day, and wash my hands and face clean three times a day, at the very least.' He said, that was *too much* to think of doing.

[24 April 1818]

Let us, now, take a survey, or rather glance, at the face, which
nature now wears. The grass begins to afford a good deal for
sheep and for my grazing English pigs, and the cows and oxen
get a little food from it. The pears, apples, and other fruit trees,
have not made much progress in the swelling or bursting of their
buds. The buds of the weeping-willow have *bursted* (for, in spite
of that conceited ass, Mr JAMES PERRY, *to burst* is a *regular verb*,
and vulgar pedants only make it irregular), and those of a *lilac*,
in a warm place, are almost *bursted*, which is a great deal better
than to say, 'almost *burst*'. Oh, the coxcomb! As if an absolute
pedagogue like him could injure me by his *criticisms*! And, as if
an error like this, even if it had been one, could have any thing
to do with my capacity for developing principles, and for simpli-
fying things, which, in their nature, are of great complexity! The
oaks, which, in England, have now their sap in *full flow*, are here
quite unmoved as yet. In the gardens in general there is *nothing
green*, while, in England, they have *broccoli* to eat, early cabbages
planted out, coleworts to eat, peas four or five inches high. Yet,
we shall have *green peas* and *loaved cabbages as soon as they will*.
We have *sprouts* from the cabbage stems preserved under cover;
the Swedish turnip is giving me *greens* from bulbs planted out in
March; and I have some *broccoli* too, just coming on for use.
*How* I have got this broccoli I must explain in my *Gardener's
Guide*; for write one I must. I never can leave this country
without an attempt to make every farmer a gardener. In the meat
way, we have beef, mutton, bacon, fowls, a calf to kill in a
fortnight's time, sucking pigs when we choose, lamb nearly fit to
kill; and all of our own breeding, or our own feeding. We kill an
ox, send three quarters and the hide to market and keep one
quarter. Then a sheep, which we use in the same way. The bacon
is always ready. Some fowls always fatting. Young ducks are just
coming out to meet the green peas. Chickens (the earliest) as big
as American Partridges (misnamed quails), and ready for the
asparagus, which is just coming out of the ground. Eggs at all
times more than we can consume. And, if there be any one, who
wants *better* fare than this, let the grumbling glutton come to that
poverty, which Solomon has said shall be his lot. And, the *great*

*thing of all*, is, that here, *every man*, even every labourer, may live as well as this, if he will be *sober* and *industrious*.

There are *two things*, which I have not yet mentioned, and which are almost wholly wanting here, while they are so amply enjoyed in England. The *singing birds* and the *flowers*. Here are many birds in summer, and some of very beautiful plumage. There are some wild flowers, and some English flowers in the best gardens. But, generally speaking, they are birds without song, and flowers without smell. The *linnet* (more than a thousand of which I have heard warbling upon one scrubbed oak on the sand hills in Surrey), the *skylark*, the *goldfinch*, the *wood-lark*, the *nightingale*, the *bullfinch*, the *blackbird*, the *thrush*, and all the rest of the singing tribe are wanting in these beautiful woods and orchards of garlands. When these latter have dropped their bloom, all is gone in the flowery way. No *shepherd's rose*, no *honeysuckle*, none of that endless variety of beauties that decorate the hedges and the meadows in England. No *daisies*, no *primroses*, no *cowslips*, no *bluebells*, no *daffodils*, which, as if it were not enough for them to charm the sight and the smell, must have names, too, to delight the ear. All these are wanting in America. Here are, indeed, birds, which bear the *name* of robin, blackbird, thrush and goldfinch; but, alas! the thing at Westminster has, in like manner, the *name* of parliament, and speaks the voice of the people, whom it pretends to represent, in much about the same degree that the blackbird here speaks the voice of its namesake in England.

*Of health*, I have not yet spoken, and though it will be a subject of remark in another part of my work, it is a matter of too deep interest to be wholly passed over here. In the first place, as to *myself*, I have always had excellent health; but, during a year, in England, I used to have a *cold* or two; a trifling sore throat; or something in that way. *Here*, I have neither, though I was more than two months of the winter travelling about, and sleeping in different beds. My family have been more healthy than in England, though, indeed, there has seldom been any serious illness in it. We have had but *one visit from any doctor*. Thus much, for the present, on this subject. I said, in the second *Register* I sent home, that this climate was *not so good as that of England*. Experience, observation, a careful attention to real facts, have convinced me that it is, *upon the whole*, a better climate;

though I tremble lest the tools of the Boroughmongers should cite this as a new and most flagrant instance of *inconsistency.* England is my country, and to England I shall return. I like it best, and shall always like it best; but, then, in the word *England,* many things are included besides climate and soil and seasons, and eating and drinking.

In the *Second Part* of this work, which will follow the first part in the course of two months, I shall take particular pains to detail all that is within my knowledge, which I think likely to be useful to persons who intend coming to this country from England. I shall take every particular of the expence of supporting a family, and show what are the means to be obtained for that purpose, and how they are to be obtained. My intending to return to England ought to *deter* no one from coming hither; because I was resolved, if I had life, to return, and I expressed that resolution before I came away. But if there are good and virtuous men, who can do no good there, and who, by coming hither can withdraw the fruits of their honest labour from the grasp of the Borough-tyrants, I am bound, if I speak of this country at all, to tell them the real truth; and this, as far as I have gone, I have now done.

# TO KEEP HIS BLOOD, AND ENJOY HIS MONEY TOO

It must be obvious, that these must be in proportion to the number in family, and to the style of living. Therefore, every one knowing how he stands in these two respects, the best thing for me to do is to give an account of the *prices* [at 1818 level] of house-rent, food, raiment, and servants; or, as they are called here, *helpers*.

In the great cities and towns house-rent is very high-priced; but, then, nobody but mad people live there except they have *business* there, and, then, they are paid back their rent in the *profits of that business*. This is so plain a matter, that no argument is necessary. It is unnecessary to speak about the expences of a *farm-house*; because, the farmer eats, and very frequently wears, his own produce. If these be high-priced, so is that part which he *sells*. Thus both ends meet with him.

I am, therefore, supposing the case of a man, who follows *no business*, and who lives upon what he has got. In England he cannot eat and drink and wear the interest of his money; for the Boroughmongers have *pawned* half his income, and they will have it, or his blood. He wishes to escape from this alternative. He wishes to keep his blood, and enjoy his money too. He would come to America; but he does not know, whether prices here will not make up for the robbery of the Borough-villains; and he wishes to know, too, *what sort of society* he is going into. Of the latter I will speak in the *next chapter*.

The price of house-rent and fuel is, when at more than three miles from New York, as low as it is at the same distance from any great city or town in England. The price of wheaten bread

is a third lower than it is in any part of England. The price of
*beef, mutton, lamb, veal, small pork, hog-meat, poultry,* is *one half
the London price*; the first as good, the two next very nearly as
good, and all the rest far, very far better than in London. The
sheep I now kill for my house are as fat as any that I ever saw
in all my life; and they have been running in *wild ground,* wholly
uncultivated for many years, all the summer. A lamb, killed the
week before last, weighing in the whole, *thirty-eight pounds,* had
five *pounds of loose fat* and *three pounds and ten ounces of suet.* We
cut a pound of solid fat from each breast; and, after that it was
too fat to be pleasant to eat. My flock being small, forty or
thereabouts of some neighbours joined them; and they have all
got fat together. I have missed the interlopers lately: I suppose
the 'Yorkers' have eaten them up by this time. What they have
fattened on except *brambles* and *cedars,* I am sure I do not know.
If any Englishman should be afraid that he will find no roast-
beef here, it may be sufficient to tell him, that an ox was killed,
last winter, at Philadelphia, the quarters of which weighed *two
thousand, two hundred, and some odd pounds,* and he was sold TO
THE BUTCHER for *one thousand three hundred dollars.* This is
proof enough of the spirit of enterprize, and of the disposition in
the public to encourage it. I believe this to have been the *fattest*
ox that ever was killed in the world. Three times as much money,
or, perhaps, ten times as much, might have been made, if the ox
had been *shown for money.* But, this the owner *would not permit*;
and he sold the ox in that condition. I need hardly say that the
owner was a Quaker. New Jersey had the honour of producing
this ox, and the owner's name was JOB TYLER.

   That there must be good *bread* in America is pretty evident
from the well known fact, that hundreds of thousands of barrels
of flour are, most years sent to England, finer than any that
England can produce. And, having now provided the two principal articles, I will suppose, as a matter of course, that a gentleman will have *a garden,* an *orchard,* and a *cow* or two; but, if he
should be able (no easy matter) to find a genteel country-house
without these conveniences, he may buy *butter,* cheaper, and
upon an average, better than in England. The garden stuff, if he
send to New York for it, he must buy pretty dear; and, faith, he
*ought* to buy it dear, if he will not have some planted and preserved.

*Cheese*, of the North River produce, I have bought as good of Mr STICKLER of New York as I ever tasted in all my life; and, indeed, no better cheese need be wished for than what is now made in this country. The average price is about *seven pence a pound* (English money) which is much lower than even *middling* cheese is in England. Perhaps, *generally speaking*, the cheese here is not so good as the better kinds in England; but, there is none here so poor as the poorest in England. Indeed the people *would not eat it*, which is the best security against its being made. Mind, I state distinctly, that as good cheese as I ever tasted, if not the best, was of American produce. I know the article well. Bread and cheese *dinners* have been the dinners of a good fourth of my life. I know the Cheshire, Gloucester, Wiltshire, Stilton, and the Parmasan; and I never tasted better than American cheese, bought of Mr STICKLER, in Broad Street, New York. And this cheese Mr STICKLER informs me is nothing uncommon in the county of Cheshire in Massachusetts; he knows at least a hundred persons himself that make it equally good. And, indeed, why should it not be thus in a country where the pasture is so rich; where the *sun* warms every thing into sweetness; where the cattle eat the grass close *under the shade of the thickest trees*; which we know well they will not do in England. Take any fruit which has grown in the shade in England, and you will find that it has not half the sweetness in it, that there is in fruit of the same bulk, grown in the sun. But, here the sun sends his heat down through all the boughs and leaves. The *manufacturing* of cheese is not yet *generally* brought, in this country, to the English perfection; but, here are all the materials, and the rest will soon follow.

*Groceries*, as they are called, are, upon an average, at far less than *half* the English price. Tea, sugar, coffee, spices, chocolate, cocoa, salt, sweet oil; all free of the Boroughmonger's *taxes* and their *pawn*, are so cheap as to be within the reach of every one. Chocolate, which is a *treat* to the *rich*, in England, is here used even by *the negroes*. Sweet oil, raisins, currants; all the things from the Levant, are at a *fourth* or *fifth* of the English price. The English people, who pay enormously to keep possession of the East and West Indies, purchase the produce even of the English possessions at a price double of that which the Americans give *for that very produce*! What a hellish oppression must that people live under! Candles and soap (quality for quality) are half the English price. Wax candles (beautiful) are at a *third* of the English price. It is no very great piece of extravagance to burn wax candles *constantly* here, and it is frequently done by genteel people, who do not make their own candles.

*Fish* I have not mentioned, because fish is not *everywhere* to be had in abundance. But, any where near the coast it is; and, it is so cheap, that one wonders how it can be brought to market for the money. Fine black-rock, as good, at least, as codfish, I have seen sold, and in cold weather too, at an *English farthing a pound*. They now bring us fine fish round the country to our doors, at an English three pence a pound. I believe they count *fifty* or *sixty sorts* of fish in New York market, as the average. Oysters, other shellfish, called *clams*. In short, the variety and abundance are such that I cannot describe them.

An idea of the state of *plenty* may be formed from these facts: nobody but the free negroes who have families ever think of eating a *sheep's head and pluck*. It is seldom that *oxen's heads* are used at home, or *sold*, and never in the country. In the course of the year hundreds of *calves' heads*, large bits and *whole joints* of meat, are left on the shambles, at New York, for any body *to take away* that will. They generally fall to the share of the *street hogs*, a thousand or two of which are constantly *fatting* in New York on the meat and fish flung out of the houses. I shall be told, that it is only in *hot weather*, that the shambles are left thus garnished. Very true; but are the shambles of *any other country* thus garnished in *hot weather*? Oh! no! If it were not for the superabundance, all the food would be sold at *some* price or other.

After bread, flesh, fish, fowl, butter, cheese and groceries, comes *fruit*. Apples, pears, cherries, peaches at a *tenth* part of the English price. The other day I met a man going to market with a waggon load of *winter pears*. He had high boards on the sides of the waggon, and his waggon held about forty or fifty bushels. I have bought very good apples this year for *four pence halfpenny* (English) a bushel, to boil for little pigs. Besides these, strawberries grow wild in abundance; but no one will take the trouble to get them. Huckleberries in the woods in great abundance, chestnuts all over the country. Four pence halfpenny (English) a quart for these latter. Cranberries, the finest fruit for tarts that ever grew, for about a dollar a bushel, and they will keep, flung down in the corner of a room, for five months in the year. As a sauce to venison or mutton, they are as good as currant jelly. Pine apples in abundance, for several months in the year, at an average of an English shilling each. Melons at an average of English eight pence. In short, what is there not in the way of fruit? All excellent of their kinds and all for a mere trifle, compared to what they cost in England.

I am afraid to speak of *drink*, lest I should be supposed to countenance the *common use* of it. But, protesting most decidedly against this conclusion, I proceed to inform those, who are not content with the *cow* for vintner and brewer, that all the materials for making people drunk, or muddle headed, are much cheaper here than in England. Beer, *good ale*, I mean, a great deal better than the common public-house beer in England; in short, good, strong, clear ale, is, at New York, eight dollars a barrel; that is, about *fourteen English pence a gallon*. Brew yourself, in the country, and it is about *seven English pence a gallon*; that is to say, *less than two pence a quart*. No Boroughmongers' tax on malt, hops, or beer! Portugal wine is about *half* the price that it is in England. French wine a *sixth part* of the English price. Brandy and Rum about the same in proportion; and the common spirits of the country are about three shillings and sixpence (English) *a gallon*. Come on, then, if you love toping; for here you may drink yourselves blind at the price of sixpence.

*Wearing apparel* comes chiefly from England, and all the *materials* of dress are as cheap as they are there; for, though there is a duty laid on the importation, the absence of taxes, and the cheap food and drink, enable the retailer to sell as low here as there. Shoes are cheaper than in England; for, though shoemakers are well paid for their labour, there is no Borough-villain to *tax the leather*. All the *India* and *French* goods are at half the English price. Here no ruffian can seize you by the throat and tear off your suspected handkerchief. Here SIGNOR WAITHMAN, or any body in that line, might have sold French gloves and shawls without being tempted to quit the field of politics as a compromise with the government; and without any breach of covenants, after being suffered to escape with only a gentle squeeze.

*Household furniture*, all cheaper than in England. *Mahogany* timber a third part of the English price. The distance shorter to bring it, and the tax next to nothing on importation. The *woods* here, the pine, the ash, the white-oak, the walnut, the tulip-tree, and many others, all excellent. The workman paid high wages but *no tax*. No Borough-villains to share in the amount of the price.

Horses, carriages, harness, all as good, as gay, and cheaper than in England. I hardly ever saw a *rip* in this country. The hackney coach horses and the coaches themselves, at New York, bear no resemblance to things of the same name in London. The former are all good, sound, clean, and handsome. What the latter are I need describe in no other way than to say, that the coaches seem fit for nothing but the fire and the horses for the dogs.

*Domestic servants!* This is a weighty article: not in the cost, however, so much as in the plague. A *good man servant* is worth *thirty pounds sterling* a year; and a *good woman servant, twenty pounds sterling a year*. But, this is not all; for, in the first place, they will hire only *by the month*. This is what they, in fact, do in England; for, there they can quit at *a month's warning*. The man will not wear *a livery*, any more than he will wear a halter round his neck. This is no great matter; for, as your neighbours' men are of the same taste, you expose yourself to no humiliation on this score. Neither men nor women will allow you to call them *servants*, and they will take especial care not to call themselves by that name. This seems something very capricious, at the least; and, as people in such situations of life, really *are* servants, according to even the sense which MOSES gives to the word, when he forbids the working of the *man servant* and the *maid servant*, the objection, the rooted aversion, to the name; seems to bespeak a mixture of *false pride* and of *insolence*, neither of which belong to the American character, even in the lowest walks of life. I will, therefore, explain the *cause* of this dislike to the name of servant. When this country was first settled, there were no people that *laboured for other people*; but, as man is always trying to throw the working part off his own shoulders, as we see by the conduct of *priests* in all ages, *negroes* were soon introduced. *Englishmen*, who had fled from *tyranny* at home, were naturally shy of calling other men their slaves; and, therefore, '*for more grace*', as Master Matthew says in the play, they called their slaves *servants*. But, though I doubt not that this device was quite efficient in quieting their own consciences, it gave rise to the notion, that *slave* and *servant* meant one and the same thing, a conclusion perfectly natural and directly deducible from the premises. Hence every *free* man and woman have rejected with just disdain the appellation of *servant*. One would think, however, that they might be reconciled to it by the conduct of some of their superiors in life, who, without the smallest apparent reluctance, call themselves *Public Servants*, in imitation, I suppose, of English ministers, and His Holiness, the Pope, who, in the excess of his humility, calls himself '*the Servant of the Servants of the Lord*'. But, perhaps, the American domestics have observed, that *Public Servant* really means *master*. Be the cause what it may, however, they continue most obstinately, to scout the name of servant; and, though they still keep a civil tongue in their head, there is not one of them that will not resent the affront with more bitterness than any other that you can offer. The man, therefore, who would deliberately offer such an affront must be a fool. But, there is an inconvenience far greater than this. People in general are so comfortably situated, that very few, and then only of those who are pushed hard, will become domestics to any body. So that, generally speaking, domestics of both sexes are far from good. They are *honest*; but they are not *obedient*. They are careless. Wanting frequently in the greater part of those qualities which make their services conducive to the neatness of houses and comfort of families. What a difference would it make in this country, if it could be supplied with nice, clean, dutiful English maid servants! As to the *men*, it does not much signify; but for the want of maids, nothing but the absence of grinding taxation can compensate. As to *bringing them with you*, it is as wild a project as it would be to try to carry the sunbeams to England. They will begin to change before the ship gets on soundings; and, before they have been here a month, you must turn them out of doors, or they will you. If, by any chance, you *find them here*, it may do; but bring them out and keep them you cannot. The best way is to put on your philosophy; never to look at this evil without, at the same time, looking at the many good things that you find here. Make the best selection you can. Give *good wages*, not too much work, and resolve, at all events, to treat them with *civility*.

However, what is this plague, compared with that of the *tax gatherer*? What is this plague compared with the constant sight of beggars and paupers, and the constant dread of becoming a pauper or beggar yourself? If your commands are not obeyed with such alacrity as in England, you have, at any rate, nobody to *command you*. You are not ordered to *stand and deliver* twenty or thirty times in the year by the insolent agent of Boroughmongers. No one comes to forbid you to open or shut up a window. No insolent set of commissioners send their order for you to dance attendance on them, to *shew cause* why they should not *double-tax you*; and, when you have shown cause, even on your oath, make you pay the tax, laugh in your face, and leave you *an appeal* from themselves to another set, deriving their authority from the same source, and having a similar interest in oppressing you, and thus laying your property prostrate beneath the hoof of an insolent and remorseless tyranny. Free, wholly free, from this tantalizing, this grinding, this odious curse, what need you care about the petty plagues of domestic servants?

However, as there are some men and some women, who can never be at heart's ease, unless they have the power of domineering over somebody or other, and who will rather be slaves themselves than not have it in their power to treat others as slaves, it becomes a man of fortune, proposing to emigrate to America, to consider soberly, whether he, or his wife, be of this taste; and, if the result of his consideration be in the affirmative, his best way will be to continue to live under the Boroughmongers, or, which I would rather recommend, hang himself at once.

# AMERICAN MANNERS:
## A GUIDE FOR IMMIGRANTS

The manners, customs and character of the people are, generally speaking, the same as those of the people of England. The French call this people *Les Anglo-Américains*; and, indeed, what are they else? Of the manners and customs somewhat peculiar to America I have said so much, here and there, that I can hardly say any thing here upon these matters. But, as *society* is naturally a great thing with a gentleman, who thinks of coming hither with his wife and children, I will endeavour to describe the society that he will find here. To give *general* descriptions is not so satisfactory as it is to deal a little in particular instances; to tell of what one has seen and experienced. This is what I shall do; and, in this chapter I wish to be regarded as addressing myself to a most worthy and public-spirited gentleman of moderate fortune, *in Lancashire*, who, with a large family, now balances whether he shall come, or stay.

Now, then, my dear sir, this people contains very few persons very much raised in men's estimation, above the general mass; for, though there are some men of immense *fortunes*, their wealth does very little indeed in the way of purchasing even the outward signs of respect; and, as to *adulation*, it is not to be purchased with love or money. Men, be they what they may, are generally called by their *two names*, without any thing prefixed or added. I am one of the greatest men in this country at present; for people in general call me *Cobbett*, though the Quakers provokingly persevere in putting the *William* before it, and my old friends in Pennsylvania, use even the word *Billy*, which, in the very sound of the letters, is an antidote to everything like thirst for distinction.

Fielding, in one of his romances, observes, that there are but few cases, in which a husband can be justified in availing of the right which the law gives him to bestow manual chastisement upon his wife, and that one of these, he thinks, is, when any pretensions to *superiority of blood* make their appearance in her language and conduct. They have a better cure for this malady here; namely: silent, but, *ineffable contempt.*

It is supposed, in England, that this equality of estimation must beget a general coarseness and rudeness of behaviour. Never was there a greater mistake. No man likes to be treated with disrespect; and, when he finds that he can obtain respect only by treating others with respect, he will use that only means. When he finds that neither haughtiness nor wealth will bring him a civil word, he becomes civil himself; and, I repeat it again and again, this is a country of *universal civility*.

The causes of *hypocrisy* are the fear of loss and the hope of gain. Men crawl to those, whom, in their hearts, they despise, because they fear the effects of their ill-will and hope to gain by their good-will. The circumstances of all ranks are so easy here, that there is no cause for hypocrisy; and the thing is not of so fascinating a nature, that men should love it for its own sake.

The boasting of wealth, and the endeavouring to disguise poverty, these two acts, so painful to contemplate, are almost total strangers in this country; for, no man can gain adulation or respect by his wealth, and no man dreads the effects of poverty, because no man sees any dreadful effects arising from poverty.

That *anxious eagerness to get on*, which is seldom unaccompanied with some degree of *envy* of more successful neighbours, and which has its foundation first in a *dread of future want*, and next in a *desire to obtain distinction by means of wealth*; this anxious eagerness, so unamiable in itself, and so unpleasant an inmate of the breast, so great a sourer of the temper, is a stranger to America, where accidents and losses, which would drive an Englishman half mad, produce but very little agitation.

From the absence of so many causes of uneasiness, of envy, of jealousy, of rivalship, and of mutual dislike, *society*, that is to say, the intercourse between man and man, and family and family, becomes easy and pleasant; while the universal plenty is the cause of universal hospitality. I know, and have ever known, but little of the people in the cities and towns in America; but, the difference between them and the people in the country can only be such as is found in all other countries. As to the manner of living in the country, I was, the other day, at a gentleman's house, and I asked the lady for *her bill of fare for the year*. I saw *fourteen* fat hogs, weighing about *twenty score a piece*, which were to come *into the house* the next Monday; for here they slaughter *them all in one day*. This led me to ask, 'Why, in God's name, what do you eat in a year?' The bill of fare was this, for this present year: about *this same quantity of hog-meat*; *four beeves*; and *forty-six fat sheep*! Besides the *sucking pigs* (of which we had then one on the table), besides *lambs*, and besides the produce of *seventy hen fowls*, not to mention good parcels of *geese*, *ducks* and *turkeys*, but, not to forget a garden of three quarters of an acre and *the butter of ten cows*, not one ounce of which is ever *sold*! What do you think of that? Why, you will say, this must be some *great overgrown farmer*, that has swallowed up half the country; or some nabob sort of merchant. Not at all. He has only *one hundred and fifty four acres of land* (all he consumes is of the produce of this land), and he lives in the same house that his English-born grandfather lived in.

When the hogs are killed, the house is full of work. The sides are salted down as pork. The hams are smoked. The lean meats are made into sausages, of which, in this family, they make about *two hundred weight*. These latter, with broiled fish, eggs, dried beef, dried mutton, slices of ham, tongue, bread, butter, cheese, short cakes, buckwheat cakes, sweet meats of various sorts, and many other things, make up the *breakfast* fare of the year, and, a dish of *beef steakes* is frequently added.

When one sees this sort of living, with the houses *full of good beds*, ready for the guests as well as the family to sleep in, we cannot help perceiving, that this is that *English Hospitality*, of which we have *read* so much; but, which Boroughmongers' taxes and pawns have long since driven out of England. This American way of life puts one in mind of FORTESCUE'S fine description of the happy state of the English, produced by their *good laws*, which kept every man's property sacred, even from the grasp of the king.

Every inhabitant is at his Liberty fully to use and enjoy whatever his Farm produceth, the Fruits of the Earth, the Increase of his Flock, and the like: All the Improvements he makes, whether by his own proper Industry, or of those he retains in his Service, are his own to use and enjoy without the Lett, Interruption, or Denial of any: If he be in any wise injured, or oppressed, he shall have his *Amends* and satisfaction against the party offending: Hence it is, that the Inhabitants are Rich in Gold, Silver, and in all the Necessaries and Conveniences of Life. They drink no Water, unless at certain Times, upon a Religious Score, and by Way of doing Penance. They are fed, in great Abundance, with all sorts of Flesh and Fish, of which they have Plenty every where; they are cloathed throughout in good Woollens; their Bedding and other Furniture in their Houses are of wool, and that in great store. They are well-provided with other sorts of Household Goods, and necessary Implements for Husbandry: Every one, according to his Rank, hath all Things *which conduce to make Life easy and happy.* They are not sued at Law but before the Ordinary Judges, where they are treated with Mercy and Justice, according to the Laws of the Land; neither are they impleaded in Point of Property, or arraigned for any Capital Crime, how heinous soever, but before the King's Judges, and according to the Laws of the Land. These are the Advantages consequent from that *Political Mixt Government* which obtains in *England.*

This passage, which was first pointed out to me by SIR FRANCIS BURDETT, describes the state of England four hundred years ago; and this, with the *polish* of modern times added, is now the state of the Americans. Their forefathers brought the 'English Hospitality' with them; for, when they left the country, the infernal *Boroughmonger Funding system* had not begun. The STUARTS were *religious* and *prerogative* tyrants; but they were not, like their successors, the Boroughmongers, taxing, plundering tyrants. Their quarrels with their subjects were about mere *words*: with the Boroughmongers it is a question of purses and strong-boxes, of goods and chattels, lands and tenements. *'Confiscation'* is their word; and you must submit, be hanged, or flee. They take away men's property at their pleasure, *without any appeal to any tribunal.* They appoint *Commissioners* to seize what they choose. There is, in fact, *no law* of property left. The bishop-begotten and hell-born system of Funding has stripped England of every vestige of what was her ancient character. Her hospitality along with her freedom have crossed the Atlantic; and here they are to shame our ruffian tyrants, if they were sensible of shame, and to give shelter to those who may be disposed to deal them distant blows.

It is not with a little bit of dry toast, so neatly put in a rack; a bit of butter so round and small; a little milk pot so pretty and so empty; an egg *for you*, the host and hostess *not liking eggs*. It is not with looks that seem to say, 'don't eat too much, for the taxgatherer is coming'. It is not thus that you are received in America. You are not much *asked*, not much *pressed*, to eat and drink; but, such an abundance is spread before you, and so hearty and so cordial is your reception, that you instantly lose all restraint, and are tempted to feast whether you be hungry or not. And, though the *manner* and *style* are widely different in different houses, the *abundance* every where prevails. This is the strength of the government: a happy people: and no government ought to have any other strength.

But, you may say, perhaps, that plenty, however great, is not *all* that is wanted. Very true: for the *mind* is of more account than the carcass. But, here is mind too. These repasts, amongst people of any figure, come forth under the superintendance of industrious and accomplished housewifes, or their daughters, who all *read a great deal*, and in whom that gentle treatment from parents and husbands, which arises from an absence of racking anxiety, has created an habitual, and even an hereditary *good humour*. These ladies can converse with you upon almost any subject, and the ease and gracefulness of their behaviour are surpassed by those of none of even our best-tempered English women. They fade at an earlier age than in England; but, till then, they are as beautiful as the women in *Cornwall*, which contains, to my thinking, the prettiest women in our country. However, young or old, blooming or fading, well or ill, rich or poor, they still preserve their *good humour*.

> *But, since, alas! frail beauty must decay,*
> *Curl'd, or uncurl'd, since locks will turn to grey;*
> *Since painted, or not painted, all shall fade,*
> *And she who scorns a man must die a maid;*

*What, then, remains, but well our pow'r to use,*
*And keep* good humour *still, whate'er we lose?*
*And, trust me, dear, good-humour can prevail,*
*When flights and fits, and screams and scolding fail.*

This beautiful passage, from the most beautiful of poets, which ought to be fastened in large print upon every lady's dressing table, the American women, of all ranks, seem to have by heart. Even amongst the very lowest of the people, you seldom hear of that torment, which the old proverb makes the twin of a smoky house.

There are very few really *ignorant* men in America of native growth. Every farmer is more or less of a *reader*. There is no *brogue*, no *provincial dialect*. No class like that which the French call *peasantry*, and which degrading appellation the miscreant spawn of the Funds have, of late years, applied to the whole mass of the most useful of the people in England, those who do the work and fight the battles. And, as to the men, who would naturally form *your* acquaintances, they, I know from experience, are as kind, frank, and sensible men as are, on the general run, to be found in England, even with the power of selection. They are all well-informed; modest without shyness; always free to communicate what they know and never ashamed to acknowledge that they have yet to learn. You never hear them *boast* of their possessions, and you never hear them *complaining* of their wants. They have all been *readers* from their youth up; and there are few subjects upon which they cannot converse with you, whether of a political or scientific nature. At any rate, they always *hear* with patience. I do not know that I ever heard a native American interrupt another man while he was speaking. Their *sedateness* and *coolness*, the *deliberate* manner in which they say and do every thing, and the *slowness* and *reserve* with which they express their assent; these are very wrongly estimated, when they are taken for marks of a *want of feeling*. It must be a tale of woe indeed, that will bring a tear from an American's eye; but any trumped up story will send his hand to his pocket, as the ambassadors from the beggars of France, Italy and Germany can fully testify.

However, you will not, for a long while, know what to do for want of the *quick responses* of the English tongue, and the *decided* tone of the English expression. The *loud voice*; the *hard squeeze* by the hand; the *instant assent or dissent*; the *clamorous joy*; the *bitter wailing*; the *ardent friendship*; the *deadly enmity;* the *love that makes people kill themselves*; the *hatred that makes them kill others*. All these belong to the characters of Englishmen, in whose minds and hearts every feeling exists in the *extreme*. To decide the question, which character is, upon the whole, *best*, the American or the English, we must appeal to some *third party*. But, it is no matter: we cannot change our natures. For my part, who can, in nothing, think or act by halves, I must belie my very nature, if I said I did not like the character of my own countrymen best. We all like our own parents and children better than other people's parents and children; not because they *are* better, but because they are *ours*; because they belong to us and we to them, and because we must *resemble* each other. There are some Americans that I like full as well as I do any man in England; but, if, nation against nation, I put the question home to my heart, it instantly decides in favour of my countrymen.

You must not be offended if you find people here take but little interest in the concerns of England. Why should they? BOLTON F——R cannot hire spies to entrap them. As matter of curiosity, they may contemplate such works as those of FLETCHER; but, they cannot *feel* much upon the subject; and they are not insincere enough to express much.

There is one thing in the Americans, which, though its proper place was further back, I have reserved, or rather *kept back*, to the last moment. It has presented itself several times; but I have turned from the thought, as men do from thinking of any mortal disease that is at work in their frame. It is not covetousness; it is not niggardliness; it is not insincerity; it is not enviousness; it is not cowardice, above all things: it is DRINKING. Aye, and that too, amongst but too many men, who, one would think, would loathe it. You cannot go into hardly any man's house, without being asked to drink wine, or spirits, even *in the morning*. They are quick at meals, are little eaters, seem to care little about what they eat, and never talk about it. This, which arises out of the universal abundance of good and even fine eatables, is very amiable. You are here disgusted with none of those *eaters* by *reputation* that are found, especially amongst *the parsons*, in England: fellows that *unbutton* at it. Nor do the Americans *sit and tope much after dinner*, and talk on till they get into nonsense and *smut*, which last is a sure mark of a silly and, pretty generally, even of a base mind. But, they *tipple*; and the infernal spirits they tipple too! The scenes that I witnessed at Harrisburgh I shall never forget. I almost wished (God forgive me!) that there were Boroughmongers here to *tax* these drinkers: they would soon reduce them to a moderate dose. Any nation that feels itself uneasy with its fulness of good things, has only to resort to an application of Boroughmongers. These are by no means nice feeders or of contracted throat: they will suck down any thing from the poor man's pot of beer to the rich man's lands and tenements.

The Americans preserve their gravity and quietness and good-humour even in their drink; and so much the worse. It were far better for them to be as noisy and quarrelsome as the English drunkards; for then the odiousness of the vice would be more visible, and the vice itself might become less frequent. Few vices want an *apology*, and drinking has not only its apologies but its *praises*; for, besides the appellation of *generous wine*, and the numerous songs, some in very elegant and witty language, from the pens of debauched men of talents, drinking is said to be necessary, in certain cases at least, *to raise the spirits*, and *to keep out cold*. Never was anything more false. Whatever intoxicates must *enfeeble* in the end, and whatever enfeebles must *chill*. It is very well known, in the Northern countries, that, if the cold be such as to produce danger of *frost-biting*, you must take care *not to drink strong liquors*.

To see this beastly vice in *young men* is shocking. At one of the taverns at Harrisburgh there were several as fine young men as I ever saw. Well-dressed, well educated, polite, and everything but *sober*. What a squalid, drooping, sickly set they looked *in the morning!*

Even little boys at, or under, *twelve* years of age, go into *stores*, and tip off their *drams!* I never struck a child, in anger, in my life, that I recollect; but, if I were so unfortunate as to have a son to do this, he having had an example to the contrary in me, I would, if all other means of reclaiming him failed, whip him like a dog, or, which would be better, make him an out-cast from my family.

However, I must not be understood as meaning, that this tippling is *universal* amongst gentlemen; and, God be thanked, the *women* of any figure in life do by no means give into the practice; but, abhor it as much as well-bred women in England, who, in general, no more think of drinking strong liquors, than they do of drinking poison.

I shall be told, that men in the *harvest field* must have *something* to drink. To be sure, where perspiration almost instantly carries off the drink, the latter does not remain so long to burn the liver, or whatever else it does burn. But, I much question the utility even here; and I think, that, in the long run, a water-drinker would beat a spirit-drinker at anything, provided both had plenty of good food. And, besides, *beer*, which does not *burn*, at any rate, is within every one's reach in America, if he will but take the trouble to brew it.

A man, at Botley, whom I was very severely reproaching for getting drunk and lying in the road, whose name was JAMES ISAACS, and who was, by the by, one of the hardest workers I ever knew, said, in answer: 'Why, now, sir, NOAH and LOT were two very good men, you know, and yet they loved *a drop of drink.*' 'Yes, you drunken fool,' replied I, 'but you do not read that *Isaac* ever got drunk and rolled about the road.' I could not help thinking, however, that the BIBLE SOCIETIES, with the wise Emperor Alexander and the Holy Alliance at their head, might as well (to say nothing about the *cant* of the thing) leave the Bible to work its own way. I had seen ISAACS dead drunk, lying stretched out, by my front gate, against the public highway; and, if he had followed the example of NOAH, he would not have endeavoured to excuse himself in the modest manner that he did, but would have affixed an *everlasting curse on me and my children to all generations.*

The soldiers, in the regiment that I belonged to, many of whom served in the American war, had a saying, that the *Quakers* used the word *tired* in place of the word *drunk*. Whether any of them do ever get *tired* themselves, I know not; but, at any rate they most resolutely set their faces against the common use of spirits. They forbid their members to retail them; and, in case of disobedience, they *disown* them.

However, there is no remedy but the introduction of *beer*, and, I am very happy to know, that beer is, every day, becoming more and more fashionable. At Bristol in Pennsylvania, I was pleased to see excellent beer in clean and nice pewter pots. Beer does not kill. It does not eat out the vitals and take the colour from the cheek. It will make men 'tired', indeed, by midnight; but it does not make them half dead in the morning. We call wine the *juice of the grape*, and such it is with a proportion of *ardent spirits*, equal, in Portugal wine, to a *fifth* of the wine; and, therefore, when a man has taken down a bottle of Port or of Madeira, he has nearly *half a pint* of ardent spirits in him. And yet how many foolish mothers give their children Port wine to *strengthen* them! I never like your *wine-physicians*, though they are great favourites with but too many patients. BONIFACE, in the *Beaux Stratagem*, says that he has eaten his ale, drunk his ale, worked upon his ale, and slept upon his ale, for forty years, and that he has grown fatter and fatter; but, that his wife (God rest her soul!) would not take it *pure*: she would adulterate it with brandy; till, at last, finding that the poor woman was never well, he put a tub of her favourite by her bedside, which, in a short time, brought her '*a happy release*' from this 'state of probation', and carried her off into *the world of spirits*. Whether Boniface meant this as a *pun*, I do not know; for, really, if I am to judge from the *practice* of many of the vagrant fanatics, I must believe, that, when they rave about the *spirit's entering them*, they mean that which goes out of a glass down their throat. Priests may make what they will of their devil: they may make him a reptile with a forked tongue, or a beast with a cloven hoof; they may, like Milton, dress him out with seraphic wings; or like Saint Francis, they may give him horns and tail: but, I say that the devil, who is the strongest tempter and who produces the most mischief in the world, approaches us in the shape of *liquid*, not melted brimstone, but wine, gin, brandy, rum, and whiskey. One comfort is, however, that *this* devil, of whose existence we can have no doubt, who is visible and even tangible, we can, if we will, without the aid of priests, or, rather, in spite of them, easily and safely set at defiance. There are many wrong things which men do against the general and natural bent of their minds. Fraud, theft, and even murder, are frequently, and most frequently, the offspring of *want*. In these cases, it is a choice of evils; *crime* or *hunger*. But drinking to excess is a man's own act; an evil deliberately sought after; an act of violence committed against reason and against nature; and that, too, without the smallest temptation, except from that vicious appetite, which he himself has voluntarily created.

You, my dear sir, stand in need of no such lectures as this, and the same is, I hope, the case with the far greater part of my readers; but, if it tend, in the smallest degree, to check the fearful growth of this tree of unmixed evil; if it should make the bottle less cherished even in one small circle; nay, if it keep but one young man in the world in the paths of sobriety, how could my time have been better bestowed?

# AMERICA'S RURAL SPORTS

There are persons, who question *the right* of man to pursue and destroy the wild animals, which are called *game*. Such persons, however, claim the right of killing *foxes* and *hawks*; yet, these have as much right to live and to follow their food as *pheasants* and *partridges* have. This, therefore, in such persons, is *nonsense*.

Others, in their mitigated hostility to the sports of the field, say, that it is *wanton* cruelty to shoot or hunt; and that we *kill* animals from the farmyard only because their flesh is *necessary to our own existence*. PROVE THAT. No: you cannot. If you could, it is but the *'tyrant's* plea'; but you cannot: for we know that men can, and do, live without animal food, and, if their labour be not of an exhausting kind, live well too, and longer than those who eat it. It comes to this, then, that we kill hogs and oxen because we *choose* to kill them; and, we kill game for precisely the same reason.

A third class of objectors, seeing the weak position of the two former, and still resolved to eat flesh, take their stand upon this ground: that sportsmen send game off *wounded* and leave them in *a state of suffering*. These gentlemen forget the operations performed upon calves, pigs, lambs and sometimes on poultry. Sir ISAAC COFFIN prides himself upon teaching the English ladies how to make *turkey-capons*! Only think of the separation of calves, pigs, and lambs, at an early age, from their mothers! Go, you sentimental eaters of veal, suckling pig and lamb, and hear the mournful lowings, whinings, and bleatings; observe the anxious listen, the wistful look, and the drooping tear, of the disconsolate dams; and, then, while you have the carcasses of their young ones under your teeth, cry out, as soon as you can empty your mouths a little, against the *cruelty* of hunting and shooting. Get up from dinner (but take care to stuff well first), and go and drown the puppies of the bitch, and the kittens of the cat, lest they should share a little in what their mothers have guarded with so much fidelity; and, as good stuffing may tend to make you restless in the night, order the geese to be picked alive, that, however your consciences may feel, your bed, at least, may be easy and soft. Witness all this with your own eyes; and then go weeping to bed, at the possibility of a hare having been terribly frightened without being killed, or of a bird having been left in a thicket with a shot in its body or a fracture in its wing. But, before you go upstairs, give your servants orders to be early at market for fish, fresh out of the water; that they may be *scaled*, or *skinned alive*! A truce with you, then, sentimental eaters of flesh: and here I propose the terms of a lasting compromise with you. We must, on each side yield something: we sportsmen will content ourselves with merely *seeing the hares skip and the birds fly*; and you shall be content with the flesh and fish that come from cases of *natural death*, of which, I am sure, your compassionate disposition will not refuse us a trifling allowance.

Nor have even the *Pythagoreans* a much better battery against us. Sir RICHARD PHILLIPS, who once rang a peal in my ears against shooting and hunting, does, indeed, eat neither *flesh*, *fish*, nor *fowl*. His abstinence surpasses that of a Carmelite, while his bulk would not disgrace a Benedictine monk, or a Protestant dean. But, he forgets, that his *shoes* and *breeches* and *gloves* are made of the skins of animals: he forgets that he *writes* (and very eloquently too) with what has been cruelly taken from a fowl; and that, in order to cover the *books* which he has had made and sold, hundreds of flocks and scores of droves must have perished: nay, that, to get him his *beaver-hat*, a beaver must have been *hunted* and *killed*, and, in the doing of which, many beavers may have been *wounded* and left to pine away the rest of their lives; and, perhaps many little orphan beavers, left to lament the murder of their parents. BEN LEY was the only real and sincere Pythagorean of modern times, that I ever heard of. He protested, not only against eating the flesh of animals, but also against robbing their backs; and, therefore, his dress consisted wholly of *flax*. But, even he, like Sir Richard Phillips, eat milk, butter, cheese, and eggs; though this was cruelly robbing the hens, cows, and calves; and, indeed causing the murder of calves. In addition, poor little BEN forgot the materials of *book-binding*; and it was well he did; for else, his Bible would have gone into the fire!

Taking it for granted, then, that sportsmen are as good as other folks on the score of *humanity*, the sports of the field, like everything else done in the fields, tend to produce, or preserve *health*. I prefer them to all other pastime, because they produce *early rising*; because they have no tendency to lead young men into vicious habits. It is where men *congregate* that the vices haunt. A hunter or a shooter may also be a gambler and a drinker; but, he is *less likely* to be fond of the two latter, if he be fond of the former. Boys will take to *something* in the way of pastime; and, it is better that they take to that which is innocent, healthy, and manly, than that which is vicious, unhealthy, and effeminate. Besides, the scenes of rural sports are necessarily at *a distance from cities and towns*. This is another great consideration; for though great talents are wanted to be *employed* in the *hives of men*, they are very rarely *acquired* in these hives: the surrounding objects are too numerous, too near the eye, too frequently under it, and too artificial.

For these reasons I have always encouraged my sons to pursue these sports. They have, until the age of fourteen or fifteen, spent their time, by day, chiefly amongst horses and dogs, and in the fields and farmyard; and their candlelight has been spent chiefly in reading books about hunting and shooting and about dogs and horses. I have supplied them plentifully with *books* and *prints* relating to these matters. They have *drawn* horses, dogs, and game themselves. These things, in which they took so deep an interest, not only engaged their attention and wholly kept them from all taste for, and even all knowledge of, *cards* and other senseless amusements; but, they led them *to read and write of their own accord; and, never in my life have I set them a copy in writing nor attempted to teach them a word of reading.* They have learnt to read by looking into books about dogs and game; and they have learnt to write by imitating my writing, and by writing endless letters to me, when I have been from home, about their dogs and other rural concerns. While the Borough-tyrants had me in Newgate for two years, with a thousand pounds fine, for having expressed my indignation at their flogging of Englishmen, in the heart of England, under a guard of Hanoverian sabres, I received *volumes of letters* from my children; and, I have them now, from

the *scrawl* of *three years*, to the neat and beautiful hand of thirteen. I never told them of any *errors* in their letters. All was well.
The best evidence of the utility of their writing, and the strongest
encouragement to write again, was *a very clear answer from me*,
in a very precise hand, and upon very nice paper, which they
never failed promptly to receive. They have all written to me
*before they could form a single letter*. A little bit of paper, with
some ink-marks on it, folded up by themselves, and a wafer stuck
in it, used to be sent to me, and it was *sure* to bring the writer
a very, very kind answer. Thus have they gone on. So far from
being a *trouble* to me, they have been all *pleasure* and *advantage*.
For many years they have been so many *secretaries*. I have *dictated* scores of registers to them, which have *gone to the press
without my ever looking at them*. I dictated registers to them at
the age of *thirteen*, and even of *twelve*. They have, as to *trustworthiness*, been grown persons, at eleven or twelve. I could leave
my house and affairs, the paying of men, or the going from home
on business, to them at an age when boys in England, in general,
want servants to watch them to see that they do not kill chickens,
torment kittens, or set the buildings on fire.

Here is a good deal of *boasting*; but, it will not be denied,
that I have *done a great deal* in a short public life, and I see no harm
in telling my readers of any of the means, that I have employed;
especially as I know of few greater misfortunes than that of
breeding up things to be *schoolboys all their lives*. It is not, that
I have so many wonders of the world: it is that I have pursued
a rational plan of education, and one that any man may pursue,
if he will, with similar effects. I remembered, too, that I myself
had had a sportsman-education. I ran after the hare-hounds at the
age of *nine or ten*. I have many and many a day left the rooks to
dig up the wheat and peas, while I followed the hounds; and
have returned home at dark-night, with my legs full of thorns
and my belly empty to go supperless to bed, and to congratulate
myself if I escaped a flogging. I was *sure* of these consequences;
but that had not the smallest effect in restraining me. All the
lectures, all the threats, vanished from my mind in a moment
upon hearing the first cry of the hounds, at which my heart used
to be ready to bound out of my body. I *remembered* all this. I
traced to this taste my contempt for card-playing and for all
childish and effeminate amusements. And, therefore, I resolved

to leave the same course freely open to my sons. This is *my plan* for education: others may follow what plan they please.

This [chapter] will be a head without a body; for, it will not require much time to give an account of the rural sports in America. The general taste of the country is to *kill* the things in order to have them to *eat*, which latter forms no part of the *sportsman*'s objects.

There cannot be said to be anything here, which we, in England, call *hunting*. The deer are hunted by *dogs*, indeed, but the hunters do not *follow*. They are *posted* at their several stations to *shoot* the deer as he passes. This is only one remove from the *Indian* hunting. I never saw, that I know of, any man that had *seen a pack of hounds* in America, except those kept by old JOHN BROWN, in Bucks County, Pennsylvania, who was the only *hunting Quaker* that I ever heard of, and who was grandfather of the famous General Brown. In short, there is none of what we call hunting; or, so little, that no man can expect to meet with it.

No *coursing*. I never saw a greyhound here. Indeed, there are no *hares* that have the same manners that ours have, or any thing like their fleetness. The woods, too, or some sort of cover, except in the singular instance of the *plains* in this island, are too near at hand.

But, of *shooting* the variety is endless. Pheasants, partridges, woodcocks, snipes, grouse, wild-ducks of many sorts, teal, plover, rabbits.

There is a disagreement between the north and the south as to the *naming* of the two former. North of New Jersey the pheasants are called partridges, and the partridges are called quails. To the south of New Jersey, they are called by what I think are their proper names, taking the English names of those birds to be proper. For, pheasants do not remain in *coveys*; but, mix, like common fowls. The intercourse between the males and females is promiscuous, and not by *pairs*, as in the case of partridges. And these are the manners of the American pheasants, which are found by ones, twos and so on, and never in *families*, except when *young*, when, like chickens, they keep with the old hen. The American *partridges* are not *quails*; because quails are *gregarious*. They keep in *flocks*, like *rooks* (called *crows* in America), or like *larks*, or *starlings*; of which the reader will remember a remarkable instance in the history of the migration of those grumbling vagabonds, the Jews, soon after their march from HOREB, when the quails came and settled upon each other's backs to a height of two cubits, and covered a superficial space of two days' journey in diameter. It is a well known fact, that quails *flock*: it is also well known, that partridges do not, but that they keep in *distinct families*, which we call *coveys* from the French *couvée*, which means the eggs or brood which a hen *covers* at one time. The American partridges live in coveys. The cock and hen *pair* in the spring. They have their brood by *sitting alternately* on the eggs, just as the English partridges do; the young ones, if none are killed, or die, remain with the old ones till spring; the covey always live within a small distance of the same spot; if frightened into a state of separation, they *call* to each other and re-assemble; they roost all together in a round ring, as close as they can sit, the tails inward and the heads outward; and are, in short, in all their *manners*, precisely the same as the English partridge, with this exception, that they will sometimes alight on a rail or a bough, and that, when the hen sits, the cock, perched at a little distance, makes a sort of periodical whistle, in a monotonous, but very soft and sweet tone.

The size of the pheasant is about the *half* of that of the English. The plumage is by no means so beautiful; but, the flesh is far more delicate. The size of the partridge bears about the same proportion. But its plumage is more beautiful than that of the English, and its flesh is more delicate. Both are delightful, though rather difficult, shooting. The pheasant does not *tower*, but darts through the trees; and the partridge does not rise boldly, but darts away at no great height from the ground. Some years they are more abundant than other years. This is an abundant year. There are, perhaps, fifty coveys within half a mile of my house.

The *woodcocks* are, in all respects, like those in England, except that they are about three-fifths of the size. They *breed* here; and are in such numbers, that some men kill twenty brace, or more in a day. Their haunts are in marshy places, or woods. The shooting of them lasts from the fourth of July till the *hardish frosts* come. The last we killed this year was killed on the 21st of November. So that here are *five months* of this sport; and pheasants and partridges are shot from September to April.

The *snipes* are called *English snipes*, which they resemble in all respects, and are found in great abundance in the usual haunts of snipes.

The *grouse* is precisely like the Scotch grouse. There is only here and there a place where they are found. But they are, in those places, killed in great quantities in the fall of the year.

As to *wild-ducks* and other water-fowl, which are come at by lying in wait, and killed most frequently swimming, or sitting, they are slaughtered in whole flocks. An American counts the cost of powder and shot. If he is *deliberate* in everything else, this habit will hardly forsake him in the act of *shooting*. When the sentimental flesh-eaters hear the report of his gun, they may begin to pull out their white handkerchiefs; for death follows his pull of the trigger, with, perhaps, even more certainty than it used to follow the lancet of DOCTOR RUSH.

The *plover* is a fine bird, and is found in great numbers upon the plains, and in the cultivated fields, of this island, and at a mile from my house. Plovers are very *shy* and *wary*; but they have ingenious enemies to deal with. A waggon, or carriage of some sort, is made use of to approach them; and then they are easily killed.

*Rabbits* are very abundant in some places. They are killed by shooting; for all here is done with the *gun*. No reliance is placed upon a dog.

As to *game-laws* there are none, except those which appoint the *times* for killing. People go where they like, and, as to wild animals, shoot what they like. There is the Common Law, which forbids *trespass*, and the Statute Law, I believe, of *malicious trespass*, or trespass *after warning*. And these are more than enough; for nobody, that I ever hear of, *warns people off*. So that, as far as *shooting* goes, and that is the sport which is the most general favourite, there never was a more delightful country than this island. The sky is so fair, the soil so dry, the cover so convenient, the game so abundant, and the people, go where you will, so civil, hospitable, and kind.

# GOVERNMENT, LAWS
# AND RELIGION

MR PROFESSOR CHRISTIAN, who has written great piles of *Notes* on Blackstone's Commentaries, and whose Notes differ from those of the Notewriters on the Bible, in this, that the latter only tend to add darkness to that which was sufficiently dark before, while the professor's Notes, in every instance, without a single exception, labour most arduously, and not always without success, to render that obscure, which was before clear as the sun now is in Long Island, on this most beautiful 5th of December, 1818: this professor, who, I believe, is now a *Judge*, has, in his Note 126 on Book I, drawn what he calls 'a *distinction*' between *Political* and *Civil* Liberty, which distinction contains as to ideas, manner, and expressions, a complete specimen of what, in such a case, a writer ought to avoid.

Leaving definitions of this sort to such conceited bunglers as the professor, I will just give a *sketch* (for it can be nothing more) of the *Government* and *Laws* of this country.

The country is divided into *States*. Each of these States has its own separate government, consisting of a *governor, legislative body*, and *judiciary department*. But, then, there is a *General Government*, which is, in fact, the government of the whole *nation*; for, it alone can do anything with regard to *other nations*. This General Government consists of a *President*, a *Senate*, a *House of Representatives*, all which together are called the *Congress*. The President is elected for *four years*, the Senate for *four years*, and the House of Representatives for *two years*.

In most of the State-Governments, the election is *annual* for the *House of Representatives*. In some the governor and the Senate are elected for a longer period, not exceeding *four years* in any case. But, in some, the whole, governor, Senate, and Representatives, are elected ANNUALLY; and this last appears now to be the *prevailing* taste.

The *suffrage*, or *qualification of electors*, is very various. In some States every free man; that is, every man who is not *bondman* or *slave*, has a vote. In others, the payment of *a tax* is required. In others, a man must be *worth a hundred pounds*. In Virginia a man must be a freeholder.

This may serve to show how little Mr JERRY BENTHAM, the new mentor of the Westminster Telemachus, knows about the political part of the American governments. Jerry, whose great, and, indeed, *only* argument, in support of *annual parliaments* and *universal suffrage*, is, that *America* is so *happy* under *such a system*, has, if we were to *own him*, furnished our enemies with a complete answer; for, they have, in order to silence him, only to refer to the *facts* of his argument of happy experience. By *silencing* him, however, I do not mean, the stopping of his tongue, or pen; for nothing but mortality will ever do that. This everlasting babbler has aimed a sort of stiletto stroke at me; *for what* God knows, except it be to act a consistent part, by endeavouring to murder the man whom he has so frequently robbed, and whose facts and thoughts, though disguised and disgraced by the robber's quaint phraseology, constitute the better part of his book. Jerry, who was made a Reformer, by PITT'S *refusal to give him a contract to build a penitentiary, and to make him prime administrator of penance*, that is to say, Beggar-Whipper General, is a very proper person to be toasted by those, who have plotted and conspired against Major Cartwright [the propagandist for Reform and organizer of Hampden Clubs]. Mr Brougham *praises* Jerry: that is enough!

In the *four New England States*, the qualification was *a hundred pounds*. But, one of those States, CONNECTICUT, has, to her great honour, recently set an example worthy of the imitation of the other three. A new constitution has, during this year, been formed in that State, according to which all the elections are to be *annual*; and, as to the *suffrage*, I will give it in the words of the instrument itself: 'Every male white citizen of the United States, who shall have gained a settlement in this state, attained the age of twenty-one years, and resided in the town (that is *parish* in the English meaning) in which he may offer himself to be admitted to the privilege of being an elector, at least six months preceding, *and have a freehold estate of the yearly value of seven dollars in this State*; OR, having been *enrolled in the militia*, shall have performed military duty therein for the term of one year, next preceding the time he shall offer himself for admission, or, being liable thereto, shall have been, by authority of law, altogether excused therefrom; OR, shall *have paid a State Tax* within the year next preceding the time he shall present himself for admission, and shall sustain a good moral character, shall, on his taking the oath prescribed, *be an elector.*'

And then, the proof of bad moral character, is, 'a conviction of *bribery, forgery, perjury, duelling, fraudulent bankruptcy, theft,* or other offences, for which an infamous punishment is inflicted.' By *forgery* is not, of course, contemplated, *puff-out* forgery; for that, as an act of resistance of *oppression*, is fully justifiable: it is not only not an immoral, but it is a *meritorious* act. The *forgery* here meant is forgery committed against honest men, who, when they *promise to pay*, mean to pay, and do pay when called upon. *Bribery* is very properly set at the head of the disqualifications; but, what a nest of villains it would exclude in England! *White* men are mentioned, but another clause, admits all the Blacks *now* free, though it shuts out future *comers* of that colour, or of the yellow hue; which is perfectly just; for, Connecticut is not to be the receptacle of those, whom other States may choose to release from slavery, seeing that she has now *no slaves of her own.*

Thus, then, this *new* Constitution; a constitution formed by the *steadiest* community in the whole world; a constitution dictated by the most *ample experience*, gives to the people, as to the *three branches* of the government (the *governor, Senate,* and *Representatives*) precisely what we reformers in England ask as to only *one* branch of the three. Whoever *has a freehold* worth a guinea and a half a year, though he pay no tax, and though he be not enrolled in the militia, has a vote. Whoever *pays a tax*, though he be not enrolled in the militia, and have no freehold, has a vote. Whoever is enrolled in the militia, though he have no freehold and pay no tax, has a vote. So that nothing but beggars, paupers, and criminals, can easily be excluded: and, you will observe, if you please, Messrs Boroughmongers, that the State taxes are *all direct*, and so contemptible in amount, as not to be, all taken together, enough to satisfy the maw of a *single sinecure place-man* in England; and that the Electors choose, and annually too, *king, Lords, and Commons.* Now, mind, this change has been deliberately made by the most deliberate people that ever lived on the earth. New England is called, and truly, 'the Land of *Steady Habits*'; but, a Connecticut man is said to be a *'full-blooded Yankee'*, and Yankee means *New Englander.* So that, here are the *steadiest* of the *steady* adopting, after all their usual deliberation and precaution, in a time of profound tranquillity, and without any party spirit or delusion, the plan of us *'wild* and *mad'* Reformers of Old England. Please God, I will, before I go home, perform a pilgrimage into this State!

In *Virginia*, and the States where negro slavery exists, the slaves are *reckoned amongst the population in apportioning the seats in the General Congress.* So that, the slaves do not vote; but, their *owners have votes for them.* This is what Davis Giddy, Wilberforce, and the Spawn of the *Green Room*, call *virtual representation.* And this, to be sure, is what Sir FRANCIS BURDETT, in his speech at the Reading Dinner, meant by *universal* INTERESTS! From *universal suffrage*, he came down to *general suffrage*: this was only *nonsense*; but, *universal* INTERESTS is down-right boroughmongering. Well may he *despair* of doing any *good* in the House of Commons! *Universal interests* is the Virginian plan; and, *in that state of things*, by no means unwise or unjust; for, it is easier to *talk* about freeing black slaves, than it is to *do* it. The *planters* in the Southern States are not to blame for having slaves, until some man will show how they are to get rid of them. No one has yet discovered the means. *Virtual representation*, or, in other words, *universal interests*, is as good a thing as anyone can devise for those States; and, if Sir FRANCIS will but boldly declare, that the people of England *must necessarily remain slaves*, his joining of Davis Giddy and Canning, will be very consistent. Let him black the skins of the people of England, and honestly call a part of them his property, and then he will not add the meanest to the most dastardly apostacy.

The right of suffrage in America is, however, upon the whole, sufficient to guard the people against any general and long-existing abuse of power; for, let it be borne in mind, that *here* the people elect *all* the persons, who are to exercise power; while, even if our Reform were obtained, there would still be *two branches out of the three*, over whom the people would have no direct control. Besides, in England, Ireland, and Scotland, there is an *Established Church*; a richly endowed and powerful hierarchy; and this, which is really a *fourth* branch of the government, has nothing to resemble it in America. So that, in this country, the whole of the government may be truly said to be in the hands of the people. The people are, in reality as well as in name, *represented*.

The consequences of this are, first, that, if those who are chosen do not behave well, they are *not chosen a second time*; second, that there are no *sinecure place-men* and *place-women*, *grantees, pensioners without services*, and big place-men who swallow the earnings of two or three thousand men each; third, that there is no military staff to devour more than the whole of a government ought to cost; fourth, that there are no proud and insolent grasping Boroughmongers, who make the people toil and sweat to keep them and their families in luxury; fifth, that seats in the Congress are not like stalls in Smithfield, bought and sold, or hired out; sixth, that the members of Congress do not sell their votes at so much a vote; seventh, that there is no waste of the public money, and no expences occasioned by the bribing of electors, or by the hiring of spies and informers; 8th, that there are no shootings of the people, and no legal murders committed, in order to defend the government against the just vengeance of an oppressed and insulted nation. But, all is harmony, peace and prosperity. Every man is zealous in defence of the laws, because every man knows that he is governed by laws, to which he has really and truly given his assent.

As to the nature of the laws, the *Common Law* of England is the *Common Law of America*. These States were formerly *Colonies of England*. Our Boroughmongers wished to tax them *without their own consent*. But, the Colonies, standing upon the ancient Laws of England, which say that *no man shall be taxed without his own consent*, resisted the Boroughmongers of that day; overcame them in war; cast off all dependence, and became free and independent States. But, the great man, who conducted that Revolution, as well as the people in general, were too wise to cast off the excellent laws of their forefathers. They, therefore, declared, that the *Common Law* of England should remain, being subject to such modifications as might be necessary in the new circumstances in which the people were placed. The *Common*

*Law* means, *the ancient and ordinary usages and customs of the land* with regard to the means of *protecting property and persons* and of *punishing crimes.* This law is no *written* or *printed* thing. It is more ancient than books. It had its origin in the hearts of our forefathers, and it has lived in the hearts of their sons, from generation to generation. Hence it is emphatically called *the Law of the Land.* Juries, judges, courts of justice, sheriffs, constables, head-boroughs, haywards, justices of the peace, and all their numerous and useful powers and authorities, make use of this *Law of the Land.* The Boroughmongers would fain persuade us, that it is *they* who have *given* us this Law, *out of pure generosity.* But, we should bear in mind, that this law is more ancient, and far more ancient, than the titles of even the most ancient of their families. And, accordingly, when the present Royal Family were placed upon the throne, there was a solemn *declaration* by the parliament in these words: 'The Laws of England are the *Birthright* of the People of England'. The Boroughmongers by giving new powers to justices of the peace, and judges, setting aside the trial by jury in many cases, both of property and person, even before the present horrible acts; and by a thousand other means, have, by *Acts of Parliament,* greatly despoiled us of the *Law of the Land*; but, never have they given us any one good in addition to it.

The Americans have taken special care to prevent the like encroachments on their rights: so that, while they have courts of justice, juries, judges, sheriffs, and the rest, as we have; while they have all the *good* part of the laws now in force in England, they have none of the *bad.* They have none of that *Statute Law* of England, or *Act of Parliament Law,* which has robbed us of a great part, and the *best* part of our 'Birthright'.

It is, as I said before, not my intention to go much into particulars here; but, I cannot refrain from noticing, that the People of America, when they came to settle their new governments, took special care to draw up specific *Constitutions,* in which they forbade any of their future law-makers to allow of any *Titles of Nobility,* any *Privileged Class,* any *Established Church,* or, to *pass any law* to give to anybody *the power of imprisoning men otherwise than in due course of Common Law,* except in cases of actual *invasion* or *open rebellion.* And, though actual invasion took place several times during the late war; though the Capital City was in possession of our troops, no such law was passed. Such is the effect of that confidence, which a good and just government has in the people whom it governs!

There is one more particular, as to the laws of America, on which, as it is of very great importance, I think it right to remark. The uses, which have been made of the *Law of Libel* in England are well known. In the first place, the *Common Law* knows of no such offence as that of *criminal libel*, for which so many men, have been so cruelly punished in England. The crime is an invention of late date. The Common Law punished men for *breaches of the peace*, but no *words*, whether written or spoken, can be a breach of the peace. But, then some Boroughmonger judges said, that words might *tend to produce* a breach of the peace; and that, therefore, it was *criminal* to use such words. This, though a palpable stretch of law, did, however, by usage, become law so far as to be acted upon in America as well as in England; and, when I lived in the State of PENNSYLVANIA, eighteen years ago, the chief justice of that State, finding even this law not sufficiently large, gave it another stretch to make it fit me. Whether the legislature of that State will repair this act of injustice and tyranny remains yet to be seen.

The State of NEW YORK, in which I now live, awakened, probably by the act of tyranny, to which I allude, has taken care, by an act of the State, passed in 1805, to put an end to those attacks on the press by charges of *constructive libel*, or, at least, to make the law such, that no man shall suffer from the preferring of any such charges unjustly.

The principal effect of this twisting of the law was, that, whether the words published were *true* or *false* the *crime* of publishing was *the same*; because, whether true or false, they *tended to a breach of the peace!* Nay, there was a Boroughmonger judge in England, who had laid it down as *law*, that the *truer* the words were, the *more criminal* was the libel; because, said he, a breach of the peace was more likely to be produced by telling *truth* of *a villain*, than by telling *falsehood* of a *virtuous* man. In point of fact, this was true enough, to be sure; but what an infamous doctrine! What a base, what an unjust mind must this man have had!

The State of New York, ashamed that there should any longer be room for such miserable quibbling; ashamed to leave the liberty of the press exposed to the changes and chances of a doctrine so hostile to common sense as well as to every principle of freedom, passed an *act*, which makes the *truth* of any publication a *justification* of it, provided the publisher can shew, that the publication was made with *good motives* and *justifiable ends*; and who can *possibly* publish *truth* without being able to show *good motives* and *justifiable ends?* To expose and censure tyranny, profligacy, fraud, hypocrisy, debauchery, drunkenness: indeed, all sorts of wickedness and folly; and to do this in the world of *truth*, must tend, *cannot fail to tend*, to check wickedness and folly, and to strengthen and promote virtue and wisdom; and these, and *these only*, are the uses of the press. I know it has been said, for I have heard it said, that this is going *too far*; that it would tend to lay open the *private affairs of families*. And what then? Wickedness and folly should meet their *due* measure of censure, or ridicule, be they found where they may. If the faults of private persons were too trifling to deserve public notice, the mention of them would give the parties no pain, and the publisher would be despised for his tittle-tattle; that is all. And if they were of a nature so grave as for the exposure of them to give the parties *pain*, the exposure would be *useful*, as a warning to others.

Amongst the persons whom I have heard express a wish, to see the press what they called *free*, and at the same time to extend the restraints on it, with regard to persons in their private life, *beyond the obligation of adherence to truth*, I have never, that I know of, met with one, who had not some *powerful motive of his own* for the wish, and who did not feel that he had some vulnerable part about himself. The common observation of these persons, is, that *public men are fair game*. Why *public* men only? Is is because *their* wickedness and folly affect the public? And, how long has it been, I should be glad to know, since bad example in private life has been thought of no consequence to the public? The press is called 'the *guardian* of the *public morals*'; but, if it is to meddle with none of the vices or follies of individuals in private life, how is it to act as the guardian of the morals of the whole community? A press perfectly free, reaches these vices, which the *law* cannot reach without putting too much power into the hands of the magistrate. Extinguish the press, and you must let the magistrate into every private house. The experience of the world suggests this remark; for, look where you will, you will see virtue in all the walks of life hand in hand with freedom of discussion, and vice hand in hand with censorships and other laws to cramp the press. England, once so free, so virtuous and so happy, has seen misery and crimes increase and the criminal laws multiply in the exact proportion of the increase of the restraints on the press and of the increase of the severity in punishing what are called libels. And, if this had not taken place it would have been very wonderful. Men who have the handling of the public money, and who know that the parliament is such as to be *silenced*, will be very apt to squander that money; this squandering causes heavy taxes; these produce misery amongst the greater number of the people; this misery produces crimes; to check these new penal laws are passed. Thus it is in England, where new hanging places, new and enlarged jails, prisons on the water, new modes of transporting, a new species of police officers, a new species of justices of the peace, troops employed regularly in aid of the magistrate, and at last, spies and blood-money bands, all proclaim a real revolution in the nature of the government. If the *press* had continued *free*, these sad effects of a waste of the public money never could have taken place; for, the wasters of that money would have been so exposed as to be unable to live under the odium which the exposure would have occasioned; and, if the parliament had not checked the waste and punished the wasters, the public indignation would have destroyed parliament. But, with a muzzled press, the wasters proceeded with the consciousness of impunity. Say to any individual man when he is twenty years of age: 'You shall do just what you please with all the money of other people that you can, by any means, all your life long, get into your hands, and no one shall ever be permitted to make you accountable, or even to write or speak against you for any act of fraud, oppression, or waste.' Should you expect such an individual to act honestly and wisely? Yet, this, in fact, is what a Boroughmonger parliament and the new Law of Libel say to every set of ministers.

Before I quit this subject of *Libel*, let me observe, however, that *no juryman*, even as the law now stands *in England*, is in *conscience* bound to find any man guilty on a charge of *criminal* libel, unless the *evidence prove* that the pretended libeller has been actuated by an *evil motive*, and unless it be also *proved by evidence*, that his words, spoken or written, were *scandalous* and *malicious*. Unless these things *be clearly proved by evidence*, the juryman, who finds a man *guilty*, is a base, *perjured villain*; and ought to be punished as such.

The State of Connecticut, in her new Constitution, before mentioned, has put this matter of libel on the true footing; namely; 'In *all* prosecutions and indictments for *libel* the TRUTH *may be given in evidence*, and the jury shall have the right to determine *the law and the facts.*' Thus, then, common sense has, at last, got the better; and TRUTH can, in this State at least, in no case be a *legal crime*. But indeed, the press has NOW *no restraint* in America, other than that imposed by TRUTH. Men publish what they please, so long as they do not publish falsehoods; and even in such cases, they are generally punished by the public contempt. The press is, therefore, *taken altogether*, what the magistrate always ought to be: '*a terror to evil doers*, and a *reward to those who do well.*' But, it is not *the name* of REPUBLIC that secures these, or any other of the blessings of freedom. As gross acts of tyranny may be committed, and as base corruption practised, under *that name* as under the name of *absolute monarchy*. And, it becomes the people of America to guard their minds against ever being, in any case, *amused with names*. It is *the fair representation of the people* that is the cause of all the good; and, if this be obtained, I, for my part, will never quarrel with anybody about *names*.

*Taxes* and *Priests*; for these always lay on heavily together. On the subject of taxes, I have, perhaps, spoken sufficiently clear before; but, it is a great subject. I will, on these subjects, address myself more immediately to *my old neighbours of Botley*, and endeavour to make them understand, what America is as to taxes and priests.

Worried, my old neighbours, as you are by tax-gatherers of all descriptions from the County-Collector, who rides in his coach and four down to the petty Window-Peeper, the little miserable spy, who is constantly on the look-out for you, as if he were a thief-catcher and you were thieves; devoured as you are by these vermin, big and little, you will with difficulty form an idea of the state of America in this respect. It is a state of such blessedness, when compared with the state of things in England, that I despair of being able to make you fully comprehend what it is. Here a man may make new windows, or shut up old windows, as often as he pleases, without being compelled under a penalty to give notice to some insolent tax-gathering spy. Here he may keep as many horses as he likes, he may ride them or drive them at his pleasure, he may sell them or keep them, he may lend them or breed from them; he may, as far as their nature allows, do the same with regard to his dogs; he may employ his servants in his house, in his stables, in his garden, or in his fields, just as he pleases; he may, if he be foolish enough, have armorial bearings on his carriage, his watch-seals, on his plate, and, if he likes, on his very buckets and porridge pots; he may write his receipts, his bills, his leases, his bonds, and deeds upon unstamped paper; his wife and daughters may wear French gloves and lace and French and India silks; he may purchase or sell lands and may sue at law for his rights: and all these, and a hundred other things, without any dread of the interloping and insolent interference of a tax-gatherer or spy of any description. Lastly, when he dies, he can bequeath his money and goods and houses and lands to whomsoever he pleases; and he can close his eyes without curses in his heart against a rapacious band of place-men, pensioners, grantees, sinecure holders, staff-officers, Borough-jobbers, and blood-money spies, who stand ready to take from his friends, his relations, his widow, and his children, a large part of what he leaves, under the name of a tax upon legacies.

But, you will ask, 'are there *no taxes* in America?' Yes; and taxes, or public contributions of some sort, there must be in every civilized state; otherwise *government* could not exist, and without government there could be no security for property or persons. The taxes in America consist principally of *custom duties imposed on goods imported into the country*. During the late war, there were taxes on several things in the country; but, they were taken off at the peace. In the cities and large towns, where *paving* and *lamps* and *drains* and *scavengers* are necessary, there are, of course, direct contributions to defray the expence of these. There are also, of course, *county rates* and *road rates*. But, as the money thus raised is employed for the immediate benefit of those who pay, and is expended amongst themselves and under their own immediate inspection, it does not partake of the nature of *a tax*. The taxes or duties, on goods imported, yield a great sum of money; and, owing to the persons employed in the collection being appointed for their integrity and ability, and not on account of their connection with any set of bribing and corrupt Borough-mongers, the whole of the money thus collected is fairly applied to the public use, and is amply sufficient for all the purposes of government. The *army*, if it can be so called, costs but a mere trifle. It consists of a few men, who are absolutely necessary to keep forts from crumbling down, and guns from rotting with rust. The navy is an object of care, and its support and increase a cause of considerable expence. But the government, relying on the good sense and valour of a people, who must hate or disregard themselves before they can hate or disregard that which so man-ifestly promotes their own happiness, has no need to expend much on any species of warlike preparations. The government could not stand a week, if it were hated by the people; nor, indeed, *ought* it to stand an hour. It has the hearts of the people with it, and, therefore, it need expend nothing in *blood-money*, or in *secret services* of any kind. Hence the *cheapness* of this govern-ment; hence the small amount of the *taxes*; hence the ease and happiness of the People.

Great as the distance between you and me is, my old neigh-bours, I very often think of you; and especially when I buy *salt*, which our neighbour Warner used to sell us for 19s. a bushel, and which I buy here for 2s. 6d. This salt is made you know, down somewhere by Hambel. This very salt; when brought here from England, has all the charges of freight, insurance, wharfage, storage, to pay. It pays, besides, one third of its value in duty to the American Government before it be landed here. Then, you will observe, there is the *profit* of the American Salt Merchant, and then that of the shop-keeper who sells me the salt. And, after all this, I buy that very Hampshire salt for 2s. 6d. a bushel, English measure. What a government, then, must that of the Boroughmongers be! The salt is a gift of God. It is thrown on the shore. And yet, these tyrants will not suffer us to use it, until we have paid *them* 15s. a bushel for liberty to use it. They will not suffer us to use the salt, which God has sent us, until we have given them 15s. a bushel for them to bestow on themselves, on their families and dependants, in the payment of the interest of the Debt, which they have contracted, and in paying those, whom they hire to shoot at us. Yes; England is a fine country; it is a glorious country; it contains an ingenious, industrious, a brave and warm-hearted people; but, it is now disgraced and enslaved: it is trodden down by these tyrants; and we must free it. We cannot, and we will not die their slaves.

Salt is not the only one of the English articles that we buy cheaper here than in England. *Glass*, for instance, we buy for half the price that you buy it. The reason is, that you are compelled to pay a *heavy tax*, which is not paid by us for the same glass. It is the same as to almost everything that comes from England. You are compelled to pay the Boroughmongers a heavy tax on your *candles* and *soap*. You dare not *make* candles and soap, though you have the fat and the ashes in abundance. If you attempt to do this, you are taken up and imprisoned; and, if you resist, soldiers are brought to shoot you. This is *freedom*, is it? Now, we, *here*, make our own candles and soap. Farmers sometimes *sell* soap and candles; but they never *buy* any. A labouring man, or a mechanic buys a sheep now and then. Three or four days' work will buy a labourer a sheep to weigh sixty pounds, with seven or eight pounds of loose fat. The meat keeps very well, in winter, for a long time. The wool makes stockings. And the loose fat is made into candles and soap. The year before I left Hampshire, a poor woman at Holly Hill had *dipped* some *rushes* in grease to use instead of candles. An exciseman found it out; went and ransacked her house; and told her, that, if the rushes had had *another dip*, they would have been *candles*, and she must have gone to jail! Why, my friends, if such a thing were told here, nobody would believe it. The Americans could not bring their minds to believe, that Englishmen would submit to such atrocious, such degrading tyranny.

I have had living with me *an Englishman*, who smokes tobacco; and he tells me, that he can buy as much tobacco here for *three cents*; that is, about *three English half-pence*, as he could buy in England for *three shillings*. The *leather* has *no tax* on it here; so that, though the shoemaker is paid a high price for his labour, the labouring man gets his shoes very cheap. In short, there is no *excise* here; no *property tax*; no *assessed taxes*. We have no such men here as Chiddel and Billy Tovery to come and take our money from us. No window-peepers. No spies to keep a look-out as to our carriages and horses and dogs. Our dogs that came from Botley now run about free from the spying of tax-gatherers. We may wear hair-powder if we like without paying for it, and a boy in our house may whet our knives without our paying two pounds a year for it.

But, then, we have not the honour of being covered over with the dust, kicked up by the horses and raised by the carriage-wheels of such men as Old GEORGE ROSE and OLD GARNIER, each of whom has pocketted more than *three hundred thousand pounds* of the public, that is to say, the people's money. There are no such men here. Those who receive public money here, do something for it. They earn it. They are no richer than other people. The *judges* here are plain-dressed men. They go about with no sort of parade. They are dressed, on the bench, like other men. The lawyers the same. Here are no black gowns and scarlet gowns and big foolish-looking wigs. Yet, in the whole world, there is not so well-behaved, so orderly, so steadily a people; a people so *obedient to the law*. But, it is *the law only* that they will *bow* to. They will bow to nothing else. And, they bow with reverence to the law, because they know it to be just, and because it is made by men, whom they have all had a hand in choosing.

And, then, think of the *tithes!* I have talked to several farmers here about the tithes in England; and, they *laugh*. They sometimes almost make me angry; for they seem, at last, not to believe what I say, when I tell them, that the English farmer gives, and is compelled to give, the parson a tenth part of his whole crop and of his fruit and milk and eggs and calves and lambs and pigs and wool and honey. They cannot believe this. They treat it as a sort of *romance*. I sometimes almost wish them to be farmers in England. I said to a neighbour the other day, in half anger: 'I wish your farm were at Botley. There is a fellow there, who would soon let you know, that your fine apple-trees do not belong to you. He would have his nose in your sheep-fold, your calf-pens, your milk-pail, your sow's-bed, if not in the sow herself. Your daughters would have no occasion to hunt out the hen's nests; he would do that for them.' And then I gave him a proof of an English parson's vigilance by telling him the story of Baker's peeping out *the name*, marked on the sack, which the old woman was wearing as a petticoat. To another of my neighbours, who is very proud of the circumstance of his grandfather being an *Englishman*, as, indeed, most of the Americans are, who are descended from Englishmen: to this neighbour I was telling the story about the poor woman at Holly Hill, who had nearly dipped her rushes once too often. He is a very grave and religious man.

He looked very seriously at me, and said, that *falsehood* was *falsehood*, whether in jest or earnest. But, when I invited him to come to my house, and told him, that I would show him the acts which the Borough-men had made to put us in jail if we made our own soap and candles, he was quite astonished. 'What!' said he, 'and is *Old England really come to this*! Is the land of our forefathers brought to this state of abject slavery! Well, Mr Cobbett, I confess, that I was always for King George, during our revolutionary war; but, I believe, all was for the best; for, if I had had my wishes, he might have treated us as he now treats the people of England!' '*He!*' said I. '*It is not he*; he, poor man, does nothing to the people, and never has done anything to the people. *He* has no power more than you have. None of his family have any. All put together, they have not a thousandth part so much as I have; for I am able, though here, to annoy our tyrants, to make them less easy than they would be; but, these tyrants care no more for the Royal Family than they do for so many posts or logs of wood.' And then I explained to him who and what the Boroughmongers were, and how they oppressed us and the king too. I told him how they disposed of the Church livings, and, in short, explained to him all their arts and all their cruelties. He was exceedingly shocked; but was glad, at any rate to know the *truth*.

When I was, last winter, in the neighbourhood of Harrisburgh in Pennsylvania, I saw some *hop-planters*. They grow prodigious quantities of hops. They are obliged to put their hills so wide apart, that they can have only four hundred hills upon an acre; and yet they grow three thousand pounds of hops upon an acre, with no *manure* and with once ploughing in the year. When I told them about the price of hops in England, and about the difficulty of raising them, they were greatly surprised; but, what was their astonishment, when I told them about the hop-poles of CHALCRAFT at Curbridge! The hop is naturally a weed in England as well as in America. Two or three vines had come up out of Chalcraft's garden hedge, a few years ago. Chalcraft put *poles* to them; and, there might be a pound or two of hops on these poles. Just before the time of gathering, one of the spies called *excisemen* called on Chalcraft and asked him why he did not *enter* his hops. Chalcraft did not understand; but, answered, he meant to *take them in* shortly, though he did not think they were yet quite ripe. 'Ay,' said the exciseman, 'but I mean, when do you mean to enter them at the *excise office?*' Chalcraft did not know (not living in a hop-country) that he had already incurred a *penalty* for not reporting to the tyrants that he had hops growing in his garden hedge! He did not know, that he could not gather them and put them by without giving notice, under a *penalty of fifty pounds.* He did not know, that he could not receive this little gift of God without paying money to the Boroughmongers in the shape of tax: and, to the parson in the shape of tithe, or, to give a tenth of the hops to the parson, and not dare pick a single hop till he had sent *notice to the parson!* What he did, upon this occasion, I have forgotten; but, it is likely that he let the hops stand and rot, or cut them down and flung them away as weeds. Now, poor men in England are told to be *content* with rags and hungry bellies, for that is *their lot*; that 'it has pleased Divine Providence to place them in that state'. But, here is a striking instance of the falsehood and blasphemy of this doctrine; for, providence had sent Chalcraft the hops, and he had put poles to them. Providence had brought the hops to perfection; but then came the Boroughmongers and the parson to take from this poor man this boon of a benevolent Maker. What, did God order a tax with all its vexatious regulations, to be imposed upon what he had freely given to this poor man? Did God ordain that, in addition to this tax, a *tenth* should be yielded to a parson, who had solemnly vowed at his ordination, that he believed himself called, not by the love of tithes, but by '*the Holy Ghost*, to take on him the *cure of souls*', and to '*bring stray sheep into the fold of the Lord?*' Did God ordain these things? Had it *pleased God* to do this? What impunity, what blasphemy, then, to ascribe to Providence the manifold sufferings occasioned by the Borough-mongers' taxes and parson's tithes!

But, my Botley neighbours, you will exclaim, 'No *tithes!* Why, then, there can be no *churches* and no *parsons!* The people must know nothing of God or Devil; and must all go to hell!' By no means, my friends. Here are plenty of churches. No less than three Episcopal (or English) Churches; three Presbyterian Churches; three Lutheran Churches; one or two Quaker Meeting-houses; and two Methodist Places; all within *six miles* of the spot where I am sitting. And, these, mind, not poor shabby churches; but each of them larger and better built and far hand-

somer than Botley Church, with the churchyards all kept in the
neatest order, with a head-stone to almost every grave. As to the
Quaker Meeting-house, it would take Botley Church into its
belly, if you were first to knock off the steeple.

Oh, no! Tithes are not necessary to promote *religion*. When
our parsons, such as Baker, talk about *religion*, or *the church*,
being in danger; they mean, that the *tithes* are in danger. They
mean, that they are in danger of being compelled to work for
their bread. This is what they mean. You remember, that, at our
last meeting at Winchester, they proposed for us to tell the Prince
Regent, that we would *support the church*. I moved, to leave out
the word *church*, and insert the word *tithes*; for, as there were
many presbyterians and other dissenters present, they could not,
with clear consciences, pledge themselves to support *the church*.
This made them *furious*. It was lifting up the *mask*; and the
parsons were enraged beyond measure.

Oh, no! *Tithes* do not mean *religion*. Religion means *a reverence
for God*. And, what has this to do with tithes? Why cannot you
reverence God, without Baker and his wife and children eating
up a tenth part of the corn and milk and eggs and lamb and pigs
and calves that are produced in Botley parish? The parsons, in
this country, are supported by those who choose to employ them.
A man belongs to what congregation he pleases. He pays what is
required by the rules of the congregation. And, if he think that
it is not necessary for him to belong to any congregation, he pays
nothing at all. And, the consequence is, that all is harmony and
good neighbourhood. Here are not disputes about religion; or, if
they be, they make no noise. Here is no ill-will on this account.
A man is never asked what religion he is of, or whether he be of
any religion at all. It is a matter that nobody interferes in. What
need, therefore, is there of an *Established* Church. What need is
there of tithes? And, why should not that species of property be
taken for *public use*? That is to say, as far as it has anything to do
with religion? I know very well, that tithes do not operate as many
people pretend; I know that those who complain most about
them have the least right to complain; but, for my present purpose,
it is sufficient to shew, that they have nothing to do with *religion*.

If, indeed, the Americans were wicked, disorderly, criminal
people, and, of course, a miserable and foolish people: then we
might doubt upon the subject: then we might possibly suppose,

that their wickedness and misery arose, in some degree, at least, from the *want of tithes*. But, the contrary is the fact. They are the most orderly, sensible, and least criminal people in the whole world. A common labouring man has the feelings of a man of honour; he never thinks of violating the laws; he crawls to no-body; he will call every man *sir*, but he will call no man *master*. When he utters words of respect towards anyone, they do not proceed from fear or hope, but from civility and sincerity. A native American labourer is never *rude* towards his employer, but he is never *cringing*.

However, the best proof of the inutility of an Established Church is the absence of *crimes* in this country, compared to the state of England in that respect. There have not been three *felonies* tried in this country since I arrived in it. The court-house is at two miles from me. An Irishman was tried for forgery in the summer of 1817, and the whole country was alive to go and witness the novelty. I have not heard of a man being hanged in the whole of the United States since my arrival. The Borough-mongers, in answer to statements like these, say that this is a *thinly inhabited* country. This very country is *more thickly settled than Hampshire*. The adjoining country, towards the city of New York is much more thickly settled than Hampshire. New York itself and its immediate environs contain nearly two hundred thousand inhabitants, and after London, is, perhaps, the first commercial and maritime city in the world. Thousands of sailors, ship-carpenters, dockyard people, dray-men, boat-men, crowd its wharfs and quays. Yet, never do we hear of hanging; scarcely ever of a robbery; men go to bed with scarcely locking their doors; and never is there seen in the streets what is called in England, *a girl of the town*; and, what is still more, never is there seen in those streets a *beggar*. I wish you, my old neighbours, could see this city of New York. Portsmouth and Gosport, taken together, are miserable holes compared to it. Man's imagination can fancy nothing so beautiful as its bay and port, from which two immense rivers sweep up on the sides of the point of land, on which the city is. These rivers are continually covered with vessels of various sizes bringing the produce of the land, while the bay is scarcely less covered with ships going in and out from all parts of the world. The city itself is a scene of opulence and industry: riches without insolence, and labour without grudging.

*The Tontine Coffee House, on the corner of Wall Street and Water Street, New York City*

*Cobbett's house at Botley in Hampshire*

Government, Laws and Religion 219

What Englishman can contemplate this brilliant sight without feeling some little pride that this city bears an English name? But, thoughts of more importance ought to fill his mind. He ought to contrast the ease, the happiness, the absence of crime which prevail here with the incessant anxieties, the miseries and murderous works in England. In his search after causes he will find them nowhere but in the *government*: and, as to an established church, if he find no sound argument to prove it to be an evil: at the very least he must conclude, that it is *not a good*; and, of course that property to the amount of five millions a year is very unjustly as well as unwisely bestowed on its clergy.

Nor, let it be said, that the people here are of a better natural disposition than the people of England are. How can it be? They are, the far greater part of them, the immediate descendants of Englishmen, Irishmen, and Scotsmen. Nay, in the *city* of New York it is supposed, that a full half of the labour is performed by natives of Ireland, while men of that Island make a great figure in trade, at the bar, and in all the various pursuits of life. They have their Romish Chapels there in great brilliancy; and they enjoy 'Catholic Emancipation' without any petitioning or wrangling. In short, blindfold an Englishman and convey him to New York, unbind his eyes, and he will think himself in an English city. The same sort of streets; shops precisely the same; the same beautiful and modest women crowding in and out of them; the same playhouses; the same men, same dress, same language: he will miss by day only the nobility and the beggars, and by night only the street-walkers and pickpockets. These are to be found only where there is an *established* clergy, upheld by what is called the *state*, and which means, in England, *the Borough-mongers*.

Away, then, my friends, with all cant about *the church* and the church being *in danger*. If the church, that is to say, the *tithes*, were completely *abolished*; if they, and all the immense property of the church, were taken and applied to public use, there would not be a sermon or a prayer the less. Not only the Bible but the very Prayer-book is in use here as much as in England, and, I believe, a great deal *more*. Why give the five millions a year, then, to parsons and their wives and children? Since the English, Irish and Scotch, are so good, so religious, and so moral *here* without glebes and tithes; why not use these glebes and tithes for other purposes seeing they are possessions which can legally be disposed of in another manner?

But, the fact is, that it is the circumstance of the church being *established by law* that makes it *of little use* as to real religion, and as to morals, as far as they be connected with religion. Because, as we shall presently see, this establishment forces upon the people, parsons whom they cannot respect, and whom indeed, they must *despise*; and, it is easy to conceive, that the moral precepts of those, whom we despise on account of their immorality, we shall never much attend to, even supposing the precepts themselves to be good. If a precept be self-evidently good; if it be an obvious duty which the parson inculcates, the inculcation is useless to us, because, whenever it is wanted to guide us, it will occur without the suggestion of anyone; and, if the precept be not self-evidently good, we shall never receive it as such from the lips of a man, whose character and life tell us we ought to suspect the truth of everything he utters. When the matters as to which we are receiving instructions are, in their nature, wholly dissimilar to those as to which we have witnessed the conduct of the teacher, we may reasonably, in listening to the precept, disregard that conduct. Because, for instance, a man, though a very indifferent Christian, may be a most able soldier, seaman, physician, lawyer, or almost anything else; and what is more, may be honest and zealous in the discharge of his duty in any of these several capacities. But, when the conduct, which we have observed in the teacher, belongs to the same department of life as the precept which he is delivering, if the one differ from the other we cannot believe the teacher to be sincere, unless he, while he enforces his precept upon us, acknowledge his own misconduct. Suppose me, for instance, to be a great liar, as great a liar, if possible, as STEWART of the COURIER, who has said that I have been 'fined 700 dollars for writing against the American Government', though I never was prosecuted in America in all my life. Suppose me to be as great a liar as STEWART, and I were to be told by a parson, whom I knew to be as great a liar as myself, that I should certainly go to hell if I did not leave off lying. Would his words have any effect upon me? No: because I should conclude, that if he thought what he said, he would not be such a liar himself. I should rely upon the parson generally, or I should not. If I did, I should think myself safe until I out-lied him; and, if I did not rely on him generally, of what use would he be to me?

Thus, then, if men be *sincere* about religion; if it be not all a mere matter of form, it must always be of the greatest consequence, that the example of the teacher correspond with his teaching. And the most likely way to insure this, is to manage things so that he may in the first place be selected by the people, and, in the second place, have no rewards in view other than those which are to be given in consequence of his perseverance in a line of good conduct.

And thus it is with the clergy in America, who are duly and amply rewarded for their diligence, and very justly respected for the piety, talent, and zeal which they discover; but, who have no tenure of their places other than that of the will of the congregation. Hence, it rarely indeed happens, that there is seen amongst them an impious, an immoral, or a despicable man. Whether the teaching of even these reverend persons have any very great *effect* in producing virtue and happiness amongst men is a question upon which men may, without deserving to be burnt alive, take the liberty to differ; especially since the world has constantly before its eyes a society, who excel in all the Christian virtues, who practise that simplicity which others teach, who, in the great work of charity, really and truly hide from the left hand that which the right hand doeth; and who know nothing of bishop, priest, deacon, or teacher of any description. Yes, since we have the Quakers constantly before our eyes, we may, without deserving to be burnt alive, question the utility of paying any parsons or religious teachers at all. But, the worst of it is, we are apt to confound things; as we have, by a figure of speech, got to call a *building a church*, when a church really means a body of people; so we are apt to look upon the *priest as being religious*, and especially when we call him *the reverend*; and, it often sadly occurs, that no two things can be wider from each other in this quality. Some writer has said, that he would willingly leave to the clergy everything above the tops of the chimneys; which, perhaps, was making their possessions rather too ethereal; but, since our law calls them *spiritual persons*; since they profess, that 'their kingdom is not of this world', and, since those of our church have solemnly declared, that they believe themselves to be called to the ministry 'by the Holy Ghost': it is, I think, a little out of character for them to come poking and grunting and grumbling about after our eggs, potatoes, and sucking pigs.

However, upon the general question of the utility or non-utility of paid religious teachers, let men decide for themselves; but if teachers be to be paid, it seems a clear point, to my mind, that they should be paid upon the American plan: and this, I think, must be obvious to everyone, who is able to take a view of the English clergy. They are appointed by the absolute will of the Boroughmongers. They care nothing for the good will of their congregation or parish. It is as good to them to be hated by their parishioners as to be loved by them. They very frequently never even *see* their parish more than once in four or five years. They solemnly declare at the altar, that they believe themselves called by the Holy Ghost to take on them the *cure of souls*; they get possession of a living; and leave the cure of souls to some *curate*, to whom they give a tenth part, perhaps, of the income. Many of them have *two livings*, at thirty miles distance from each other. They live at neither very frequently; and, when they do they only add to the annoyance which their curate gives.

As to their general character and conduct; in what public transaction of pre-eminent scandal have they not taken a part? Who were most intimate with Mrs CLARKE, and most busy in her commission dealing affairs? Clergymen of the Church of England. This is notorious. Miss TOCKNER tells of the *two livings* given to PARSON GURNEY for his electioneering works in Cornwall. And, indeed all over the country, they have been and are the prime agents of the Boroughmongers. Recently they have been the tools of Sidmouth for gagging the press in the country parts of the kingdom. *Powis* and *Guillim* were the prosecutors of Messrs Pilling and Melor; and for which if they be not made to answer, the kingdom ought to be destroyed. They are the leading men at Pitt Clubs all over the country; they were the foremost to defend the peculation of Melville. In short, there has been no public man guilty of an infamous act, of whom they have not taken the part; and no act of tyranny of which they have not been the eulogists and the principal instrument.

But, why do I attempt to describe Parsons to *Hampshire men*? You saw them all assembled in grand cohort the last time that I saw any of you. You saw them at *Winchester*, when they brought forward their lying address to the Regent. You saw them on that

day, and so did I; and in them I saw a band of more complete
blackguards than I ever before saw in all my life. I then saw
Parson Baines of Exton, standing up in a chair and actually
spitting in Lord Cochrane's poll, while the latter was bending his
neck out to speak. Lord Cochrane looked round and said, 'By
G— sir, if you do that again I'll knock you down.' 'You be
d—d,' said Baines, 'I'll spit where I like.' Lord Cochrane struck
at him; Baines jumped down, put his two hands to his mouth in a
huntsman-like way, and cried 'whoop! whoop!' till he was actually
black in the face. One of them trampled upon my heel as I was
speaking. I looked round and begged him to leave off. 'You be
d—d,' said he, 'you be d—d, Jacobin.' He then tried to press on
me, to stifle my voice, till I clapped my elbow into his ribs and
made 'the spiritual person' hiccup. There were about twenty of
them mounted upon a large table in the room; and there they
jumped, stamped, halloed, roared, thumped with canes and um-
brellas, squalled, whistled, and made all sorts of noises. As Lord
Cochrane and I were going back to London, he said that, so
many years as he had been in the navy, he never had seen a band
of such complete blackguards. And I said the same for the army.
And, I declare, that, in the whole course of my life, I have never
seen any men, drunk or sober, behave in so infamous a manner.
Mr PHILLIPS, of Eling (now Doctor Phillips) whom I saw
standing in the room, I tapped on the shoulder, and asked
whether he was not ashamed. Mr LEE, of the College; Mr OGLE,
of Bishop's Waltham; and DOCTOR HILL of Southampton: these
were exceptions. Perhaps there might be some others; but the
*mass* was the most audacious, foul, and atrocious body of men I
ever saw. We had done nothing to offend them. We had proposed
nothing to offend them in the smallest degree. But, they were
afraid of our *speeches*; they knew they could not answer us; and
they were resolved, that, if possible, we should not be heard.
There was one parson, who had his mouth within a foot of Lord
Cochrane's ear, all the time his lordship was speaking, and who
kept on saying: '*You lie! you lie! you lie! you lie!*' as loud as he
could utter the words.

BAKER, the Botley parson, was extremely busy. He acted the
part of buffoon to LOCKHART. He kept capering about behind
him, and really seemed like a merry andrew rather than a *spiritual
person.*

Such is the character of the great body of Hampshire parsons. I know of no body of men so despicable, and yet, what sums of public money do they swallow! It now remains for me to speak more particularly of BAKER, he who, for your sins I suppose, is fastened upon you as your parson. But what I have to say of this man must be the subject of another letter. That it should be the subject of any letter at all may well surprise all who know the man; for not one creature knows him without despising him. But, it is not Baker, it is the scandalous priest, that I strike at. It is the impudent, profligate, hardened priest that I will hold up to public scorn.

When I see the good and kind people here going to church to listen to some decent man of good moral character and of sober quiet life, I always think of you. You are just the same sort of people as they are here; but, what a difference in the clergyman! What a difference between the sober, sedate, friendly man who preaches to one of these congregations, and the greedy, chattering, lying, backbiting, mischief-making, everlasting plague, that you go to hear, and are *compelled* to hear, or to stay away from the church. Baker always puts me in mind of the magpie.

> *The magpie, bird of chatt'ring fame,*
> *Whose tongue and hue bespeak his name;*
> *The first a* squalling clam'rous clack,
> *The last made up of white and black;*
> *Feeder alike on* flesh *and* corn,
> *Greedy alike at eve and morn;*
> *Of all the birds the* prying pest,
> *Must needs be* Parson *o'er the rest.*

Thus I began a fable, when I lived at Botley. I have forgotten the rest of it. It will please you to hear that there are *no magpies* in America; but, it will please you still more to hear, that no men that resemble them are parsons here. I have sometimes been half tempted to believe, that the magpie first suggested to tyrants the idea of having a tithe-eating clergy. The magpie devours the corn and grain; so does the parson. The magpie takes the wool from the sheep's backs; so does the parson. The magpie devours alike the young animals and the eggs; so does the parson. The magpie's clack is everlastingly going; so is the parson's. The magpie repeats by rote words that are taught it; so does the parson. The magpie is always skipping and hopping and peeping into other's nests; so is the parson. The magpie's colour is partly black and partly white; so is the parson's. The magpie's greediness, impudence, and cruelty are proverbial; so are those of the parson. I was saying to a farmer the other day, that if the Boroughmongers had a mind to ruin America, they would another time, send over five or six good large flocks of magpies, instead of five or six of their armies; but, upon second thought, they would do the thing far more effectually by sending over five or six flocks of their parsons, and getting the people to receive them and cherish them as the *bulwark* of *religion*.

# ON SETTLING IN THE WEST
## An Open Letter to Morris Birkbeck

North Hempstead, Long Island
10 December 1818

MY DEAR SIR,

I have read your two little books, namely, the *Notes on a Journey in America*, and the *Letters from the Illinois*. I opened the books, and I proceeded in the perusal with *fear and terembling* [*sic*]; not because I supposed it possible for you to put forth an *intended* imposition on the world; but, because I had sincere respect for the character and talents of the writer; and because I knew how enchanting and delusive are the prospects of enthusiastic minds, when bent on grand territorial acquisitions.

My apprehensions were, I am sorry to have it to say, but too well founded. Your books, written, I am sure, without any intention to deceive and decoy, and without any even the smallest tincture of base self-interest, are, in my opinion, calculated to produce great disappointment, not to say misery and ruin, amongst our own country people (for I will, in spite of your disavowal, still claim the honour of having you for a countryman), and great injury to America by sending back to Europe accounts of that disappointment, misery and ruin.

It is very true, that you decline *advising* anyone to go to the ILLINOIS, and it is also true, that your description of the *hardships* you encountered is very candid; but still, there runs throughout the whole of your *Notes* such an account as to the *prospect*, that is to say, the *ultimate effect*, that the book is, without your either wishing or perceiving it, calculated to deceive and decoy. You do indeed describe difficulties and hardships: but, then, you *overcome* them all with so much ease and gaiety, that you make them disregarded by your English readers, who, sitting by their fire-sides, and feeling nothing but the gripe of the Boroughmongers and the tax-gatherer, merely cast a glance at your hardships and fully participate in all your enthusiasm. You do indeed fairly describe the rugged roads, the dirty hovels, the fire in the woods to sleep by, the pathless ways through the wilderness, the dangerous crossings of the rivers; but, there are the beautiful meadows and rich lands at *last*; there is the *fine freehold domain* at *the end*! There are the giants and the enchanters to encounter; the slashings and the rib-roastings to undergo; but then, there is, *at last*, the lovely languishing damsel to repay the adventurer.

The whole of your writings relative to your undertaking, address themselves directly to *English Farmers*, who have property to the amount of two or three thousand pounds, or upwards. Persons of this description are, not by your express words, but by the natural tendency of your writings, *invited*, nay, strongly invited, to emigrate with their property to the Illinois Territory. Many have already acted upon the invitation. Many others are about to follow them. I am convinced, that their doing this is unwise, and greatly injurious, not only to them, but to the character of America as a country to emigrate to, and, as I have, in the first part of this work, promised to give, as far as I am able, a *true* account of America, it is my duty to state the *reasons* on which this conviction is founded; and, I address the statement to you in order, that, if you find it erroneous, you may, in the like public manner, show wherein I have committed error.

We are speaking, my dear sir, of English Farmers possessing each two or three thousand pounds sterling. And, before we proceed to inquire, whether such persons ought to emigrate to the *West* or to the *East*, it may not be amiss to inquire a little, whether they ought to *emigrate at all*! Do not start, now! For, while I am very certain that the emigration of *such persons* is not, in the end, calculated to produce benefit to America, as a nation, I greatly doubt of its being, *generally speaking*, of any benefit to the emigrants themselves, if we take into view the chances of their speedy relief at home.

Persons of advanced age, of settled habits, of deep rooted

prejudices, of settled acquaintances, of contracted sphere of movement, do not, to use Mr GEORGE FLOWER'S expression, *transplant well.* Of all such persons, farmers transplant worse; and, of all farmers, English farmers are the worst to transplant. Of some of the *tears,* shed in the ILLINOIS, an account reached me several months ago, through an eye-witness of perfect veracity, and a very sincere friend of freedom, and of you, and whose information was given me, unasked for, and in the presence of several Englishmen, every one of whom, as well as myself, most ardently wished you success.

It is nothing, my dear sir, to say, as you do, in the Preface to the *Letters from the Illinois,* that, 'as little would I encourage the emigration of the tribe of *grumblers,* people who are petulant and discontented under the *everyday* evils of life. Life has its petty miseries in *all situations* and climates, to be mitigated or cured by the continual efforts of an elastic spirit, or to be borne, if incurable, with cheerful patience. But the *peevish emigrant* is perpetually comparing the *comforts* he has quitted, but never could enjoy, with the *privations of his new allotment.* He overlooks the *present good,* and broods over the evil with *habitual perverseness;* whilst in the recollection of the past, he dwells on the good only. Such people are always *bad associates,* but they are an *especial nuisance* in an infant colony.'

Give me leave to say, my dear sir, that there is too much *asperity* in this language, considering who were the objects of the censure. Nor do you appear to me to afford, in this instance, a very happy illustration of the absence of that *peevishness,* which you perceive in others, and for the yielding to which you call them a *nuisance;* an appellation much too harsh for the object and for the occasion. If you, with all your elasticity of spirit, all your ardour of pursuit, all your compensations of fortune in prospect, and all your gratifications of fame in possession, cannot with patience hear the wailings of some of your neighbours, into what source are they to dip for the waters of content and good-humour?

It is no *everyday evil* that they have to bear. For an English farmer, and, more especially, an English farmer's wife, after crossing the sea and travelling to Illinois, with the consciousness of having expended a third of their substance, to purchase, as yet, nothing but sufferings; for such persons to boil their pot in the gipsy-fashion, to have a mere board to eat on, to drink whisky or pure water, to sit and sleep under a shed far inferior to their English cowpens, to have a mill at twenty miles distance, an apothecary's shop at a hundred, and a doctor nowhere: these, my dear sir, are not, to *such people* '*everyday* evils of life'. You, though in your little 'cabin' have your *books*, you have your name circulating in the world, you have it to be given, by and by, to a city or county; and, if you fail of brilliant success, you have still a sufficiency of fortune to secure you a safe retreat. Almost the whole of your neighbours must be destitute of all these sources of comfort, hope, and consolation. As they *now are*, their change is, and must be, for the worse; and, as *to the future*, besides the uncertainty attendant, everywhere, on that which is to come, they ought to be excused, if they, at their age, despair of seeing days as happy as those that they have seen.

It were much better for *such people* not to emigrate at all; for while they are *sure* to come into a state of some degree of suffering, they leave behind them the *chance* of happy days; and, in my opinion, a *certainty* of such days. I think it next to impossible for any man of tolerable information to believe, that the present tyranny of the seat-owners can last another two years. As to *what change* will take place, it would, perhaps, be hard to say: but, that *some great change* will come is certain; and, it is also certain, that the change *must be for* the better. Indeed, one of the motives for the emigration of many is said to be, that they think a *convulsion* inevitable. Why should such persons as I am speaking of fear a convulsion? Why should they suppose, that they will suffer by a convulsion? What have *they* done to provoke the rake of blanket-teers? Do they think that their countrymen, all but themselves, will be transformed into prowling wolves? This is precisely what Boroughmongers wish them to believe; and, believing it, they *flee* instead of remaining to assist to keep the people down as the Boroughmongers wish them to do.

Being here, however, they, as you say, *think only of the good they have left behind them, and of the bad they find here*. This is no fault of theirs: it is the natural course of the human mind; and this you ought to have known. You yourself acknowledge, that England, '*was never so dear to you as it is now in recollection*: being no longer under its base oligarchy, I can think of my native country and her *noble institutions*, apart from her *politics*.' I may ask you, by the way, what *noble institutions* she has, which are not of a *political nature?* Say the *oppressions of her tyrants*, say that you can think of her and love her renown and her famous political institutions, apart from those oppressions, and then I go with you with all my heart; but, so thinking, and so feeling, I cannot say with you, in your *Notes*, that England is to me *matter of history*, nor with you, in your *Letters from the Illinois*, that 'where *liberty* is, there is *my country*'.

But, leaving this matter, for the present, if English farmers must emigrate, why should they encounter *unnecessary* difficulties? Coming from a country like a garden, why should they not stop in another *somewhat resembling* that which they have lived in before? Why should they, at an expence amounting to a large part of what they possess, prowl two thousand miles at the hazard of their limbs and lives, take women and children through scenes of hardship and distress not easily described, and that too, to live like gipsies at the end of their journey, for, at least, a year or two, and, as I think I shall shew, without the smallest chance of their *finally* doing so well as they may do in these Atlantic States? Why should an English farmer and his family, who have always been jogging about a snug homestead, eating regular meals, and sleeping in warm rooms, push back to the Illinois, and encounter those hardships which require all the habitual disregard of comfort of an American backwoods-man to overcome? Why should they do this? The undertaking is hardly reconcileable to reason in an Atlantic *American* farmer who has half a dozen sons, all brought up to use the axe, the saw, the chisel and the hammer from their infancy, and everyone of whom is a ploughman, carpenter, wheelwright and butcher, and can work from sunrise to sunset, and sleep, if need be, upon the bare boards. What, then, must it be in an English farmer and his family of helpless mortals? Helpless, I mean, in this scene of such novelty and such difficulty? And what is his *wife* to do; she who has been torn from all her relations and neighbours, and from everything that she liked in the world, and who, perhaps, has never, in all her life before, been *ten miles* from the cradle in which she was nursed? An American farmer mends his plough, his waggon, his tackle of all sorts, his household goods, his shoes; and, if need be, he *makes* them all. Can our people do all this, or any part of it? Can they live without bread for months? Can they live without beer? Can they be otherwise than miserable, cut off, as they must be, from all intercourse with, and hope of hearing of, their relations and friends? The truth is, that this is not *transplanting*, it is *tearing up and flinging away*.

*Society!* What society can these people have? 'Tis true they have nobody to envy, for nobody can have any thing to enjoy. But there may be, and there must be, mutual complainings and upbraidings; and every unhappiness will be traced directly to him who has been, however unintentionally, the cause of the unhappy person's removal. The very foundation of your plan necessarily contained the seeds of discontent and ill-will. A *colony* all from the same country was the very worst project that could have been fallen upon. You took upon yourself the *charge* of MOSES without being invested with any part of his *authority*; and absolute as this was, he found the charge so heavy, that he called upon the Lord to share it with him or to relieve him from it altogether. Soon after you went out, an Unitarian priest, upon my asking what you were going to do in that wild country, said, you were going to form a community, who would be 'content to worship *one* *God*'. 'I hope not,' said I, 'for he will have plagues enough without adding a priest to the number.' But, perhaps I was wrong: for AARON was of great assistance to the leader of the Israelites.

As if the inevitable effects of disappointment and hardship were not sufficient, you had, too, a sort of *partnership* in the *leaders*. This is *sure* to produce feuds and bitterness in the long run. Partnership-sovereignties have furnished the world with numerous instances of poisonings and banishments and rottings in prison. It is as much as merchants, who post their books every Sunday, can do to get along without quarrelling. Of man and wife, though they are flesh of flesh and bone of bone, the harmony is not always quite perfect, except in France, where the husband is the servant, and in Germany and Prussia, where the wife is the slave. But, as for a partnership sovereignty without disagreement, there is but one single instance upon record; that, I mean, was of the *two kings of Brentford*, whose cordiality was, you know, so perfect, that they both smelt to the same nosegay. This is, my dear sir, no bantering. I am quite serious. It is impossible that separations should not take place, and equally impossible that the neighbourhood should not be miserable. This is not the way to settle in America. The way is, to go and *sit yourself down amongst the natives*. They are already settled. They can *lend* you what you want to borrow, and happy they are always to do it. And, which is the great thing of all great things, you have their *women* for *your women to commune with!*

RAPP, indeed, has done great things; but RAPP has the authority of Moses and that of Aaron united in his own person. Besides, Rapp's community observe in reality the celibacy, which monks and nuns pretend to, though I am not going to take my oath, mind, that none of the tricks of the convent are ever played in the tabernacles of *Harmony*. At any rate, Rapp secures the *effects* of celibacy; first, an absence of the expence attending the breeding and rearing of children, and, second, unremitted labour of woman as well as man. But, where, in all the world is the match of this to be found? Where else shall we look for a society composed of persons willing and able to forego the gratification of the most powerful propensity of nature, for the sake of getting money together? Where else shall we look for a band of men and women who love money better than their own bodies? Better than their *souls* we find people enough to love money; but, who ever before heard of a set that preferred the love of money to that of their own bodies? Who, before, ever conceived the idea of putting a stop to the procreation of children, for the sake of saving the expence of bearing and breeding them? This society, which is a perfect prodigy and monster, ought to have the image of MAMMON in their place of worship; for that is the object of their devotion, and not the God of nature. Yet the persons belonging to this unnatural association are your nearest neighbours. The masculine things here, called women, who have imposed barrenness on themselves, out of a pure love of gain, are the nearest neighbours of the affectionate, tender-hearted wives and mothers and daughters, who are to inhabit your colony, and who are, let us thank God, the very reverse of the petticoated Germans of Harmony.

In such a situation, with so many circumstances to annoy, what happiness can an English family enjoy in that country, so far distant from all that resembles what they have left behind them? 'The fair Enchantress, *Liberty*,' of whom you speak with not too much rapture, they would have found in any of *these states*, and, in a garb, too, by which they would have *recognised*

her. Where they now are, they are *free* indeed; but their freedom
is that of the wild animals in your woods. It is not *freedom*, it is
*no government*. The GIPSIES, in England, are *free*; and anyone,
who has a mind to live in a cave, or cabin, in some hidden recess
of our *Hampshire forests*, may be *free* too. The English farmer, in
the Illinois, is, indeed, beyond the reach of the Boroughmongers;
and so is the man that is in the grave. When it was first proposed,
in the English ministry, to *drop quietly* the title of *King of France*
in the enumeration of our king's titles, and, when it was stated
to be an expedient *likely to tend to a peace*, Mr WINDHAM, who
was then a member of the Cabinet, said: 'As this is a measure of
*safety*, and as, doubtless, we shall hear of others of the same cast,
what think you of *going under ground at once?*' It was a remark
enough to cut the liver out of the hearers; but Pitt and his
associates had no livers. I do not believe, that any twelve jour-
neymen, or labourers, in England would have voted for the adop-
tion of this mean and despicable measure.

If, indeed, the Illinois were the *only* place out of the reach of
the Borough-grasp; and, if men are resolved to get out of that
reach; then, I should say, Go to Illinois, by all means. But, as
there is a country, a settled country, a free country, full of kind
neighbours, full of all that is good, and when this country is to
be *traversed* in order to *get at* the acknowledged hardships of the
Illinois, how can a sane mind lead an English farmer into the
expedition?

It is the enchanting damsel that makes the knight encounter
the hairbreadth scapes, the sleeping on the ground, the cooking
with cross-sticks to hang the pot on. It is the *prairie*, that pretty
French word, which means green grass bespangled with daisies
and cowslips! Oh, God! What delusion! And that a man of sense;
a man of superior understanding and talent; a man of honesty,
humanity, and lofty sentiment, should be the cause of this delusion; I, my dear sir, have seen *prairies* many years ago, in America, as fine as yours, as fertile as yours, though not so extensive.
I saw those prairies settled on by American loyalists, who were
carried, with all their goods and tools to the spot, and who were
furnished with four years' provisions, all *at the expence of England*; who had the lands *given them*; tools *given them*; and who
were thus seated down on the borders of creeks, which gave them
easy communication with the inhabited plains near the sea. The

settlers that I particularly knew were Connecticut men. Men with families of sons. Men able to do as much in a day at the works necessary in their situation as so many Englishmen would be able to do in a week. They began with a *shed*; then rose to a *log house*; and next to a *frame house*; all of their own building. I have seen them manure their land with *salmon* caught in their creeks and with *pigeons* caught on the land itself. It will be a long while before you will see such beautiful *corn-fields* as I saw there. Yet nothing but the danger and disgrace which attended their return to Connecticut *prevented their returning*, though there they must have begun the world anew. I saw them in their log huts, and saw them in their frame houses. They had overcome all their difficulties as settlers; they were under a government which required neither tax nor service from them; they were as happy as people could be as to ease and plenty; but, still, they *sighed for Connecticut*; and especially the *women*, young as well as old, though we, gay fellows with worsted or silver lace upon our bright red coats, did our best to make them happy by telling them entertaining stories about Old England, while we drank their coffee and grog by gallons, and eat their fowls, pigs and sausages and sweetmeats, by wheelbarrow loads; for, though we were by no means *shy*, their hospitality far exceeded our appetites. I am an old hand at the work of settling in wilds. I have, more than once or twice, had to begin my nest and go in, like a bird, making it habitable by degrees; and, if I, or if such people as my old friends above-mentioned with everything found for them and brought to the spot, had difficulties to undergo, and *sighed for home* even after all the difficulties were over, what must be the lot of an English Farmer's family in the Illinois?

All this I told you, my dear sir, in London just before your departure. I begged of you and Mr Richard Flower, both, not to think of the Wildernesses. I begged of you to go within a day's ride of some of these great cities, where your ample capital and your great skill could not fail to place you upon a footing, at least, with the richest amongst the most happy and enlightened Yeomanry in the world; where you would find everyone to praise the improvements you would introduce, and nobody to envy you anything that you might acquire. Where you would find society as good, in all respects, as that which you had left behind you. Where you would find neighbours ready prepared for you far more generous and hospitable than those in England *can* be, loaded and pressed down as they are by the inexorable hand of the Borough-villains. I offered you a letter (which, I believe, I sent you), to my friends the PAULS. 'But', said I, 'you want no letter. Go into Philadelphia, or Bucks, or Chester, or Montgomery County; tell any of the Quakers, or anybody else, that you are an English farmer, come to settle amongst them; and, I'll engage that you will instantly have friends and neighbours as good and as cordial as those that you leave in England.'

At this very moment, if this plan had been pursued, you would have had a beautiful farm of two or three hundred acres. Fine stock upon it feeding on Swedish turnips. A house overflowing with abundance; comfort, ease, and, if you choose, elegance, would have been your inmates; *libraries*, public and private within your reach; and a communication with England much more quick and regular than that which you now have even with Pittsburgh.

You say, that 'Philadelphians *know nothing* of the western countries'. Suffer me, then, to say, that you know nothing of the *Atlantic States*, which, indeed, is the only apology for your saying, that the *Americans have no mutton fit to eat*, and regard it *only as a thing fit for dogs*. In this island *every* farmer has sheep. I kill *fatter* lamb than I ever *saw* in England, and the *fattest* mutton I ever saw, was in company with Mr Harline, in Philadelphia Market last winter. At BRIGHTON, near Boston, they produced, at a cattle shew this fall, an ox of *two-thousand seven-hundred pounds* weight, and sheep much finer, than you and I saw at the Smithfield Show in 1814. Mr Judge Lawrence of this county, has kept, for seven years, an average of *five hundred Merinos* on his farm of *one hundred and fifty acres*, besides raising twenty acres of corn and his usual pretty large proportion of grain! Can your western farmers beat that? Yes, in extent, as the surface of five dollars beats that of a guinea.

However, happiness is in the *mind*; and, if it be necessary to the gratification of your mind to inhabit a wilderness and be the owner of a large tract of land, you are right to seek and enjoy this gratification. But, for the plain, plodding *English farmer*, who simply seeks safety for his little property, with some addition to it for his children; for such a person to *cross* the Atlantic states in search of safety, tranquillity and gain in the Illinois, is, to my mind, little short of madness. Yet, to this mad enterprize is he allured by your captivating statements, and which statements become decisive in their effects upon his mind, when they are reduced to *figures*. This, my dear sir, is the part of your writings, which has given me most pain. You have not *meant to deceive*; but you have first practised a deceit upon yourself, and then upon others. All the disadvantages you *state*; but, then, you accompany the statement by telling us how *quickly* and how *easily* they will be *overcome*. Salt, Mr HULME finds, even at ZANES-VILLE, at *two dollars and a half a bushel*; but, you tell us, that it *soon will be* at three quarters of a dollar. And thus it goes all through.

I am happy, however, that you have given us *figures* in your account of what an English farmer may do *with two thousand pounds*. It is alluring, it is fallacious, it tends to disappointment, misery, ruin and broken hearts; but it is open and honest in intention, and it affords us the means of detecting and exposing the fallacy. Many and many a family have returned to New England after having emigrated to the West in search of *fine estates*. They, able workmen, exemplary livers, have returned to labour in their native States amongst their relations and old neighbours; but, what are our poor ruined countrymen to do, when they become pennyless? If I could root my country from my heart, common humanity would urge me to make an humble attempt to dissipate the charming delusions, which have, without your perceiving it, gone forth from your sprightly and able pen, and which delusions are the more dangerous on account of your justly high and well-known character for understanding and integrity.

After this, it appears unnecessary for me to notice any other part of this Transalleganian romance, which I might leave to the admiration of the Edinburgh Reviewers, whose knowledge of these matters is quite equal to what they have discovered as to the Funding System and Paper Money. But when I think of the flocks of poor English Farmers, who are tramping away towards an imaginary, across a real land of milk and honey, I cannot lay down the pen, till I have noticed an item or two of the *produce*.

The farmer is to have 100 acres of Indian corn, the first year. The minds of you gentlemen who cross the Allegany seem to expand, as it were, to correspond with the extent of the horizon that opens to your view; but, I can assure you, that if you were to talk to a farmer on this side of the mountains of a field of corn of a hundred acres during the first year of a settlement, with grassy land and hands scarce, you would frighten him into a third-day ague. In goes your corn, however! 'Twenty more: kill 'em!' Nothing but ploughing: no harrowing; no marking; and only a horse-hoeing, during the summer, at *a dollar an acre*. The planting is to cost only *a quarter of a dollar an acre*. The planting will cost a *dollar an acre*. The horse-hoeing in your grassy land, *two dollars*. The *hand-hoeing*, which must be *well* done, or you will have no corn, *two dollars*; for in spite of your teeth, your rampant natural grass will be up before your corn, and a man must go to *a thousand hills* to do *half an acre a day*. It will cost *two dollars* to harvest a hundred bushels of *corn ears*. So that here are about 400 dollars of expences on the corn alone, to be added. A *trifle*, to be sure, when we are looking through the Transalleganian glass, which diminishes out-goings and magnifies incomings. However, here are four hundred dollars.

In goes the plough for wheat? 'In him again! Twenty more!' But, this is in *October*, mind. Is the corn off? It may be; but, where are the *four hundred waggon loads of corn stalks*? A prodigiously fine thing is this forest of fodder, as *high* and as *thick* as an English coppice. But, though it be of *no use* to *you*, who have the *meadows without* bounds, this coppice must be *removed*, if you please, before you plough for wheat!

Let us pause here, then; let us look at the *battalion*, who are at work; for, there must be little short of a Hessian battalion. Twenty men and twenty horses *may* husk the corn, cut and cart the stalks, plough and sow and harrow for the wheat; twenty two-legged and twenty four-legged animals *may* do the work in the proper time; but, if they do it, they must work *well*. Here is a goodly group to look at, for an English farmer, without a penny in his pocket; for all his money is *gone long ago*, even according to your own estimate; and, here, besides the expence of cattle and tackle, are 600 dollars, in bare wages, to be paid in a month! You and I both have forgotten the *shelling* of the corn, which, and putting it up, will come to 50 dollars more at the least, leaving the price of the barrel to be paid for by the purchaser of the corn.

But, what did I say? *Shell* the corn? It must go into the *cribs* first. It cannot be shelled *immediately*. And it must not be thrown into *heaps*. It must be put into *cribs*. I have made out an estimate of the expence of the cribs for *ten thousand bushels* of corn ears: that is the crop; and the cribs will cost 570 dollars! Though, mind, the farmer's *house, barn, stables, waggon-house*, and all, are to cost but 1500 dollars! But, the third year, our poor simpleton is to have 200 acres of corn! 'Twenty more: kill 'em!' Another 570 dollars for cribs!

However, crops now come tumbling on him so fast, that he must struggle hard not to be stifled with his own superabundance. He has now got 200 acres of corn and 100 acres of wheat, which latter he has, indeed, had one *year before*! Oh, madness! But to proceed. To get in these crops and to sow the wheat, first taking away 200 acres of *English coppice* in stalks, will, with the *dunging* for the wheat, require, at least, *fifty good men*, and *forty good horses or oxen*, for *thirty days*. Faith! when farmer Simpleton sees all this (in his *dreams* I mean), he will think himself a farmer of the rank of JOB, before Satan beset that example of patience, so worthy of imitation, and so seldom imitated.

Well, but Simpleton must bustle to *get in* his wheat. *In*, indeed! What can *cover* it, but the canopy of heaven? A *barn*! It will, at *two English waggon loads of sheaves to an acre*, require a barn a hundred feet long, fifty feet wide, and twenty-three feet high up to the eaves; and this barn, with two proper floors, will cost more than *seven thousand dollars*. He will put it in *stacks*; let him add six men to his battalion then. He *will thrash it in the field*; let him add ten more men! Let him, at once, send and press the Harmonites into his service, and make RAPP march at their head, for, never will he by any other means get in the crop; and, even then, if he pay fair wages, he will lose by it.

After the crop is in and the seed sown, in the fall, what is to become of Simpleton's men till corn ploughing and planting time in the spring? And, then, when the planting is done, what is to become of them till harvest time? Is he, like BAYES, in the Rehearsal, to lay them down when he pleases, and when he pleases make them rise up again? To hear you talk about these crops, and, at other times to hear you advising others to bring labourers from England, one would think you, for your own part, able, like CADMUS, to make men start up out of the earth. How would one ever have thought it possible for infatuation like this to seize hold of a mind like yours?

When I read in your Illinois Letters, that you had *prepared* horses, ploughs, and other things, *for putting in a hundred acres of corn in the spring*, how I pitied you! I saw all your plagues, if you could not see them. I saw the grass choking your plants; the grubs eating them; and you fretting and turning from the sight with all the pangs of sanguine baffled hope. I expected you to have *ten bushels*, instead of *fifty*, upon an acre. I saw your confusion, and participated in your mortification. From these feelings I was happily relieved by the Journal of our friend HULME, who informs the world, and our countrymen in particular, that you had not, in *July last, any corn at all growing*!

Thus it is to reckon one's chickens before they are hatched: and thus the Transalleganian dream vanishes. You have been deceived. A warm heart, a lively imagination, and I know not what caprice about republicanism, have led you into sanguine expectations and wrong conclusions. Come, now! Confess it like yourself; that is, like a man of sense and spirit: like an honest and fair-dealing John Bull. To err belongs to all men, great as well as little; but, to be ashamed to confess error, belongs only to the latter.

Great as is my confidence in your candour, I can, however, hardly hope wholly to escape your anger for having so decidedly condemned your publications; but, I do hope, that you will not be so unjust as to impute my conduct to any base self-interested motive. I have no private interest, I can have no such interest in endeavouring to check the mad torrent towards the West. I *own* nothing in these States, and never shall; and whether English farmers put on into misery and ruin, or stop here in happiness and prosperity, to me, as far as private interest goes, it must be the same. As to the difference in our feelings and notions about *country*, about *allegiance*, and about *forms of government*, this may exist without any, even the smallest degree of personal dislike. I was no hypocrite in England; I had no views farther than those which I professed. I wanted nothing for myself but the fruit of my own industry and talent, and I wished nothing for my country but its liberties and laws, which say, that the people shall be *fairly represented*. England has been very happy and *free*; her greatness and renown have been surpassed by those of no nation in the world; her wise, just, and merciful laws form the basis of that freedom which we here enjoy, she has been fertile beyond all rivalship in men of learning and men devoted to the cause of freedom and humanity; her people, though proud and domineering, yield to no people in the world in frankness, good faith, sincerity, and benevolence: and I cannot but know, that this state of things has existed, and that this people has been formed, under a government of king, Lords, and Commons. Having this powerful argument of experience before me, and seeing no reason why the thing should be otherwise, I have never wished for republican government in England; though, rather than that the present tyrannical oligarchy should continue to trample on king and people, I would gladly see the whole fabric torn to atoms, and trust to chance for something better, being sure that nothing could be worse. But, if I am not a republican; if I think my duty towards England indefeasible; if I think that it becomes me to abstain from any act which shall seem to say I abandon her, and especially in this her hour of distress and oppression; and, if, in all these points, I differ from you, I trust that to this difference no part of the above strictures will be imputed, but that the motive will be fairly inferred from the act, and not the act imputed unfairly to any motive. I am, my dear sir, with great respect for your talents as well as character,

Your most obedient,
And most humble servant,
WM COBBETT

# EPILOGUE: AMERICA REMEMBERED

## (*1830*)

# THE HAPPINESS OF THE
# AMERICANS

---

The weather has been beautiful ever since last Thursday morning; but, there has been a white frost every morning, and the days have been coldish. *Here*, however, I am quite at home in a room, where there is one of my *American fire-places*, bought, by my host, of MR JUDSON OF KENSINGTON, who has made many a score of families comfortable, instead of sitting shivering in the cold. At the house of the gentleman, whose house I am now in, there is a good deal of *fuel-wood*; and here I see, in the parlours, those fine and cheerful fires that make a great part of the happiness of the Americans. But, these fires are to be had only in this sort of fire-place. Ten times the fuel; nay, no quantity, would effect the same object, in any other fire-place. It is equally good for *coal* as for wood; but, for *pleasure*, a wood fire is the thing. There is, round about almost every gentleman's or great farmer's house, more wood suffered to rot every year, in one shape or another, than would make (with this fire-place) a couple of rooms constantly warm, from October to June. *Here*, peat, turf, saw-dust, and wood, are burnt in these fire-places.

*Rural Rides, 26 October 1825*

# SOURCES FOR THE TEXT

*When I am asked what books a young man or young woman ought to read, I always answer let him or her read all the books that I have written.*

In his long career as author and journalist Cobbett published more than a hundred books or pamphlets and, usually in his own journals, some thousands of articles. Not infrequently he plagiarized himself, borrowing from his earlier writings, sometimes *verbatim*, often with the text amended to suit the thrust of the new argument upon which he was launched, but almost always without acknowledgment.

The selections reproduced in this edition follow generally the earliest-known version but, where it seems appropriate to the flow of the narrative, a later variant has been interpolated.

The following are the principal sources for the text:

### YOUTH RECALLED
This section is taken in its entirety from *The Life and Adventures of Peter Porcupine*, 1796.

### COBBETT IN CANADA
There is no sequential narrative of Cobbett's career as a soldier, though it was a topic to which, throughout his life, he was forever returning in recollection. The text for most of this section has been pieced together from many sources but principally from *The Life and Adventures of Peter Porcupine*, *Advice to Young Men*, 1829, and from articles in *The Political Register*. The chapter titles are the editor's.

Only 'The Court Martial' is reprinted virtually in the form in which it was originally accessible. It was published in June 1809 in *Cobbett's Weekly Political Register* as part of an open letter addressed 'To The Independent People of Hampshire', and as answer to a government-inspired pamphlet which had been designed to bring Cobbett into disrepute by resurrecting, in scabrous and inaccurate form, the long-forgotten details of his court martial. The version here presented excises only those parts of his reply in which Cobbett dismisses *seriatim* the various charges raised against him before the court.

### PHILADELPHIA JOURNALIST

| | |
|---|---|
| 'Paul Hedgehog Presents Peter Porcupine' | First published by Cobbett in 1795 in Philadelphia and later reproduced in *Porcupine's Works*, Vol. IV. 1801 |
| 'Mrs Cobbett' | *Advice to Young Men* |
| 'A Cheating, Lying, Roguish Gang' | Cobbett Mss. |
| 'A Bone to Gnaw for the Democrats' | Published by Thomas Bradford in Philadelphia, 1795 |
| 'Remarks against Peter Porcupine' | Published by Cobbett as 'Remarks of the Pamphlets Lately Published Against Peter Porcupine' in *The Political Censor* for September 1796, and reprinted in Vol. IV of *Porcupine's Works* |
| 'This Modern Judas, Talleyrand' | First published by Cobbett in *The Political Censor* for May 1797, and reprinted in Vol. V of *Porcupine's Works* |
| 'The Scare-crow' | *The Scare-crow:* being an infamous letter sent to Mr John Oldden, threatening Destruction to his House, and Violence to the Person of his Tenant, William Cobbett; |

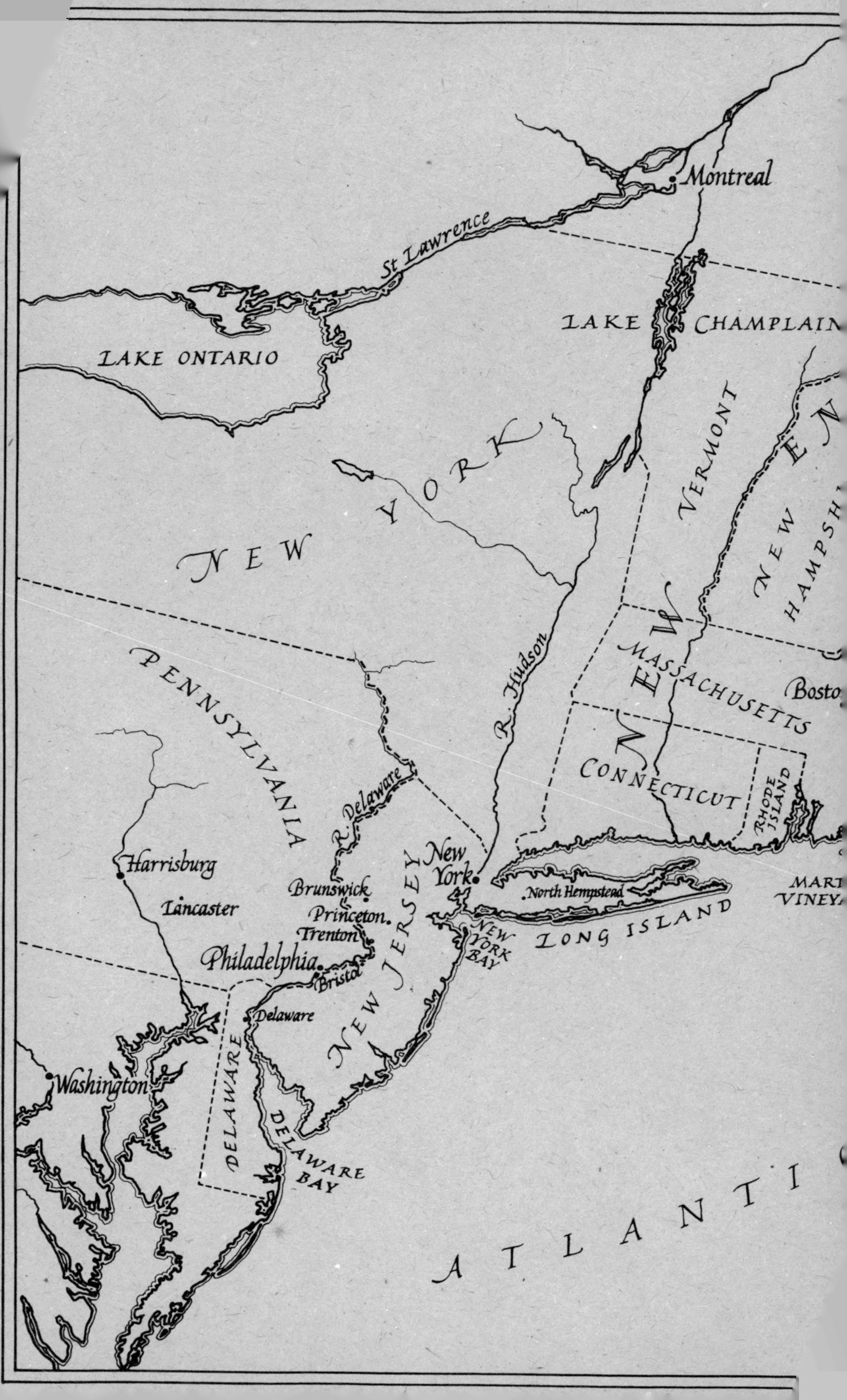

Montreal
St Lawrence
LAKE ONTARIO
LAKE CHAMPLAIN
NEW YORK
VERMONT
NEW HAMPSHIRE
NEW ENGLAND
MASSACHUSETTS
Boston
CONNECTICUT
RHODE ISLAND
R. Hudson
PENNSYLVANIA
R. Delaware
Harrisburg
Lancaster
Brunswick
Princeton
Trenton
Philadelphia
Bristol
New York
North Hempstead
LONG ISLAND
NEW YORK BAY
NEW JERSEY
Delaware
DELAWARE
DELAWARE BAY
Washington
ATLANTIC